Forensic Linguistics

Language in Society

GENERAL EDITOR
Peter Trudgill, Chair of English Linguistics,
University of Fribourg

ADVISORY EDITORS
J. K. Chambers, Professor of Linguistics,
University of Toronto

Ralph Fasold, Professor of Linguistics,
Georgetown University

William Labov, Professor of Linguistics,
University of Pennsylvania

Lesley Milroy, Professor of Linguistics,
University of Michigan, Ann Arbor

Forensic Linguistics

An Introduction to Language in the Justice System

John Gibbons

Blackwell Publishing

© 2003 by John P. Gibbons

350 Main Street, Malden, MA 02148-5018, USA
108 Cowley Road, Oxford OX4 1JF, UK
550 Swanston Street, Carlton South, Melbourne, Victoria 3053, Australia
Kurfürstendamm 57, 10707 Berlin, Germany

First published 2003 by Blackwell Publishing Ltd

Library of Congress Cataloging-in-Publication Data

Gibbons, John, 1946–
    Forensic linguistics : an introduction to language in the justice system /
John Gibbons.
        p. cm. – (Language in society ; 32)
    Includes bibliographical references and index.
    ISBN 0-631-21246-9 (hc. : alk. paper) – ISBN 0-631-21247-7 (pbk. :
alk. paper)
    1. Law – Language. 2. Law – Terminology. 3. Forensic linguistics.
4. English language – Semantics.   I. Title. II. Language in society (Oxford,
England) ; 32.

K213 .G53 2002
340'.14–dc21

                                                                    2002070942

A catalogue record for this title is available from the British Library.

Set in 10.5 on 12.5 pt Ehrhardt
by Ace Filmsetting Ltd, Frome, Somerset
Printed and bound in the United Kingdom
by MPG Books Ltd, Bodmin, Cornwall

For further information on
Blackwell Publishing, visit our website:
http://www.blackwellpublishing.com

Contents

Series Editor's Preface

The term 'applied linguistics' is sometimes used to refer simply to the application of the findings of linguistic research to the teaching and learning of foreign languages. Obviously, however, the findings of research carried out by people working in linguistics can be employed towards the solution of very many more real-world problems than just this. The Blackwell's journal *International Journal of Applied Linguistics*, for instance, recognizes this fact by publishing papers on an enormous range of applications of linguistics, in very many different societal spheres, in addition to foreign and second language teaching and learning. One major development in recent decades in applied linguistics in this more correct and general sense has been in the growth of forensic linguistics. This involves the application of linguistic research – in sociolinguistic areas such as discourse analysis, dialectology, linguistic variation and stylistics, as well as in phonetics, syntax and other core linguistic areas – to different societal issues connected with the law. As John Gibbons says, the law is an overwhelmingly linguistic institution. This book is written by an author who is not only a linguist and sociolinguist but also someone who is actually enormously experienced himself in the practice of forensic linguistics – someone, that is, who has been personally (and very skilfully) involved in applying linguistics, and knowledge about language generally, in society, to matters connected with the law. This book is very much a work in language and society. And John Gibbons' expert knowledge emerges on every page of this wide-ranging, comprehensive and timely volume.

Peter Trudgill
Fribourg
Switzerland

Examples and Conventions

Wherever possible, examples are taken from authentic legal texts and exchanges. In the case of transcriptins of spoken language, if they are not referenced otherwise, the police examples are from transcripts of NSW Police records of interview, and the court examples are from transcripts of trials in NSW courts. Most of these are from cases in which I was involved as an expert witness, and all have concluded. I would like to thank Sandra Hale for facilitating access to some additional courtroom material, and Philip Hall for some additional police material.

The conventions used are the following (and where necesary original transcripts have been modified to maintain consistency). Transcripts of the words used by participants have been left unchanged.

J	Judge or magistrate
C	Counsel
DC	Counsel for the Defence
PC	Counsel for the Prosecution
W	Witness
P	Police Officer
G	Corrective Service Officer (Gaoler)
I	Interpreter

( )	an optional element, or a translation
x^y	x precedes y
x·y	x may precede or follow y (. . . is unordered relative to . . .)
x/y	x or y

select a or b:

$$\rightarrow \left[\begin{array}{l} a \\ \\ b \end{array} \right.$$

select both a and b:

$$\rightarrow \left\{ \begin{array}{l} a \\ \\ b \end{array} \right.$$

Introduction: The Law and Language

Few professions are as concerned with language as is the law.

Tiersma (1993)

Introduction

Law forms the framework within which we manage our daily lives, including our family lives, housing and transport, study and work. Our relationships with partners and children are hemmed about by the law. Buying or renting a home is done by means of a legally binding contract. Indeed nowadays the act of renting or buying does not have a formal existence until the legal document is signed, so the legal process constitutes the act of buying or renting. Similarly, in using transport we are entering a contractual arrangement with the provider of the transport. Work and study are regulated by a large body of legislation. In summary, the law is important to us, because it permeates and to some degree constructs many aspects of modern life.

Law also represents a society's value system, in that it attempts to impose both rights and obligations, proscribing and punishing behaviour that goes against a society's norms. Such values are not universal. While infanticide is forbidden in most countries, in some cultures in times of extreme food shortage infanticide is practised and tolerated.

The law is an overwhelmingly linguistic institution. Laws are coded in language and the concepts that are used to construct the law are accessible only through language. Legal processes such as court cases, police investigations and the management of prisoners take place overwhelmingly through language. In particular the contracts which regulate our relationships with partners, employers and providers are mainly language documents. For instance Tiersma (1999: 1–2) mentions tickets to park or to ride a subway, where the contract entered into is 'printed in tiny letters on the back' and 'all too often it is virtually incomprehensible to those most affected by it'.

In a similar vein, Davies (forthcoming) describes a contract presented by removal men for signature when they come to move the contents of a house and which is unintelligible to non-lawyers. It is, therefore, not only the law that permeates our lives, but the language of the law, and it does so in ways that are not always problem free.

This chapter will set the framework for the rest of the book by outlining the major types of legal systems found around the world: traditional, Shari'ah, Roman Law and Common Law. It will briefly describe some of the main people involved in Common Law, because a book such as this is forced to use terms such as barrister and magistrate, which are not universally understood. It will also establish a model of communication which will form an underlying principle of organization in many of the chapters that follow. The chapter finishes with a brief outline of the rest of the book. The abbreviations and conventions that will be used are described in the preliminary pages.

Legal Systems

The legal systems of modern states generally consist of four major elements – a code of laws, a court system, a police service and prisons. There are often other ancillary elements such as law firms and probationary services. In modern legal systems, the first distinction required is that between criminal law and civil law. *Criminal law*, as the name implies, is concerned with crimes such as embezzlement, robbery, rape and murder. It usually pits a representative of the government – the prosecution – against the accused or their representatives – the defence. Criminal law has been the main focus of much of the work on language and the law, particularly court proceedings.

Civil law is for the most part not concerned with crimes as such, but includes 'private law' – areas such as contract law, the framework of rules within which citizens are expected to operate their personal and business dealings; and torts, offences like negligence and defamation, sometimes providing a machinery for settling disputes. It pits the person or company that initiates the legal action – the plaintiff, against the other party – the defence.

In modern nations there is also a substantial amount of government regulation at both local and national level for individuals and businesses, which operate in a legal fashion. The regulation on food and its preparation is an important everyday example. National regulation often works through tribunals. In Australia, for instance, there is a Refugee Review Tribunal that examines the cases of people wishing to be accepted as refugees.

All these elements operate within the legal system of the particular country, and it is these legal systems which will now be briefly introduced.

Traditional law

Law developed long before writing as part of the regulatory system of most societies. Such oral legal systems are the predecessors of all modern legal systems, and they persist in orate cultures, and in ancillary ways in some literate cultures. They are usually discussed in anthropology under the rubric of 'traditional law'.

There are a number of formal legal systems that operate around the world – for a useful survey see David and Brierly (1985). The most important, in terms of the numbers of persons subject to these systems, are Shari'ah, the Roman system, and Common Law. Often these coexist with traditional forms of law, or with local systems for the mediation of disputes, either combining with them to form a local variant, or running in parallel.

Shari'ah

This is the Islamic system, which developed from the notion that the Holy Qur'an offers not only moral guidance, but also all the fundamental guidance that is needed to run a society. It has been supplemented by substantial Islamic scholarship since the time of Mohammed. In many Islamic societies it is not the only system of law in use – some have versions of Roman or Common Law, sometimes with a parallel system of Islamic courts which handle family law and moral issues such as adultery. In other Islamic states the criminal law is a form of Shari'ah, while contract law has been adapted from Roman Law. Even that most Islamic of societies, Saudi Arabia, has a non-Islamic traffic code. I will not be discussing Shari'ah law in detail, as it is difficult to grasp without a knowledge of Arabic. For more information see Coulson (1971), Schacht (1982) and De Seife (1994).

Roman Law

As the name implies, this is the system of law which was developed by the ancient Romans. It is also known as the Inquisitorial system, Continental Law and (confusingly) as Civil Law. It forms the basis of the legal systems in almost all of continental Europe, including Eastern Europe. As a consequence of European colonialism and influence, it has spread to many other parts of the world, including much of South America, Africa, East and South-East Asia, parts of the Middle East and Scotland. In Japan and China there is a coexistence between more traditional forms of social control (such as the resolution of differences through discussion and compromise, and public confession) and variants of Roman Law. Japan adopted the German system virtually intact. China uses Roman Law for criminal matters, but has recently adapted Common Law for contract law.

Roman Law differs conceptually from the Common Law system with which most English speakers are familiar, in that there is no presumption of innocence. Rather than the prosecution and defence attempting to establish different versions of events, the proceedings are **inquisitorial**, and the judge or judges question witnesses and examine evidence in an attempt to discover the truth of the matter and reach a verdict. In criminal cases where the police bring a suspect for trial, the judge's role is more like that of a prosecutor, and the position of the defence is weaker than in the Common Law system, since judges act as both decision makers and investigators. Much of the evidence is likely to be in written form, and oral elements such as questioning of witnesses or discussion among judges may not be recorded. Courtroom proceedings differ from those of Common Law as a consequence – indeed many witnesses are interviewed by a court official, and their testimony is presented in the form of a statement prepared by that official. Counsel may be allowed to give questions to the court official, but these are used at the official's discretion. It is common for judges to base their decisions primarily on the written evidence and a summary prepared by court officials. However there has been a move in some Roman Law countries towards the use of oral proceedings that are fully recorded, involving the introduction of public prosecutors, and reducing the role of judges to that of decision makers. The reasons given for this have to do with establishing greater transparency and accountability in the legal system. This has happened in Italy, Argentina, Chile and Germany, to my knowledge.

Historically the legal system of the ancient Romans was oral. However the emperor Justinian, fairly late in the history of the Roman Empire, arranged for its recording as the Justinian Code. It was this written form that was inherited by the continental Europeans, especially as Latin remained the educated lingua franca of Europe for almost another thousand years. A crucial influence on the development of Roman Law was its revision in France under Napoleon in the form of the Napoleonic Code. Roman Law has taken distinctive paths in the many countries where it is used.

There are many characteristics of the language of the law that are shared with the Common Law system; for further detail see Watson (1991). A more inquisitorial approach is used in English language legal systems in certain circumstances, mainly Royal (and other) Commissions and in such bodies as the Hong Kong Independent Commission Against Corruption, and in tribunals such as small claims courts. In Australia at the Federal Level there are Senate Inquiries and in the USA there is the Grand Jury.

Common Law

This system is also known as the Adversarial System and (misleadingly) as Anglo-American Law. This system of law will be the main focus of this book since English is its language, although an effort will be made to avoid excessive anglo-centrism by introducing comparison material from other languages and legal systems, mostly in Romance languages because my own language competencies are strongest in those. Where English is the language of the law, Common Law is the system most used, particularly in the USA, most of Canada, Britain (apart from Scotland), Australia and New Zealand, and in many other countries as a consequence of British, Australian, American and New Zealand colonialism and influence. Importantly it is used in India and other parts of South Asia, much of anglophone Africa, parts of the Middle East, and in many countries in the Pacific such as Papua New Guinea, Singapore, Malaysia and Pacific island nations, for example Samoa. Only the briefest introduction to this extraordinarily complex subject can be given here. An approachable short survey can be found in Robinson (1994), and more detail is available, for example, in P. Harris (1984) or Derham et al. (1991).

In criminal law, one distinctive characteristic is the **presumption of innocence** until proven guilty, placing the burden of proving guilt **beyond reasonable doubt** on the prosecution, working on the basis that it is better to risk a guilty person being unpunished than an innocent person being punished. In civil matters however decisions are made on **the balance of the probabilities**, sometimes also referred to as **preponderance of evidence**. Another defining characteristic is the **adversarial** proceedings in the courtroom, which take the form of a ritualized battle between the prosecution and the defence, trying to prove conflicting cases. A third important characteristic is the use of **juries** in higher courts – a panel of fellow citizens empowered to decide in a criminal case whether it has been proved beyond reasonable doubt that the accused person has committed the crime, or in a civil case whether the preponderance of evidence has shown that the defendant is liable. In the USA there is a constitutional right to a jury trial in certain circumstances. All three of these measures are intended to reduce the abuse of power in the courtroom and put people on a similar footing.

A fourth distinctive characteristic of Common Law is that judges' decisions concerning the interpretation and application of a point of law, and the reasoning behind them can be recorded. When another judge rules on the same point of law, these previous judgments (**precedent**) may be raised and taken into account. This is sometimes called 'judge made law'. In Roman Law systems precedent also plays a role, but a much smaller one than in Common Law systems.

In Australia and the USA, there are both state and national legal systems, and most serious criminal law is a state responsibility; England and Wales have a single system. In general, higher courts can serve as courts of appeal for lower courts.

Concerning the ranking of courts, in most English speaking countries there is a Supreme or High Court which serves as the final court of appeal; there are intermediate Appeal Courts; a system of major criminal and civil courts that use jury trials; and local, district or magistrates' courts for lesser matters that do not use juries. There are also tribunals, for example in Australia the Consumer Claims Tribunal, many of which deal with regulations rather than legislation. In higher criminal courts juries decide guilt or innocence, but the judge decides the penalty if the accused is found guilty. It is often assumed that jury trials are the norm in the Common Law system, perhaps as a consequence of television courtroom dramas. In reality, most cases take place in lower courts, where less serious cases are heard. In a local or magistrates' court which deals with criminal matters, a judge or magistrate decides both guilt or innocence and any subsequent penalty. In minor criminal cases, the police case is often accepted without serious challenge, and the judge's main role is passing sentence. Small claims courts for civil law proceedings similarly have only a judge presiding.

The law in Common Law countries is created initially by the legislature – a term which relates to the law-making role of parliaments. However, as noted earlier, a particular characteristic of Common Law is that judges' interpretations of the law are recorded and serve as the basis for future decision making by other judges.

The origins of the Common Law system mainly lie in the oral legal systems introduced by the Germanic invaders of the British Isles following the collapse of Roman rule. Much of the language of the Common Law system consists of Germanic-based Old English. Another early influence on Common Law was the Ecclesiastical Courts, which used the literate lingua franca of Europe, medieval Latin. Many Latin words have become part of the Common Law vocabulary. In 1066 Britain was invaded by the Normans, who spoke their particular variety of French. Norman French was the language of the legal system for many years after it had disappeared from everyday use. Once again there were many contributions to the vocabulary of the language of the law. When the American colonies were founded, the Common Law system was established in the New World. However American independence meant that American society, its language and legal system subsequently evolved separately from their English equivalents, resulting in two varieties of legal English. There are also minor variations in the legal language used in other Common Law based jurisdictions caused by differences in culture, for example in countries such as Kenya, Canada, Malaysia and India. Courtroom proceedings under Common Law still reflect their oral origins, since trials depend predominantly upon oral rather than written evidence, in part because witnesses are subject to oral examination in court. Other Common Law procedures, such as jury instructions, are usually oral. In Roman Law systems the written heritage is reflected in a much greater dependence on written evidence.

The Individuals Involved in Common Law Courts

Judges

Normally, in a jury trial, the judge advises the jury on the law, but the jury decides guilt or liability. The judge can influence the jury's decision in the 'summing up' (this happens to a lesser degree in the USA). The judge then decides the penalty or damages. Most civil disputes, lesser criminal matters, all appeals and all matters before Supreme Courts are heard without a jury, so the judge(s) decide(s) both the verdict and any penalty or damages.

Magistrates

Magistrates decide lesser criminal and civil matters without a jury. In some jurisdictions they are called 'judge' not magistrate, and may act as a panel, not alone.

Solicitors

The term 'solicitors' is used for general legal professionals, who do most legal work other than arguing in the higher courts. They do not exist in all Common Law jurisdictions.

Barristers

Barristers are the lawyers who argue cases in court. They are 'admitted to the bar' on the basis of specialist training and experience. Sometimes they are referred to as 'Counsel'.

The distinction between solicitors and barristers holds in England and Wales, New South Wales and Queensland. In many other jurisdictions there is no distinction between solicitors and barristers – lawyers may play both roles.

Other courtroom personnel

There are a range of other people who play a role in courts such as ushers, stenographers and clerks.

Clarifying terms

Testimony is directed towards both the judge and the jury in jury trials, but only to a judge or magistrate in lower courts. In courts of appeal the testimony can be directed to a panel of judges. To cover all these contingencies I shall use the expression 'judge (and jury)' as a form of shorthand. The term 'judge' will often be used to refer to both judges and magistrates.

Communication

Legal communication includes **non-verbal semiotic systems** (e.g. gesture, illustrations), and a **linguistic** aspect. These non-verbal and linguistic systems are used to negotiate meaning, including propositional meaning, social/interpersonal meaning and functional meaning (the last includes 'speech acts'). This inevitably involves a construal of the social and physical world – the legal view of the world is unique and particular. Such construal is therefore pragmatically related to socio-cultural and physical **context**. As the notion of construal implies, a third aspect of communication is the world view/knowledge of the participants in the communication, including their **social schemas** and **physical world schemas**, in other words their pre-existing shared and differing understandings (before the communicative act) of social and material worlds, particularly the topic of the communication. An important part of this knowledge consists of their command of the above elements of the communication process i.e. their **communicative ability**.

Looking first at the linguistic aspects, an effort will be made here to hold down the level of linguistic technicality. Where linguistic terms are used, they are generally explained. The descriptive framework will I hope be accessible to people with a limited linguistics background, and it attempts to avoid excessive dependence on any particular theory, although the influence of my former colleague Michael Halliday will be evident. Linguistic descriptions often work with four major levels: (1) pronunciation or writing (the 'grapho-phonic' level); (2) words (the lexical level); (3) grammar (the clause and sentence level); (4) discourse (mostly above the level of the sentence). The descriptions given here will roughly follow this model of language. 'Sociolinguistic' and 'register' descriptions reveal the impact of social factors and functions upon the way these four levels of language are used. Legal language is often described as a register (Kurzon 1997), since it has recognizable and distinct patterns in the deployment of the linguistic resources available at all these levels.

The nature of the levels of the linguistic system will be illustrated throughout the rest of this book, but it is worth elaborating slightly at this point. Looking at this chapter as a language sample, it is organized at the

discourse level. There are headings and paragraphs. Ideas develop through the chapter in a way that I trust is coherent. At the **grammatical** level, the previous sentence has a fairly complex structure with a main clause 'Ideas develop through the chapter in a way', and a relative clause 'that I trust is coherent' that modifies 'way'. This is the level of grammatical structure or **syntax**. Notice that there is also a final -s on 'Ideas' – this is the phenomenon of word changes called **morphology**, which is also usually treated as part of the grammar system. Languages such as Italian or Swahili have rich morphological systems.

The sentence also consists of **words**, which contain their own level of meaning and patterns of organization. Common linguistic terms are *lexis*, and the adjective *lexical*. As we shall see in subsequent chapters, the lexical and grammatical levels interact to a substantial degree, leading some linguists to conflate the two levels, referring to **lexico-grammar**. Next we have the marks on paper that you are looking at, which constitute the **grapho-phonic** level. There are letters, gaps between words, punctuation and capitalization, and distinctive layout on the page which allows the reader to differentiate paragraphs, headings, etc.. Each of these writing conventions assists in the communication of the meaning of the text, and removing any one of them would make it more difficult to understand. If you are blind, then you may be feeling dents in the paper which represent letters, or you may be hearing this book presented as speech sounds. Speech and writing are different surface manifestations of (almost) the same underlying language, each mode having its particular potential and problems.

At the **register** level, this book is clearly an academic text – it uses words such as 'phenomenon' and expressions such 'patterns of organization' which are not common in everyday conversation or in the language of young children. Its **field** is mainly linguistic, as can be seen in the use of terms such as 'lexico-grammar' and 'morphological', but legal expressions are also used. The register then is academic, in the field of linguistics. Another register decision that we make every day, is how formal our language needs to be. The technical term for the way language marks formality and social relationships is **tenor**. Register is related to the **context**. When we decide how formal our language needs to be this is done partly on the basis of who we are talking to, and on the situation. These are properties of the **immediate context**. The **wider context**, both material and cultural, is also important in communication, since our communication reflects, reproduces and creates the culture in which it is embedded.

One form of language understanding that will not be familiar to all readers, but which is widely seen as important for legal language, is that of

genre. Martin (1992) defines genre as a 'a staged goal oriented social process'. A genre is an overall plan for a discourse type, which consists of an ordered sequence of steps or stages through which people move when engaged in certain social activities. There is a clear discussion of genre in Swales (1990: chs 1–4), where many of the problems and issues involved in the genre concept are addressed. Reference to this work is strongly recommended to any reader who is not already familiar with the idea of genre. Swales' notion of genre is similar to that used here, particularly the definition of genre in Swales (1990: 58). Bhatia (1993) describes the use of genres in a range of professions, including the law. Psychological theory has addressed the issue of genre in terms of 'schemas' and 'scripts'. There is extensive exemplification of the genre notion in chapter 4.

Hasan (Halliday and Hasan 1985: 52–65) views any particular text or social activity as an instance of a discourse type or genre. An important concept from Hasan is that of 'structure potential'. In essence this means that some elements of a genre are obligatory, some are optional, and some recur and are therefore iterative. So a particular text is an individual manifestation/instantiation of a genre type, and will reveal some (but usually not all) aspects of the potential structure of that genre. This theme is also

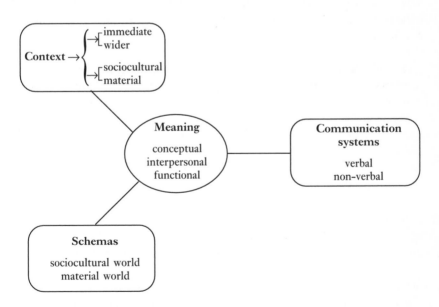

Figure I.1   Simplified model of communication

further developed in chapter 4.

These language elements constitute the verbal part of a wider process of communication. The factors which contribute to communication fall into three categories: verbal and non-verbal **communication systems**; the knowledge (or **schemas**) of both the material and the socio-cultural worlds, and the extent to which these are shared by the participants; and **context**, including the participants. These factors all contribute to the sharing of meaning between the participants. Meaning can be conceptual (to do with ideas), interpersonal (the ongoing negotiation of social relationships among the participants) or functional (getting things done). Many sentences and texts communicate all three types of meaning. This simplified model of communication is presented in figure 1.1 (the conventions used are given on p. vii). This model, which underpins the structure of many of the chapters, will be exemplified and expanded in the balance of the book.

The Subject Matter of this Book

The term *'Forensic Linguistics'* can be used narrowly to refer only to the issue of language evidence. However it is becoming accepted as a cover term for language and the law issues – the *AILA Scientific Commission on Forensic Linguistics* defines the field as follows:

> The primary objective of the *AILA Scientific Commission on Forensic Linguistics* is to support the study of the link between language and the law in all its forms. As part of this broad agenda, the Commission seeks to support the following:
>
> 1. The study of the language of the law, including the language of legal documents and the language of the courts, the police and prisons.
> 2. The study, the provision and the improvement of professional legal interpreting and translation services.
> 3. The alleviation of disadvantage produced by language in legal processes.
> 4. The provision of forensic linguistic evidence that is based on the best available linguistic expertise.
> 5. The provision of linguistic expertise in issues of legal drafting and interpretation, including plain language drafting.

The field's main journal, *Forensic Linguistics*, has papers on a wide range of language and law topics, including most of the above. This book can therefore be seen as a book on forensic linguistics broadly drawn.

The subtitle of this book, '*Language in the Justice System,*' emphasizes that coverage is not only of legislation and the courts, but also of the police and prisons. The language of legislation, regulations and of the courts is far better documented and described than the language of the police and prisons, but where possible reference is made to the language of all these major constituents of the justice system.

This book is an introduction to a range of language and law issues. Each chapter of the book could be, and sometimes has been, the subject of entire books. Therefore the coverage cannot meet the needs of specialist readers, or provide a detailed account of every aspect of the topics included or reference to every study. Instead the objective here is to provide a clear large scale mapping, forming a conceptual framework for further reading and research. It attempts to open a door on the fascinating and important relationship between language and the law in its many aspects, leaving it to readers to pursue further those elements that are of particular interest to them.

The general approach taken here is one of explanation rather than simple description – an attempt will be made to show the **reasons** for the sometimes tortured relationship between language and the law – the 'why' as well as the 'what'. The description is also 'applied linguistic' and not just linguistic, because it addresses problems (including social justice issues) that arise from the language–law interface, and canvasses possible means of addressing them. The book is not cautious: issues are confronted, and many of them, given the nature of crime and punishment, are not pleasant. The reader's indulgence is requested for disturbing material.

Since language issues in the law interact in complex ways, any division into chapters is to some degree arbitrary. Chapters 1 to 4 are broadly descriptive. Chapter 1 looks at the relationship between the spoken and written language of the law, recognizing that although legal systems have oral roots, the adoption of literacy has led to changes in the language of the law. Chapter 2 examines the language of legislation and other legal documents, and the manner in which the attempt to arrive at a precise expression of meaning has led to a specialist technical legal language. Chapter 3 looks at legal interaction, and inevitably, given the role of the law in society, how power is manifested in the language of the law. Chapter 4 deals with the way that events that are the object of legal investigation (crimes, etc.) are reconstructed linguistically in legal contexts.

The second half of the book is more socially applied. Chapter 5 discusses the difficulty of understanding legal language, and what can be done about it. Chapter 6 examines linguistic sources of disadvantage before the law, particularly for ethnic minorities, children and abused women, and chapter 7 discusses some of the major ways of addressing such disadvantage, including the use of interpreters and translators. Chapter 8 looks at legislation on language, including language crimes – linguistic acts that are illegal, such as swearing, false promises and threats. Chapter 9 looks at linguistic evidence in legal contexts. Underlying each of these chapters is the model of language and communication described in this Introduction.

1

Literacy and the Law

> The cognitive structures of the law have come to reflect written forms of consciousness.
>
> Jackson (1994)

Introduction

The language of the law can be broadly divided into two major areas – the codified and mostly written language of legislation and other legal documents such as contracts, which is largely monologic; and the more spoken, interactive and dynamic language of legal processes, particularly the language of the courtroom, police investigations, prisons and consultations among lawyers and between lawyers and their clients. I shall deal first with the codified written language of the law.

Tiersma (1999: 139–41) provides a helpful categorization of legal written texts, dividing them into three types. He proposes (Tiersma 1999: 139) that **operative documents** 'create or modify legal relations', in other words they establish the legal framework itself. This category includes legislation (acts, orders and statutes), pleadings and petitions, judgments, and private documents such as contracts and wills. A second class is **expository documents**, which explain the law, usually objectively. These might include a letter to a client or an office memorandum, and perhaps the huge volume of writing and educational material about the law. His third category is **persuasive documents**, particularly submissions designed to convince a court. Tiersma (1999: 141) notes that the latter two categories of legal writing 'tend not to be particularly formulaic or legalistic in language, although they do use fairly formal standard English'. Since we are interested in what is distinctive about the language of the law, I will concentrate mostly on operative documents here.

This chapter begins with an introduction to the oral legal systems that are the origin of all legal systems. It then tracks the changes produced in the language of the law by the move into literate systems, particularly the consequences of increased planning, decontextualization and standardization. This is illustrated by examining the differences between a modern will and an Anglo-Saxon will that stands at the point of transition from spoken to written wills. The chapter then outlines the issues involved in converting speech to writing in modern legal systems, for instance the production of transcripts, either as evidence or as court records. It ends with some speculation about turning full circle to a future where audio and video recording of speech opens up the possibility of a return to more orate legal procedures.

Oral Legal Systems

Current legal systems have their origin in societies that existed before the development of literacy. Almost all current orate societies (i.e. those in which literacy is not part of the cultural tradition) seem to have highly developed systems for handling disputes or actions that violate community norms. Such oral legal systems have been studied in considerable depth by legal anthropologists. The legal systems that operate on an oral basis are often referred to as *Customary Law*. There is a wide literature on the coexistence of Customary Law and Common Law systems.

In most orate cultures, there are specific occasions or events when Customary Law is dispensed. It is normal for those involved to have specific speech roles, roughly corresponding to litigants, mediators, arguers for a particular view and sometimes an equivalent to judge (and jury). It is not uncommon for there to be staged procedures through which Customary Law proceeding take place (legal genres). It is common for there to be a set of memorized and quoted precepts or principles by which cases are argued. The use of precedent is also not uncommon in this type of argumentation. All these are the likely antecedents of the institutionalized legal processes found in literate societies.

Forensic anthropologists have traditionally argued that there are differences between Customary Law (often discussed in terms such as 'social control') and institutionalized law. They particularly note the following characteristics : absolute liability; sorcery; magico-religious beliefs; accident. Absolute liability is the notion that people have full responsibility for other persons present – so for instance if a hunter dies during a hunting trip, the fellow hunters must take responsibility for the death. This ties in to the notion of accident. It is said that in Customary Law, the intentions of a person are irrelevant, so if one kills a person by accident it is treated in the same way as a deliberate murder (Common Law distinguishes manslaughter from murder, that is the accidentality concept is legally recognized and linguistically codified). The other area of postulated difference is in the area of sorcery and magico-religious belief. Sorcery, such as placing a curse upon a person or their possessions, is a common crime in Customary Law societies. This ties in with a range of magico-religious beliefs such as taboos, which are often also punishable. Goldman (1993, 1994) makes a very strong linguistic case for rejecting these distinctions. He documents the case of a Huli traditional trial where a wide range of arguments based upon accident and absence of liability are utilized. Since accident is part of intention, and intention is encoded in modality, it is possible to locate and reveal linguistic evidence for the use of accident as mitigation. Goldman (1994: 78) gives an example of an accidentality adverb (see figure 1.1) and goes on to discuss the use of ergative case marking to mark intention (see figure 1.2).

Goldman (1993) constructs very careful linguistic arguments based on an analysis of the legal discourse to show that the concept of accidentality is used in this Customary Law setting. There is a case for saying that Western anthropologists have been sufficiently ethno-centric to mistake

---

Evidence of a Huli concept of accident first emerged in the case of *Wanili* vs. *Ogoli* (Goldman 1986a: D.2). The dispute concerned an incident in which Wanili's teenage son Baro was drowned while out with another male friend. Wanili recounted her reactions in the following terms

[D.2. lines 140, 203]
Ibu   **tiga tiga**   *iba*   *piyagoni*   *lalu*   *piru*
he straight straight (redup) water go-3ps-PST say-SUB2 go-lsg-PST
I said 'He (Baro) **straight** drowned' and I went off

lya ilame   *iya kirali*   *honowinidago* **mememe**   *iba*   *piyadago*
we both + ERG we two people gave birth-RP **accidentally** water go-3ps-PST
We bore him together and he **accidentally** drowned

Of particular note is the counterbalance betwen the two adverbs *tiga tiga* (straight) and *mememe* (accidentally).

Figure 1.1   Extract from Huli traditional trial, illustrating an accidentality adverb
Source: Goldman 1994:78

[16] NP(A)   NP(O)
      ERG   ABS
      Kenobi one biagome   *inaga ainya*
      Kenobi wife that + ERG   1 + GEN mother + ABS
      V(tr)
      delara
      burn + CAUS-3ps-PRES

In [16] the ergatively marked NP serves to emphasise the intential actor behind some action, the 'who' of a planned transaction. The causative dimension of a reported event is thereby in focus and in reference to Gegai's death is thus highly blame implicative.

Figure 1.2   The use of ergative case marking to mark intention
Source: Goldman 1994:88

the absence of overt codification for the absence of a concept. He also argues that sorcery closely parallels the Common Law notion of intentional infliction of emotional distress, and that magico-religious beliefs are found in both oral and literate systems – note for example the offence of blasphemy in European and Shari'ah legal systems.

What orate societies lack to a significant degree is a legal register. Legal disputation is handled mostly in everyday language. It is the development of writing which permits codification of legal systems.

The Move into Literacy

The development of literacy has an impact partly through its ability to standardize. Once legal actions are committed to paper, they can be consulted and relevant elements reproduced. This leads, over time, to standard ways of performing legal functions, such as drawing up a will. It can also lead to a standardization of the steps through which a legal function must pass for its completion – in other words to the development of the standard legal **genres** (Maley 1994) discussed in chapter 4. Literacy also helps to create a legal register, in that it encourages the development, recording and long-term use and standardization of specialist legal terms (see the next chapter).

The process of codification involved the language of the law moving from largely interactive oral dispute resolution, which operated with language drawn mostly from everyday speech, to a specialized technical style of language, using the full range of resources offered by writing. It is necessary to make a brief digression at this point into the manner in which the development of the written mode influences language. Written texts, because of their composing processes and durability, tend to be better planned and less dependent on context (see for example Chafe 1985; Chafe and Tannen 1987). These distinctions between the spoken and written language – context embedding and planning – are not absolute however. A note to oneself, despite being written, can be unplanned and spontaneous, and deeply context embedded and therefore highly inexplicit, if the writer assumes that s/he will remember the context of writing. On the other hand, we have free standing and well planned oral literature. Linguists, particularly Halliday (1985) have resolved this issue by noting that there is a continuum, running from least planned and highly contextualized to most planned and context reduced. Halliday refers to this as the 'mode continuum'.

Consequences of planning

Halliday (1985) notes that one important linguistic outcome when constructing long, connected texts is that, as an understanding or issue grows steadily through a text, that growing understanding may be summarized in a noun phrase, as the starting point for the next development of the ideas.

This cumulation within the noun phrase is an important aspect of written language. Halliday shows that when ideas are first introduced they generally appear in a simple 'congruent' form – things appear as nouns, processes as verbs, attributes as adjectives, logical connections as conjunctions like 'therefore', and so on. It could be said that parts of speech have an 'unmarked' semantics. However this unmarked relationship between form and semantics can be partly lost in the need to construct connected discourse by accumulating concepts. This skewed relationship Halliday calls 'grammatical metaphor'.

The diagram from Gibbons (1999) shown in figure 1.3 gives an illustration of how in English the change to written register leads to a skewing of the relationship between the underlying semantic concepts, in this case extending beyond nominalizations. It presents two sentences which have almost the same meaning, but the first is in a simple conversational style,

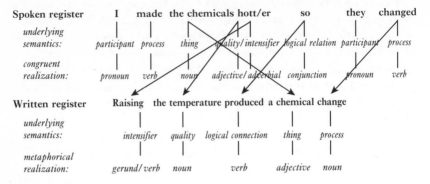

Figure 1.3   An example of grammatical metaphor in English

while the second is in a more written technical style. So in the first spoken sentence 'things' *chemicals* are realized congruently as a noun, but metaphorically in the written form as an adjective; the 'logical connection' appears congruently as a conjunction *so* in the first sentence, but metaphorically as a verb *produced* in the second, and a 'process' *change* appears as a verb in the first sentence, but metaphorically as a noun in the second. The notion of grammatical metaphor includes, but is much more powerful than 'nominalization', and the concept will be used repeatedly in this book.

In English, grammatical metaphor permits the dense packaging of information, particularly in the noun phrase. It can also entail some syntactic simplification – in the example in figure 1.3 a complex subordinating structure becomes a simple sentence. A related phenomenon in written texts is increased lexical density – there are more content words and less structure words. Other effects of planning include increased explicitness, more passives and longer sentences.

Increased explicitness in the logical structure
As a consequence of planning, and because links are made to other parts of the text rather than the outside world, the logical structure or argument is made more explicit, less of 'and' but more of 'therefore', less of 'next' but more of 'first, second, third' (see Biber 1988).

More passives
These enable us to reorganize the information flow in a text, and often works hand in hand with grammatical metaphor. One role of passives is to facilitate the placing of old information at the beginning of the sentence,

even if the old information is the logical recipient of the verb's action. An example is 'When the prisoner arrived at Court, he was jeered by a hostile crowd', where in the second half, the prisoner is old information, so he can be placed first by means of a passive, and the remainder of the clause adds information. The active version of this sentence is clumsier 'When the prisoner arrived at Court, a hostile crowd jeered him'. The unusual frequency of the use of passive constructions in legal language can be seen in the fact that the very rare construction *it is/was/has been said by . . .* for example 'it was said by Lord Justice-General Robertson' is found only seventeen times in the 100 million word British National Corpus, and of these, seven occurrences (41.2 per cent) were in legal contexts, although legal contexts constituted a very small proportion of the corpus.

Longer sentences
Another effect, which will be discussed in the next chapter, is that sentences in operative documents become very long. Indeed many operative documents cannot be read aloud with any likelihood of coherent pronunciation or adequate comprehension. They are simply too long and complex to be absorbed in speech, without the opportunities for referring to previous text that written language provides.

Consequences of decontextualization

Another major difference between face to face speech and written texts is that speech can refer to the surrounding context shared between the speakers, while written texts tend to refer to things within the text itself, or to other texts. The issue is the distance (in space time and abstraction) between the context referred to and the context of speaking, reading or writing, and also between speaker/writer and hearer/reader. As table 1.1 shows, there is a continuum between most context dependent language and abstract and decontextualized language.

The detachment from context that is a consequence of writing can lead to high levels of **autonomy** in legal texts. This is particularly important for the drafting and interpretation of legislation. A major target of legal drafters is to ensure that courts can interpret legislation on the basis of the wording of the legislation itself, without reference to the legislature or the debates that surrounded the creation of the legislation, or to any other source for judgment. This demands that the wording of legislation has a single clear meaning, and this meaning forms the basis for the interpreta-

Table 1.1 The linguistic consequences of contextualization

Contextualization	Language used	Language factors
Immediate/ context dependent In a courtroom, during examination, judge to counsel, an objection has just been raised	'sustained'	Inexplicit: who, what is sustained, the context (time, place), what is happening (short for the 'objection is sustained' – note tense)
Shared knowledge/ knowledge dependent In counsel's chambers, to another lawyer	'Judge May sustained my objection to a really coercive question today, thank heavens'	Tense changes to past as a consequence of distance in time. Some elements inserted, but others depend on knowledge Inexplicit: who is 'me' in 'my'; the context (place) and when 'today' is
No shared knowledge/ context independent Report	*31 October 2000 Local Court Number 4* Counsel Hu's objection to a coercive question from Counsel Lipovsky during cross-examination was sustained	Highly explicit Note passive and past tense
Generalized/abstracted Legal text book	Coercive questioning during cross-examination may be subject to successful challenge	Note grammatical metaphor, particularly 'questioning' 'successful' 'challenge' (compare language above) Tense changes to 'timeless present'

tion and imposition of the law. Among lawyers this is known as the **plain meaning rule**, and this notion is central to the school of legal thinking known as **textualism**. To linguists this position is open to question, since they usually do not conceive language as a simple and unambiguous means of communication. I will return to this issue in the next chapter.

The other aspect of decontextualization has to do with the different resources provided by speech and writing. In face to face speech much of the speaker's attitude to what s/he is saying is communicated by intonation, voice quality, gesture and facial expression. Emphasis and information flow is communicated to a large degree by stress, pausing and pace. Decontextualized writing has few resources to represent these non-verbal features, so in writing we tend instead to use grammar and vocabulary choices to represent them. Another noticeable characteristic of written language is that it tends to be less personal and less emotional in tone (because it is not 'face-to-face'); notice in the text above the loss of 'really' and the emotionally neutral and impersonal tone, particularly in the abstract text.

Effects of standardization

The spoken word can survive only in memory, but memory works on the basis of meaning not wording. The spoken word is usually only retained unchanged in ritualized circumstances (for instance religious rituals may retain earlier versions of the language, as in the survival of Sanskrit). Writing has the opposite effect, because written texts retain their form and wording – at a later date it is their meaning that may become open to doubt. Once something is written down, its form becomes accessible afterwards. This means that a particular wording can be reproduced exactly upon demand, in particular writing facilitates the retention of successful wordings.

In law the standardizing effect of literacy is magnified. If a form of words is admitted as adequately meeting a particular legal objective, for instance a particular wording is accepted in court as constituting a binding promise, this is a good reason to re-use the wording for subsequent promises, in fact it serves as a form of precedent. Once legal actions are committed to paper, they can be consulted, and relevant elements reproduced. In the law this has led to the development of Form Books, which provide tried and tested forms of words, which lawyers can piece together to construct operative documents. It is not in the interests of lawyers to produce new wordings, because this may expose them to challenge – according to Mellinkoff (1963: 295), 'That is the fear that freezes lawyers and their language. It is precise now. We are safe with it now. Leave us alone. Don't change. Here we stay till death or disbarment.' This can also lead in time to standard ways of constructing whole legal operative documents, such as drawing up a will. It can also lead to standardization of the steps through which a legal function must pass for its completion – in other words to the development of standard legal **genres** (see Maley 1994 and chapter 4). **Consistency** and **conservatism** are therefore characteristic features of the written language of the law, and as we have seen there are good reasons for this. One less welcome consequence can be the persistence of archaic language: this may take the form of languages that were used previously in the legal system (Latin in most European legal systems, as well as Norman French in the Common Law), or archaic elements of the current language (see the next chapter for examples).

An illustration

The consequences of the move into literacy will be exemplified by two wills. The first is the will of Wulfsige (1022–43), written at the time of the transition to literacy in Anglo-Saxon England, that is the time when wills were first being written down rather than stated orally (see figure 1.4). The analysis here is based on that of Danet and Bogoch (1994). The second will is my own (with one provision and some names removed), providing a modern comparison document (it was drawn up in the 1990s) which exemplifies the changes that long-term literacy has produced (see figure 1.5). The initial impression given by the two documents is the way the English of the law has developed over the last millennium. The elegantly simple, direct, but somewhat inexplicit language of Wulfsige's will has been replaced by complexity, wordiness, archaisms and extreme explicitness.

Turning to the detail of the two wills, the will of Wulfsige varies in its use of person. In the first paragraph Wulfsige is referred to in the third person 'his possessions' 'his soul', and so is his wife Wulfwyn 'her life' 'her death'. However at the end of the first paragraph we see a change to first person 'us both', and thereafter Wulfsige refers to himself consistently using the first person 'I' and 'my'. The modern will by contrast is **consistent**, using only the first person. What we see in Wulfsige's will in the use of the third person is the notion that the oral will was the true will, and this document is merely a report of that oral act of bequeathing. Danet and

> *[H]er switelep on pise write wam Wlsi an his aihte. þat is erst fr his soule þat ond at Wiken into seynt Eadmundes biri þa tweye deles 7 Alfric Biscop þe þridde del. buten ane gride and.XII. swine mesten þat schal habben Wlwine hire day, and after hire day into seynt Eadmundes biri 7 alle þo men fre for vunker bother soule. And ic an mine kynelouerd .II. hors. and Helm and brinie. 7 an Swerd and a goidwrecken spere. and ic an mine lauedy haif marc goldes. an mine Nifte ann ore wichte goldes. And habbe Stanhand alle þinge þe ic him bicueden habbe. and mine brother bern here owen lond. 7.ll. hors mid sadelgarun. and .I. brinie and on hakele. And se þe mine cuide awende god aimithin awende his asyne from him on domesday buten he it her þe rathere bete.*

Here is this document it is made known to whom Wulfsige grants his possessions. First, for his soul, two-thirds of the estate at *Wick* to Bury St Edmunds and the third part to Bishop Ælfic, except one yardland and mast for twelve swine which Wulfwyn shall have for life, and after her death [it shall go] to Bury St Edmunds; and all the men are to be free for the sake of the souls of us both.

And I grant to my royal lord two horses and a helmet and a coat of mail, and a sword and a spear inlaid with gold. And I grant to my lady half a mark of gold, and to my niece an ore's weight in gold. And Stanhand is to have everything which I have bequeathed to him, and my brother's children their own land, and two horses with harness, and one coat of mail and one cloak.

And he who alters my will, may Almighty God turn away his face from him on the Day of Judgment unless in this life he will quickly make amends for it.

Figure 1.4 An Anglo-Saxon will

Bogoch (1994) provide other examples of this. Wulfsige's will also begins 'Here in this document' – in other words there is a reference to the act of writing. This self-consciousness about writing has long since disappeared. Another carry over from oral wills is the curse with which Wulfsige's will ends – indicating the comparative ease with which an oral will can be misrepresented, in comparison with the stability of the written word (discussed earlier).

The act of willing itself is 'Wulfsige grants his possessions', using everyday language and not a standardized formula. In the modern will the act of willing is referred to as 'the last will and testament' 'wills and testamentary dispositions' and 'give, devise and bequeath'. These expressions will be familiar to most English speakers as the standard wording of a will. They provide a clear example of the **standardization** and **conservatism** of the

THIS IS THE LAST WILL AND TESTAMENT of me JOHN
PETER GIBBONS of _____ in the State of New South
Wales, Lecturer.
1.   I HEREBY REVOKE all former Wills and Testimentary Dispositions
heretofore made by me AND DECLARE this to be my last Will and
Testament.
2.   I GIVE DEVISE AND BEQUEATH the whole of my property of
whatsoever nature and wheresoever situate and over which I have any
power of appointment and not otherwise disposed of in the due
administration of my estate to my dear wife _____ for her sole
use and benefit absolutely AND I APPOINT her Executrix and Trustee
of this my Will.
3.   IN THE EVENT that my said wife predeceases me or dies within
one (1) month of my death then I DECLARE that the following
provisions shall take effect:
. . .
4.   I DECLARE that if any of my beneficiaries shall die leaving a child
or children him her or them surviving then such child or children shall
upon attaining the age of twenty-one (21) years take the share his her or
their parent would have taken had such parent survived me and if more
than one of such children in equal shares.

IN WITNESS WHEREOF I have hereunto set my hand to this my Will
this fifth day of July One thousand nine hundred and ninety four.

SIGNED by the Testator as and
for his last Will and Testament
in the presence of us both
present at the same time and
we at his request in his
presence and in the presence of
each other have hereunto
subscribed our names as witnesses:

Figure 1.5   A modern will (abridged)

modern language of the law. Furthermore, as Tiersma (1999) notes, every
written will is a last will, and the word 'testament' is also redundant; so are
two of the verbs in 'give devise and bequeath' (see 'doublets and triplets' in
the next chapter).

Concerning **contextualization**, Wulfsige's will depends to a large degree on assumed knowledge of the context of writing. The reader is not told who Wulfwyn is, and it is not clear whether she is the 'my lady' referred to later in the text. The modern will is totally explicit on this issue. There is a similar assumption with 'my niece' and 'my brother's children'. It is also likely that the various items left to Wulfsige's 'royal lord' were in fact specific items, not any sword, or spear inlaid with gold. Perhaps most dependent on shared knowledge is 'Stanhard is to have everything I have bequeathed to him'. The modern will is explicitly dated, while Wulfsige's and many other Anglo-Saxon wills are not. There is little grammatical metaphor in Wulfsige's will, and where it does exist the Anglo-Saxon nouns 'ainte' (possessions), 'write' (document), and 'cuiDe' (statement or will), are all strongly linked with their source verbs 'own', 'write' and 'say' (quoth) respectively. The modern will by contrast is full of grammatical metaphor: 'wills', 'testamentary', 'dispositions', 'testament', 'property', 'appointment', 'due', 'administration', 'use', 'benefit', 'executrix', 'trustee', 'beneficiary', etc. Indeed the majority of the content words are grammatically metaphorical.

Concerning **planning**, Wulfisge's will is comparatively well organized for an Anglo-Saxon will. The first part contains the 'major' provisions of the will, while the second part contains the minor legacies. Note, however, that this is not overtly signalled, making the organization of the text initially hard to grasp. By contrast the planning of the modern will is explicitly marked. First we have the numbering of the paragraphs. This is a common device in many modern legal documents. Perhaps more interesting is that the speech acts (see chapter 2) performed by each of the sections of the will are underlined and capitalized, making fully explicit the role played by each part of the document.

Legal Transcription – the Interaction of Written and Spoken Language

The move into writing is not just an historical phenomenon in the law. It is also a current reality, since most record keeping in legal settings is done in writing, while most proceedings in the Common Law system are spoken, as are proceedings in an increasing number of Roman Law countries, including Italy, Argentina, Chile and Germany. In both police stations and courtrooms, it is common for spoken language to be transcribed, and hence transformed into written language.

Legal transcription or reporting is an arena in which the issue of the differences between spoken and written language is important. It involves mainly typed police records of interview, and court records. A transcript involves the conversion of spoken language into written language. The fundamental problem is that speech and writing are different media, with different properties. As we noted previously, writing is not in general a good record of speech, since it does not conventionally include many of the features of speech, and its editing does not appear in the final version, unlike speech (see Halliday 1985, on this issue). Furthermore it is virtually impossible to accurately record in a single visual representation all the sound detail of speech, including pitch/intonation, breathiness, voice quality, accent, pausing and pace. If this were done, the transcript would in any case be virtually unreadable. Rather it is necessary to select and record those features of the oral medium which are needed to meet the particular purposes of the transcript. Sometimes an approximate representation, such as those typically found in courtroom and police transcripts, can be adequate. On other occasions the information that is lost is critical.

One possibility is to use wavelength spectrograms of speech sounds. These can be useful for speaker identification, but are useless for testimony concerning what was said, since no one other than an expert can read them, and even an expert acoustic phonetician can have problems in deciding what was said on the basis of a spectrogram. Another alternative is to do a phonetic transcription, which is capable of catching much of the pronunciation detail, although not the finer detail of pace, pitch movement and stress. Figure 6.1 shows a section of an interview with an Australian who migrated from Lebanon in adulthood. The transcription here is not as fine as is possible, but for a linguist it captures not only the words spoken, but many of the accent features of the speaker. The pauses are roughly timed in seconds.

ɔjʌs(1.5)ɷ(.3)dəmaᵊn(.3) wɔsdiswɔsdis(.5)hisɛd(.2)dʌənwaridʌ
ənwaridʌənwari(.5)jənʌaə(.2)ɔisɛi(.2)kitstəumʌtʃʌpsɛt

Figure 1.6   Version 1: phonetic transcription

The problem with this transcription is that it uses symbols that are not well-known to non-linguists, and it is therefore uninformative to lawyers and lay persons, although a form of it is used in the *Oxford English Dictionary*. I have used one or two such symbols in court, where the fine detail of a pronunciation feature was necessary as part of the evidence, carefully glossing them. However, as a means of transcribing whole interviews, it is not truly viable. The purpose to which one would put such a form of transcription is limited to details of pronunciation.

Another alternative is to use the type of phonemic transcription that is used in some dictionaries (see figure 1.7). This captures at least some of the pronunciation features lost in conventional spelling, where many of the sounds of English are not adequately represented (for instance there are more than twice as many vowel sounds as there are letters to represent them). In this case I have used the convention of using two full stops (..) for a short pause, and three (...) for a longer pause. I have also inserted gaps between words, even though these are not found in the pronunciation (although they are sometimes signalled in some of the finer detail of the pronunciation). All these render the passage capable of being pronounced with some chance of accuracy by a lay reader.

---

oi ära ... ûr ,, də man .. wos dis wos dis wos dis .. hi sed .. dōn wuri
dōn wuri dōn wuri .. yə nō .. oi sā kits tōō much upset

Figure 1.7 Version 2: *Chambers English Dictionary* transcription

This type of transcription loses the finer detail of the accent, but does show where one speech sound is substituted for another, so it could be used where there is some ambiguity in pronunciation that makes it uncertain what was actually said. It communicates more effectively to a non-linguist audience than a phonetic transcription, but it lacks the finer detail. If the issue is wording not pronunciation, then regular spelling would be more accessible. This type of transcription could be used when a broad indication of pronunciation is required.

Another form of transcription uses regular spelling, and punctuation, but retains the hesitation phenomena and repetition of the original wording (figure 1.8).

I ask, er, the man, what's this, what's this, what's this. He said, don't worry, don't worry, don't worry, you know. I say kids too much upset.

Figure 1.8 Version 3: accurate wording, regular spelling

Such a transcript is difficult to obtain, and requires some kind of audio recording that can be listened to repeatedly, otherwise much of the detail of the wording is 'edited out' subconsciously. If one is interested in a full and fairly accurate record of the wording, but not the pronunciation, of what was said, this type of transcript will serve the purpose. Transcripts of courtroom interaction or police interviews rarely target this level of detailed accuracy, and when a stenographer is producing a transcript during the language event itself, subconscious editing is likely to remove much of this detail, particularly if the stenographer is not trained. Many police records are produced during police interviews by police officers with little or no stenographic training – in my experience literally by an officer typing slowly with two fingers.

Another type of transcript that can be produced removes hesitation and repetition to arrive at a more readable (because it is more written) version (figure 1.9). Finally it is possible to produce a version in standard written language (figure 1.10).

I ask the man, "What's this." He said "Don't worry." I say "Kids too much upset."

Figure 1.9 Version 4: More written

I asked the man "What's this?" He said "Don't worry." I said "The kids will be very upset."

Figure 1.10 Version 5: Standard written

I have explored only a few of the full range of possible forms of transcription here. Another strong candidate is the type of transcription used in conversation analysis (Gardner 1994; Hutchby and Wooffitt 1998; Jefferson 1984), which provides clear transcription conventions for many meaningful elements of spoken language.

Through this range of types of transcription one can observe a tension between two incompatible and competing criteria for transcription. The first is its ability to communicate by being a 'good' written text – in a word 'readability' is a critical factor. If a transcript cannot be understood as readily as the oral language that it represents, then it is failing in its primary task of communicating what was communicated in the primary context. Furthermore less readable transcripts make greater demands upon readers, which many in the legal profession would regard as an unwarranted extra demand upon their time and energy.

The second and competing criterion is that legal transcripts purport to be 'verbatim', that is they are intended to be an exact and detailed record of the language used: in a word its 'accuracy' is a critical factor. In Versions 1–5 of the transcript (figures 1.6–1.10) there is a move from accuracy to readability. The impossibility of simultaneously meeting these criteria in a single version is demonstrated in the common practice among linguists of presenting spoken language in a detailed and accurate transcript on one line, whilst a more written and far more readable gloss is presented beneath. Speech is thus presented in two forms to meet the two criteria. This is not normally done in legal transcription.

In reality most of the transcripts produced in courtroom and police contexts, although they purport to be 'verbatim', are heavily weighted towards readability. The process of transforming speech into a readable written form can involve radical change. As Walker (1990: 204) remarks 'the written record of trials continues to be something more and something less than what happened'. In police records of longer interviews, it is common for transcripts to be far shorter than the time given to the interview. For example, in one case in which I was involved the transcript of an interview purported to be a record of 30 minutes of interview, but took less than 5 minutes to read aloud slowly. In another case two hours of interview could be read aloud slowly in less than 20 minutes (these facts when stated in court undermined faith in the fidelity of the transcripts). In many cases at least 70 per cent of the interview seems to have disappeared.

The changes that are made can be explained by reference to the factors mentioned previously: standardization, decontextualization, planning/editing and impersonal tone. Looking first at **editing**, the guidelines of the National Shorthand Reporters Association (NSRA 1983: 26) state explicitly 'To edit or not to edit is not the question; every reporter does it in greater or less degree'. Spoken language typically contains a range of features not found in written language, such as false starts, hesitations, pausal phenomena ('uhms' and 'ers', and also expressions such as 'you know'), repetition, and overlapping or simultaneous speech by two speakers (see 'Version 3' in figure 1.8 above for examples of some of these). False starts, which are common in both speech and writing, are generally edited out in written text. **Hesitations**, which occur in the process of both speech and writing, are generally not recorded in writing, because written communication normally does not take place in real time. Gibbons (1995) gives examples which compare a police record of an interview with a careful transcript of the same information from the same witness: the very frequent hesitations found in the careful transcript are almost absent in the police record. **Repetition** is generally frowned upon in writing, but in speech is an important form of emphasis. In Gibbons (1995) repetition, which is common in the careful transcript, is not found in the police record of interview. **Overlapping** is not usually possible in the written mode, since whole texts are exchanged. (However, recent developments in electronic communication such as chatrooms are leading to written communication in real time, which is breaking down such differences). In legal transcription the editing conventions of writing and readability generally predominate. Walker (1990: 223) quotes US Federal guidelines for reporters which state 'In the interests of readability, however, false starts, stutters, uhms and ahs, and other verbal tics are not normally included in transcripts' (Greenwood et al. 1983: 143). All of this reduces the amount of language that is transcribed, and deletes the information contained in pausing and in other 'verbal tics'.

In the area of **standardization**, little effort is generally made to represent dialectal or sociolectal pronunciation features. Walker (1990: 219) writes 'there is a professionwide reluctance to put into a transcript any of the features of speech that might mark a person's origins'. This of course reduces the information about the speaker available in the oral form. Weak and abbreviated forms which occur in the speech of all native speakers (Brown 1990) are generally restored to full forms, so 'gonna' becomes 'going to', and 'joo' becomes 'do you', etc. When judges or lawyers make 'grammatical errors', recorders generally correct them, while for witnesses they may not do so. The Federal guideline for reporters notes that they are expected to correct the 'ungrammatical and carelessly phrased remarks' of lawyers and judges, while 'the testimony of ignorant or illiterate witnesses should be literally rendered'. Walker (1990) argues that this can affect the impressions of witnesses gained from written transcripts, and hence the outcome of appeals. In police transcripts it is similarly noticeable that the transcription of police officers' language is more standardized than that of interviewees.

Some of this standardization is unintentional. This is particularly true when native speakers transcribe the language of second language speakers. For instance when second language speakers omit past tense endings (-*ed*) or determiners (*the, a*), native speakers tend to supply them in their comprehension, and insert them in their transcription, as shown in Gibbons (1995). This type of grammatical correction can be more far reaching and intentional however. In the same paper (Gibbons 1995: 176), the witness's limited syntactic range is greatly extended in the transcript by the use of subordination and coordination that were not part of his proficiency, replacing his pattern of strings of clauses not related by grammatical means. A solicitor, referring to police record of interview, wrote 'we would deduce from this that much of what our client had verbally stated in this interview was conveniently transcribed into better English. The Constable admitted as much.'

The **decontextualization** of written transcripts is most noticeable in the limited representation of non-verbal information. Walker's (1990) survey shows that around 90 per cent of the professional court reporters in her sample would not record laughter or tears. There are means of representing such behaviour, usually by a comment in square brackets, for example [shakes head], [turns to jury], but this is rarely done. Only when such information is needed for the interpretation of spoken language is it normally included. Little of the information carried by stress and intonation is included. Question marks are generally used when they would be expected in written language, rather than to represent a rising final tone. Emphasis may be conveyed by the use of conventions such as capitals, underlining or italics, but this is also rare. Once more, substantial information is lost. This lack of emphasis is also related to a reduction in the emotive charge that is common to written language. In Gibbons (1995: 180) there are many colourful, augmentative expressions in the comparison transcript, but almost none in the police record of interview.

Of the two competing criteria mentioned previously, it is clear that readability tends to win out over accuracy in legal transcripts. As we have seen, there are good reasons for this. There are also considerable dangers, particularly of misrepresenting the intentions of speakers, some of the information they have encoded in spoken forms, and the nature and character of both witnesses and lawyers.

Tiersma (1999: 175–9) argues that the transformation from spoken to written language means that the transcript may be regarded as having the qualities of an autonomous written text, rather than being a representation of contextualized spoken language. In court this means that the normal conventions that apply to spoken language may be ignored, and the normal implications that one would make concerning the implicit coherence of spoken language do not apply. Tiersma presents an example from a court case where the common sense conversational understanding of a transcript is replaced by a decision based on the rules of interpretation used for legal documents (see chapter 2).

Another issue that arises is that Common Law courtroom procedures are almost entirely spoken, unlike Roman Law procedures. However, the move into literacy means that the spoken language of the courtroom is often towards the written end of the mode continuum. Stygall (1994: 186–8) makes just this point about jury instructions in Indiana courtrooms, in particular that they use the storage capacity of the written language. In the case that Stygall was observing, following normal precedent, the judge read aloud the final jury instructions once only, and the jury were not provided with the written form. Yet these instructions contained seven listed considerations on which the verdict should be based. The possibility of the jury remembering these on a single hearing was remote. Furthermore, looking at grammatical metaphor, each consideration was presented in the form of a complex nominalization such as 'the value of lost time and earnings' and 'the reasonable value of each spouse's loss of society, companionship and services in the injured spouse' (*sic*) Stygall (1994: 187). This mismatch between an oral channel and a written style carries an obvious risk of poor communication.

Philips (1985) describes judges' efforts to turn the written language of their 'Bench Book' back into spoken language so that it can be understood better as speech. They reverse the move to literacy we have seen in this chapter by making the following changes: (1) recontextualization – they turn the third person language of the constitutional rights '**his** right to a jury trial' into the second person '**your** right to a jury trial', and the language becomes more interactive, using checking questions; (2) replanning – the judges break up an extremely long syntactic structure. This theme is further developed in chapter 5.

The Future

Technological changes such as the development of paper, and later of printing, played a major role in the development of literacy (Ong 1982). Recent technological developments have reduced our dependence on these technologies for recording language (for instance this book was written on a computer, and stored digitally). Even more important for the language of the law is the recording of speech on audio and video tape, and digitally on a computer. There is an increasing tendency for wills, court depositions (statements), and police interrogations to be video or audio recorded. This may form part of a societal trend towards more visual and less linguistic forms of communication, involving in particular film, television and illustrations. In the legal arena this has had the consequence of reversing some of the earlier effects of written language, of leading a movement into post-literate communication. Danet and Bogoch (1994) describe the development of the video-taped will, and mention the literate residue left in the oral will. In one example a testator points to objects and asks the camera to zoom in on them, thereby replacing a linguistic description with a contextualized visual record, making full use of the technology, and using language that is highly contextualized. Pearson and Berch (1994) describe the increasing use of video-taped depositions (sworn statements) to replace written depositions and court appearances as evidence in the American legal system. They mention specifically the usefulness of video evidence which uses charts and models, and in a medical context skeletons, and images from X-ray machines and immovable machinery. Facial expression, gestures, pausing and intonation, lost in written depositions but available in video depositions, may assist communication, although they are also more vulnerable to misinterpretation and cross-cultural misunderstanding. For example, failure to make eye contact may be seen as indicative of an evasive or unreliable witness among Westerners. In some Asian cultures, however, too much direct eye contact is viewed as aggressive and impolite. Pearson and Berch (1994) note research that shows that visual evidence is more easily remembered by jurors than linguistic evidence alone. The disadvantage over written depositions is that the witness's ethnicity and social background become more apparent, which may activate social or ethnic prejudice among jurors. In general a change to more oral and more graphic forms of communication raise hopes that communication in legal contexts can be improved – although as we shall see in chapter 5, such communication can be problematic.

2

The Pursuit of Precision

any attempt to be precise and accurate requires modification of common speech both as regards vocabulary and as regards syntax.

Russell (1975)

[legal language] diverges in many ways from ordinary speech, far more than the technical language of most other professions.

Tiersma (1999)

Introduction

Technicality

Every field of expertise develops its own language features. So photographers may talk of 'hypo' and 'single lens reflex'. On a larger scale, every major human institution, such as medicine, business, education or the law, develops not just a specialist vocabulary, but a special way of conceiving and construing the world, and a specialized language to express this understanding. Indeed, much of the difficulty that lawyers have in communicating with people who are not imbued in the law is not simply an issue of jargon, but of helping them to understand how the legal system views the social and physical world – for instance in the legal system 'justice' does not have the same meaning as the everyday common sense concept. Furthermore, there are a range of processes and institutions that are unique to the legal system, so referring to them requires a specialist language. If the specialist terms did not exist, there would be a need for long and clumsy explanations each time reference was made to the technical process or notion, so technical jargon is sometimes referred to as a form of 'shorthand'. Indeed it often makes use of short forms – either abbreviations or acronyms using the first letters of each word (such as UN for 'United Nations'). Martin (1990: 86) in talking of the language of science, writes 'scientists simply cannot do their jobs without technical discourse. Not only is it compact and therefore efficient, but, most importantly it codes an alternative perspective on reality to common sense . . . It constructs the world in a different way.' There is therefore a real need for specialist language in the conceptual realm (in Halliday's terms, to perform the ideational function) in order to be precise. Note also Tiersma's (1999: 49) comment at the start of this chapter. However, the use of technical terms for specialist concepts need not be equated with precision. Solan (1993b: 132) makes the important point that 'while a technical vocabulary can focus our attention on certain concepts, the technical words become just as unclear at the fringes as do any other words.'

Specialist language can also play a sociocultural role that is different in intent. It can mark membership of a specialist group, or club; and the lawyers' club is a particularly exclusive and prestigious club. Tiersma (1999: 3) writes 'when lawyers use these linguistic features they subtly communicate to each other that they are members of the same club or fraternity. No wonder that law students strive so hard to imitate the professors and lawyers who teach them!' Membership of in-groups is typically marked not only by the use of technical terms, but also by the use of slang, and the law is no exception. However, in-group language does not operate only to strengthen links, and assert group membership, it also operates to exclude those who are not members of the group – it is exclusive as well as inclusive language. Since lawyers are a prestigious elite group, using the language of the law can be a claim to this prestige – Mellinkoff (1963) calls the language of the law simply 'pompous'. Furthermore, if the language needed to operate within a specialist field is unintelligible to non-specialists, this creates a need for the services of a specialist to mediate between ordinary people and the specialist field. Put crudely, it makes work and money for lawyers. This I shall refer to as the 'interpersonal' use of specialist language. Criminals and prisoners have their slang also, some of it acting as specialist language to describe the special features of their activities and their lives, but also playing interpersonal roles in marking membership of the group, and perhaps also reducing outsiders' understanding when they discuss criminal activity – Halliday's 'secret language'. Such interactive and interpersonal uses of language in the law are discussed in the next chapter.

Drafting and interpretation

The distinctive features of operative documents are a product both of the forces that we examined in the previous chapter – the move to writing –

and of the issue discussed in this chapter – the pursuit of precision in legal language, which involves technicality. As we saw in chapter 1, decontextualization, a noticeable characteristic of written texts, made possible the notion that legal texts should be made clear and explicit using the internal resources of the text itself. Allied to this is the need for legal documents to be as precise and exact as possible.

Communication involves the processes of production of language and comprehension of language. (In spoken language particularly, there may be an interactive process through which participants attempt to negotiate a shared understanding.) The production of operative documents is normally referred to as **legal drafting**. The comprehension process for such texts is normally referred to as **interpretation**, although the terms **legal reasoning**, **application** and **construction** are also used to refer to aspects of the process.

Operative documents, particularly legislation, regulations and contracts, are of great importance in everyday life. Legislation codifies a society's beliefs, values and moral standards, which the justice system then imposes. Regulations can exert considerable control and exact severe penalties, whether they apply to restaurant kitchens or nuclear power stations. Contracts pervade modern life. As we noted in the introduction, work is defined by a contract; in the case of transport, tickets for a train or a parking station are contracts; a credit card or bank account requires the signing of a contract.

Because these documents are so influential, precision in their wording is very important. If their wording is too restrictive, they may place undue and unwanted limits on our lives. If their wording is too loose, this may licence undesirable behaviour or lead to unwanted outcomes. According to Bhatia (1994) **precision** is the driving force for the unique characteristics of legal documents. Precision is not necessarily extreme clarity – it may also involve selecting the appropriate level of vagueness or flexibility. Tiersma (1999: 83) gives the example of the **prudent investor rule** in many states of the USA, which requires that a trustee in charge of investing money for someone else behave like a prudent investor – a deliberately vague criterion. Crystal and Davy (1969: 211) similarly state 'on the frequent occasions on which some part of a document needs to leave room for the meaning to stretch a little, then in will come terms like *adequate, and/or, due care, intention* and *malice*'.

With regard to interpretation, its principles also have as their main objective precision in understanding. A main issue in legal construction is the 'fit' between an operative document and a particular case. Operative documents (particularly legislation) attempt to regulate defined classes of events. For example, given the wording of legislation concerning homicide, a decision may need to be made as to whether a particular killing falls into the category **murder** or **manslaughter**. Since the decision may literally be a matter of life or death for the guilty party, precision in drafting is critical to reducing the likelihood of misinterpretation.

In summary, this combination of decontextualization and the attempt to communicate no more and no less than the intended meaning requires that legal texts seek to be completely internally explicit and unambiguous. Linguists and lawyers know that this is not fully achievable, but a more reasonable target is that operative documents should pursue this objective as far as possible. This has led in turn to a set of rules and practices for the drafting and interpretation of operative documents.

This chapter has as its underlying structure the model of communication presented in the Introduction. It begins with the main linguistic manifestation of technicality – words – describing the specialist lexicon of lawyers, police and prisons; it then moves on to grammar, speech acts and discourse. The chapter finishes with a description of how the various elements of the model of communication are involved in issues of legal interpretation.

Words

In the area of words technicality is strongly marked, and precision is particularly sought. The technical meanings of words in the Common Law system has often stabilized and clarified through years of interpretation and precedent. However it is necessary to distinguish between genuine technical terms or 'terms of art' (as they are known in legal jargon), which are more accurate or more efficient when referring to legal concepts (the 'technical use' referred to above), and in-group language, utilized for interpersonal motives. Legal technicality filters down to police and prison staff, and police and prison staff have also developed professional jargons of their own.

Although much legal vocabulary is shared between Common Law countries, separate evolution has also produced some words that are more likely to be found in a particular country (while recognizing that words travel). The following abbreviations will be used to indicate this: US (United States of America); BR (England, Wales and Northern Ireland); AU

(Australia); CA (Canada). I have not encountered information on the legal language of other English speaking countries.

Lawyers

Turning first to the lawyers' lexicon, the range of legal dictionaries attests to the very large amount of technical vocabulary used by lawyers. Some of it exists to express specialist concepts, which is why a substantial proportion of this vocabulary consists of words or expressions that are not in everyday conversational use. Solan (1993b: 131–2) makes a convincing case for the value of the word *scienter* (roughly meaning 'intent to deceive') in fraud cases. He shows that the word implies a carefully defined level of intention to deceive, which may vary slightly among jurisdictions. The term therefore is useful, and replacing it with *intent to deceive* could be misleading, as well as opening the concept to challenge. Solan remarks (1993b: 132) 'the introduction of the word scienter has nothing to do with what is difficult about the law of fraud. To the contrary, it makes discussion of the law of fraud a little easier.' But he adds 'Of course I do not mean here to defend the use of every idiotic legal expression, under the rubric of a technical legal vocabulary.' Examples of other specialist terms follow:

Specialist terms
clerk of the peace
committal
a counsel
deforcement
deponent (US)
felon
interrogatory
intestate
plaintiff
remand

While the words in this list are not much used outside the legal world, there are a number of legal terms which have entered everyday language, but in the process their tightly defined legal sense may have been modified – examples are *homicide* and *assault* (which in legal language need not involve physical contact). There are also expressions that are part of legal usage but are widely known, such as *a will* and *eviction*, and the verb *to sentence*. Some of the terms used in legal language are archaisms and as such have become limited to legal contexts, even though their meaning may not be specialized. For instance rather than an adjournment being 'requested', it may be 'prayed for', rather than a previous judgment being 'consulted' it may be 'hearkened to'. Another example is *let* in the expression *without let or hindrance*.

Other written languages have tended to develop specialist legal terms – for instance Duarte i Montserrat and Martínez (1995: 117) point out that legal Spanish uses terms such as *devengar, cuarta trebeliánica* and *usucapión* that are not found in the everyday language, and other expressions have specific legal senses, for instance *testamento* (will). Likewise there is a specific legal difference between the terms *homicidio* (homicide) and *asesinato* (murder).

Perhaps most characteristic of legal language is the use of archaic deictics (old-fashioned words which point to another part of the text in which they are found, or to another place or time). Some examples of these are:

Archaic deictics
forthwith
hereafter, herein, hereof, heretofore, herewith
said, aforesaid
thence, thenceforth
thereabout, thereafter, thereat, thereby, therein, thereon, thereto, thereto, thereunto, thereupon, therewith
whereas, whereby

The argument made by lawyers for the use of archaic deictics is that they enable clearer and less ambiguous reference. Melinkoff (1963: 305–26) vigorously challenges this technical motive, calling these terms 'vague'. Other motives for using them may include interpersonal power – to give greater weight and authority to the language (see the next chapter) or simple conservatism. It should be noted however that Spanish legal language similarly uses low-frequency deictics such as the following from a Chilean contract: *en adelante* (hereafter), *presente* (present), *el mismo* (the same), *correspondiente* (aforesaid).

As a consequence of the language history of the Common Law, there are many technical terms derived directly from Latin (L) or Norman French (F). Some examples are:

Latin
decree *nisi*
order of *mittimus*
order of *certiori*
affidavit
ex parte
caveat
habeas corpus
mala fide
obiter dicta
bona gestura
in camera
noli prosequi

Norman French
breve
estoppel
judge
laches
lien
quash
void
voir dire

Some legal terminology is derived directly from Latin or French, but in form has been modified to fit into English, for example *codicil* (L) and *petty* (F).

Sometimes French or Latin is used when there is no strong technical need, as in the following examples from a recent Malaysian judgment *Sukma Darmawan Madja v. Ketua Pengarah Penjara Malaysia* [1999] 1 MLJ 266 at page 277 '. . . established by having recourse to matters**de-hors** the record', and '**Ex facie**, therefore, the sessions court did not lack jurisdiction' (emphasis added).

The degree to which such terminology is known only to lawyers varies considerably – *estoppel* is exotic, yet *judge* has become part of everyday English and its French origins are no longer apparent. Some of this Latin and French technical vocabulary has maintained its foreign credentials, while becoming part of educated everyday language in some English speaking countries, for instance *alias, de facto, bona fides* (L), in *lieu* of, *parole, venue* (F).

Terms from different languages which originally referred to the same concept, such as *child* (OE), *infant* (F) and *minor* (L) permit the functional specialization of the terms – in this case they may refer to different spreads of age for different legal purposes.

It is not only English that uses Latin for specialist legal purposes – the same is true for a number of other Western European languages. Duarte i Monserrat (1993: 49) and Duarte i Montserrat and Martínez (1995: 118) point out that Catalan and Spanish use the following Latin legal expressions among others: *iuris tantum, do ut des, ratione materiae* and *animus defendendi*. Similarly Shari'ah courts use some Quranic Arabic. Spanish also has partly modified Latinisms such as *cláusula* (clause).

Doublets and triplets
Mellinkoff (1963: 121–2) indicates that many of these legal terms appear in company – they are routinely used in sequences of two or three (doublets are also know as 'binomial expressions' and 'binomials'). Gustafsson (1984: 123) writes 'In legal English, binomials are 4–5 times more common than in other prose texts, and they are definitely a style marker in law language.' Everyday words can be transformed into legal formulae in this way. Melinkoff also points out that many doublets and triplets combine words of Old English/Germanic (OE), Latin and Norman French origins.

Examples of doublets
of sound mind (OE) *and memory* (L)
give (OE) *devise* (F) *and bequeath* (OE)
will (OE) *and testament* (F/L)
goods (OE) *and chattels* (F)
final (F) *and conclusive* (L)
fit (OE) *and proper* (F)
new (OE) *and novel* (F)
save (F) *and except* (L)
peace (F) *and quiet* (L)

These expressions are mostly centuries old, and some date from a time when it was advisable to use words of various origins either to increase intelligibility for people from different language backgrounds, or more probably it was intended to encompass previous legal usage or legal documents from both early English and Norman French.

Interestingly this phenomenon is not limited to English. Duarte i Montserrat and Martínez (1995: 115) document the following for Spanish:

Spanish doublets
visto y examinado
(seen and examined)
según mi leal saber y entender
(according to my faithful knowledge and understanding)
debo condenar y condeno
(I must condemn and I condemn)

Danet (1984) also documents the use of doublets in legal Hebrew, and suggests that their use is a product of the 'poetization' of legal language, perhaps in an attempt to make legal language sound more classically cultured and as Danet (1984: 144) says 'to create the illusion of control over the social and natural world'. Issues of power and control in language are further discussed in the next chapter. As various writers on language have observed, when an expression contains a series of synonyms, some of them are redundant, and this militates against ease of understanding.

Complex function expressions
Some legal expressions appear to replace ordinary parts of speech with more complex forms, usually complex prepositional phrases.

Swales and Bhatia (1983) claim that the simple forms are more ambiguous and less clear – that the legal expressions are part of the pursuit of precision. In many cases this is open to challenge. Similar in nature is the use of **archaic deictics** mentioned previously.

Legal expression	Everyday word	Legal expression	Everyday word
at slow speed	slowly	*during the time that*	during
in pursuance of	under	*until such time as*	until
subsequent to	after	*in order to*	to
prior to	before	*for the purpose of*	for
and additionally or alternatively	and/or	*by virtue of*	by

Short forms
Sometimes professionals wish to abbreviate longer technical terms and expressions, as a means of achieving the 'efficient communication' mentioned earlier. One way of doing this is to use the first letter of each word,

creating acronyms such as TRO (Temporary Restraining Order) and UCC (Uniform Commercial Code). This phenomenon is widespread across the literate world, and is a good example of a linguistic efficiency that often also acts as an exclusionary device, whether this is intentional or not.

Sometimes short forms are also a type of lawyer slang, for instance *a writ of fi fa* (fieri facias). In the UK, the use of a particular schedule to have someone classified as mentally ill, became abbreviated to 'having someone **scheduled**'. A related phenomenon is the practice of referring to a statute simply by its number.

Proper names

Another related phenomenon is the use of the name of a person to refer to a particular legal concept associated with that person. For example, the courts without juries which were established in Northern Ireland are referred to as *Diplock Courts* after the man whose report led to their creation. In Britain there were types of court order and warrants which were referred to by a proper name, such as an *Anton Piller* order which allowed police to enter premises. For similar reasons, in the USA the cautions or warnings given to suspects by police are called *Miranda Warnings*.

Ordinary words used with specialist meanings

One type of legal jargon that has the potential to be dangerously misleading is the use of terms which are common in everyday language but with a specialized meaning. A number of examples are shown below.

O'Toole (1994) argues that it may not be so much the formality and power of the language of the law, but its technicality and use of ordinary words with specialist meanings that causes conflict and misunderstanding between lawyers and non-lawyers.

In the case of Catalan, Duarte i Monserrat (1993: 49–50) in a similar vein, specifically mentions 'formes lingüístiques que tenen un significat dins de la llengua estàndard i un altre significat, sovint proxim però functionalment ben diferenciat' (linguistic forms that have one meaning in the standard language and another meaning, often close, but functionally well differentiated), which indicates that this phenomenon is not limited to English.

There are also some technical terms that have been developed to describe new or recent understandings that have evolved. Although they are a commonplace in the spoken language of lawyers, they may not have found their way into legal writing, particularly legislation. Examples from

Ordinary word	Technical meaning	Ordinary word	Technical meaning
action	lawsuit	*issue*	children
aggravating (US)	makes an offence more serious	*mention*	a brief hearing preparing for the full hearing
article	part of a document	*party*	one side in a court case
brief	briefing document	*pleading*	outline of a case
consideration *(particularly* *'in consideration* *of')*	recompense or payment	*real*	material (as in 'real estate')
costs	court costs	*service*	giving a legal document
diligence	a warrant to produce a witness or evidence	*stay*	a delay

the USA are *palimony* and *sidebar*. Some are still so far from being codified as to be regarded as slang, for example *wobbler* (Tiersma 1999: 137).

Slang
Lawyers have their particular slang. A small number of examples follow.

Slang	Meaning
a contest	a trial where the accused pleads 'not guilty'
a silk (BR)	King's/Queen's Counsel (*take silk* = become a QC)
a verbal (AU)	a dishonest police statement

Definitions
Words may take on a special meaning in a specific legal document by a process of **defining**. Sometimes the defined term may act as a type of 'pro-form' (see the section later in this chapter) but more usually the meaning of a word is established in order to avoid challenge. Definitions

may be given in the introduction to a legal document or, particularly in legislation, they may be given in an appendix at the end. Because definitions are so often an issue in legal cases, in some jurisictions reported judgments often have a section in the introduction concerning 'Words and Phrases' that are an issue in the case (see also *Wong Kon Poh v. New India Assurance Co Ltd* [1970] 2 MLJ 287 discussed later in this chapter).

There is however a trap in providing definitions. This can be illustrated from the case of *Sykt Telekom Malaysia Bhd v. Business Chinese Directory Sdn Bhd* [1994] 2 MLJ. This case occurred in Malaysia, where the *Telecommunication Amendment Act* 1977 strictly regulates the production of telephone directories, which in section 44 are defined as 'the book containing the alphabetical list of telephone subscribers' names and addresses'. A company had produced a 'Business Chinese Directory' in Chinese characters which included telephone numbers. By normal standards this clearly was a telephone directory. However written Chinese is not **alphabetic** – its phonetic element is minor and characters mostly represent ideas not pronunciation. Chinese dictionaries and other listings are organized according to 'radicals' – an element of the character – and the number of strokes. The case therefore failed because the directory, under the definition given above, was not a directory since it was not alphabetical. The other language issue that emerged in the case was that all evidence in the High Court in Malaysia must be available in the national language Bahasa Malaysia. Since the entire Business Chinese Directory had not been translated into Bahasa Malaysia, the directory could not be used as evidence, so the case failed on this ground too. The 'literal-mindedness' of this case, where linguistic issues of drafting and interpretation override common sense and intention, is not unusual in the law. It also provides a good illustration of the importance of language and language issues in the law.

Deeming and legal fictions

In operative documents it is common to see an *apple* redefined as a *pear* for the purpose of the document, even when the referent for the word *pear* does not include *apples* in any normal use of language. The term **deem** is often used, as in 'an apple, for the purposes of this section, is **deemed** to be a pear', which is why this practice is sometimes referred to as **deeming**.

Maley (1994: 24–6) gives the following example:

(1) A person who attempts or incites another to commit, or becomes an accessory after the fact to an offence (in this subsection called 'the principal offence') commits –

(a) if the principal offence is an indictable offence, the indictable offence, or

(b) if the principal offence is a simple offence, the simple offence, but is liable on conviction –

(c) to a fine not exceeding half of the fine, and additionally or alternatively,

(d) to imprisonment for a term not exceeding half of the term.

(Section 33, Drugs Act, Western Australia 1981)

Here 'attempting' or 'inciting' or 'becoming an accessory' are redefined as 'committing' itself, but (perversely) are subject to only half of the penalty. By definition the 'person' does not commit the offence itself, so this is a legal fiction.

Tiersma (1999: 116–19) discusses deeming under the name of **declaratory definition**, and provides the following examples.

A person (is) . . . an individual, partnership, corporation, limited liability company, association, or other group, however organized

(Consumer Legal Remedies Act, California)

The everyday meaning of *person* does not include corporations, and so on. As Tiersma (1999: 116) adds 'From a descriptive stand-point, this is nonsense'.

In another statute, *day-old poultry* is deemed to be:

any poultry of an age of 72 hours or less

(New Zealand Poultry Act, 1968)

Again, here three-day-old poultry is deemed to be 'day-old poultry'.

This phenomenon is not limited to English and the Common Law – Pardo (1994: 26) documents it for Roman Law Spanish. In the Argentine Civil Code, the section dealing with the definition of a live/dead person states in article 74 that children who die before birth 'serán considerados como si no hubiesen existido' (will be considered as if they have not existed).

Drafting and interpretation

There are a number of drafting and interpretation principles which attempt to delimit the meaning of words and grammatical constructions, that are sometimes known as legal 'canons of construction'. Essentially these are intended to prevent or resolve ambiguity. One is the **same meaning same form** principle, by which a word or expression is taken to have the same referent throughout a text, and perhaps more importantly, a synonym is expected to have a different referent. So if the nouns *shadow* and *shade* are used in an operative document, they would be expected to refer to different phenomena, rather than being stylistic variants.

Another principle is that when terms are used in a series or list, their meaning is limited or extended to things that form part of the category. For instance, following this principle, in the following list of items to be surrendered (Simpson, 1994: 430) 'all files, reports, statement, letters, diaries, notebooks, memoranda, drafts, documents and writings' the word *files* did not refer to abrasive metal tools, so no such tool needed to be produced. This principle is know as **ejusdem generis**.

The use of lists, as Solan (1995) remarks, can cause problems, because there is another principle which says that if something is not included in a list, it is thereby excluded – a principle known as **expressio unius est exclusio alterius**. To avoid falling into this trap, Tiersma (1999: 85) notes that there is now a trend to establish a category first, then give a listing which is explicitly said to be non–exhaustive, using the standardized wording *any X, including but not limited to a, b, c, d* (where *X* is a general term).

Finally, the interaction between the meaning of a text and the meaning of individual words is recognized in the principle **noscitur sociis** which says that words should be interpreted according to the linguistic and textual context in which they occur.

These canons have been rejected as being in any sense final and definitive (Solan 1993b: 37–8), but they are still regularly mentioned in the judgments and opinions given by judges, more as 'rules of thumb' than powerful principles, to be used only when there is not a plain meaning to the text.

Solan (1993a, 1995: 1075n) remarks that a major tactic used by judges and lawyers in the interpretation of word meaning is the use of dictionaries. Since they themselves claim authority on issues of the law, they grant similar authority to the compilers of dictionaries on issues of word meaning. This is a fundamentally prescriptive model of the role of linguists, and one which most linguists reject, preferring to see themselves as describers rather than prescribers. In a debate in the *Washington University Law Quarterly* (73, 3), the linguists demonstrate that modern corpus-based approaches to the meaning of words can provide a rich and detailed understanding of individual word meaning and use that is unachievable in the space available in a dictionary. This is done by tracking every occurrence in a large database (the British National Corpus for instance has more than 100 million words of text), and examining the context of use. Sadly, judges and lawyers do not appear willing to grant the same level of authority to such approaches, even though dictionary compilers are themselves linguists, often working on the same basis – particularly those compiling corpus-based dictionaries such as the *Cobuild* dictionary. Another way to examine competing meanings of words, texts or sentence structures is to perform a survey, perhaps using questionnaires – see for instance Labov and Harris (1994: 284–5).

Obviously word meaning interacts also with grammatical meaning, so there is further information of relevance in the following section on grammar.

Police

As participants in the judicial process, the police share some of the specialist legal jargon of the lawyer. They also, however, have a language to describe the concepts and practices of policing.

Slang

There are words that are more 'slangy' in nature, and can be both a means of referring to police life, and a marker of membership of police culture (see the next chapter), since many have everyday alternatives. Interestingly, many of them are shared with criminals in a form of shared criminal sub-culture. Slang can be short lived, so some of these expressions may be old hat.

Word	Meaning
bag man	police officer who collects and bags evidence at a crime scene
bang up (UK)	arrest/imprison
lock up (AU)	
blade (US, CA)	knife
brassed (AU)	robbed by another criminal
dick (US, CA not UK, AU)	plain clothes officer
fence	someone who buys and sells stolen property
(fizz) gig (AU)	informant
heater, piece (US, CA)	handgun
plod (BR)	uniformed officer
sniffer (CA)	solvent abuser

Short forms
A number of abbreviations are prevalent, frequently to make communication more efficient.

Short form	Meaning
CAD (CA)	Computer Aided Despatch
GBH (BR)	Grievous Bodily Harm
GOA	Gone On Arrival
MVA	Motor Vehicle Accident
SWAT	Special Weapons And Tactics (team)
(US, CA)	

Numbers
Familiar to any viewer of television crime dramas, is the interesting form of jargon which uses numerical radio codes, especially in the USA and Canada. There are probably two reasons for this – first the technical purpose of efficient communication, but secondly also as a means of concealing the content of police communications from casual listeners. As most professional criminals know the codes, this latter objective is achieved only in part. The police also use the section numbers of acts to refer to types of person or crime. Some examples of these are:

Word	Meaning
Code 4 (US)	I am OK
Code 8 or 10 (US)	emergency call
18-1 (CA)	a mentally unstable person, referring to a section in the Mental Health Act

Source: Cooper 1997; Chabun 1997

Prison

Enclosed communities tend to develop their own sub-culture and language, and there are few communities more enclosed than prisons. They are also, however. intensely bureaucratic and regulated institutions, and one would expect this to be demonstrated by the language of prisons. Given the social role of prisons, prison jargon often refers to sex, violence, drugs and crime, and there is offensive language – readers who dislike this should skip this section. Much of the information given here is derived from the following websites:

<http://www/sco/com/~aerick/words.htm>
<http://www.halcyon.com/scripts/dante/cgi-pvt/pe/dpp.glossary.html>
<http://www/hmprisonservice.gov.uk/life/life4.asp>

What is particularly noticeable is the multiplicity of terms for major concerns of prison life – prisoners themselves, prison guards, the personal file kept on each prisoner, periods of imprisonment, drugs, and moving in and out of cells. Particularly salient in prison language are terms to refer to solitary confinement (a major and much loathed form of punishment) – these include terms for solitary confinement itself, and for solitary confinement cells and units. There are a range of official terms, derogatory prisoner terms, and short forms for all of the above, of which only a selection is given below.

Official specialist terms
Since prisons are bureaucratic ('filing cabinets for people') there is a need for official technical terms for various aspects of prison life. However, since some of these sound pompous and euphemistic, they may also serve an interpersonal use of concealing unpleasantness or raising status.

Word	Meaning
Adjustment Center (US)	solitary confinement unit
Segregation Unit	
Administrative or *Disciplinary*	being placed in solitary confinement
Segregation	
correctional officer (US)	prison staff (guard)
correctional service officer (AU)	
warden	
prison officer (BR)	
Facility Licence (BR)	temporary release to work in the community
Recess (BR)	area of a living unit containing toilets/showers

Short forms
Short forms, particularly acronyms, are also common. They are used mainly to refer to official matters, but some are also slang.

Short form	Meaning
AC (US)	Adjustment Center
ad seg	Administrative Segregation
ARD (BR)	Automatic Release Date
chi mo	child molester
con (BR)	convicted prisoner
C & R (BR)	Control and Restraint
CUS (US)	Custody Unit Supervisor
DCR (BR)	Discretionary Conditional Release
D seg	Disciplinary Segregation
ECR (BR)	Emergency Control Room
EPRD (US)	Earliest Possible Release Date
IK	Inmate Kitchen
LWOP (US)	Life without possibility of parole
seg unit (BR)	Segregation Unit (see above)
SHU (US)	Security Housing Unit ie. Segregation Unit
UA	Urine analysis (aka *piss test*)

Numbers
Numbers can also form part of prison language. Their sources may be the offence code, a section of legislation, a particular form or of a section of prison regulations.

Word	Meaning
Code 20 (Texas)	masturbation (TDC offense code 20)
115 (California)	a rules violation report (CDC Form 115)
5150 (California)	mentally unstable (the number of a section of the California Welfare and Institutions Code)
F1150/ F2050 (BR)	prisoner's file
F2052SH (BR)	a form reporting that a prisoner is in danger of harming him/herself – hence a suicidal prisoner
Type 3 (BR)	24-hour medical facilities with a nurse

Note: DC means Department of Correction

Slang

There are a range of slang terms to refer to the realities of prison life, once again serving both specialist and interpersonal purposes. The harsh reality of prison life requires its own vocabulary. But it is also evident that use of this type of slang indicates membership of the prisoners' sub-culture, distinguishing an 'old lag' from a newcomer. It also probably acts as a 'secret language' to some degree.

Word	Meaning
beast (BR);	
rock spider (AU)	child molester
bing; the hole	solitary confinement
bird (BR)	time in prison
block (BR)	solitary confinement unit
gate money (US)	money given to prisoner on release
jacket (US)	file on an individual prisoner – by extension 'reputation'
mule (US)	person who smuggles drugs into prison
on the leg (US)	obsequious to guards
pad mate (BR)	parole panel
shank; shiv	prison weapon – usually bladed

There are so many derogatory words for prison guards that these merit a short listing of their own: *badge, cop, bull, hack, hog, pig, screw, snout.* Of these *screw* appears to be the most widely used.

This phenomenon is probably found among prisoners everywhere, for instance Gaete et al. (1999) document the sub-language COA among Chilean female prisoners. Some of the words reflect similar realities to English prisoner and criminal slang.

Word	Meaning
achaque	bringing drugs into prison
botón, yuta	police officer
carambisamba	old lag
collera	violent attack
fierro	any weapon
forever	hardened criminal
porotera	woman who has spent her childhood in institutions (reference to the 'porotos' or beans that form a large part of the diet – compare 'porridge' (BR) – time in prison)

Grammar

Specialized registers do not usually have a grammar that is distinct in major respects from the general grammar of the language. Where registers do vary it is frequently in the frequency and distribution of the use of specific aspects of grammar, although there may be some minor differences in grammatical construction. There is little evidence that the grammar of the police or prisons is different from everyday usage, with the exception that the over-elaboration in police language, described in the next chapter, spills over into grammar. Otherwise, where their grammar does vary from the normal, it is part of the patterning of legal language in general.

It is in operative documents that the distinct characteristics of legal grammar are most clearly seen. The consequences of specialization in grammar and vocabulary are important in both drafting and interpretation. Rasmussen (1995: 1055) notes 'The inevitable specialization of law leads to statutes drafted in light of legal understanding. No conception of the role of judges in interpreting statutes would suggest that judges would turn a blind eye to this prevailing practice and engage in the fiction that statutes are written in the same manner as is the daily newspaper.' Indeed, as we shall see, there are some areas in which it appears that the grammar of legal register follows slightly different rules from those of everyday language.

Drafting and interpretation

The extract shown in table 2.1 from the Victorian Companies Code will serve as a starting point by exemplifying various aspects of legal language (it should be read from top to bottom, changing columns as necessary).

If we briefly note characteristics described previously, we can see that, at the word level, the influence of literacy has produced frequent use of grammatical metaphor: *offerer, announcement, expiration, pursuant*. There are also examples of elaborate prepositional phrases: *subject to* (rather than *under*); *during the period* (rather than *when*); *pursuant to* (rather than *after*) – this is also an archaism. Another archaic usage at the end is *so varied*.

The phrases or groups tend to be long, and most of the length is a product of additional elements being added after, rather than before, the main element (the main element is in **bold** in these examples): *a **person** associated with the on-market offerer; at the expiration of the **period** during*

Table 2.1   The Companies (Acquisition of Share) (Victoria) Code, section 40 (1985)

Core	Conditions	Conditions on conditions
	subject to sub-section (3) during the period	
		commencing when a take-over announcement is made in relation to shares in a company and ending at the expiration of the period during which the offers constituted by the announcement remain open
the on-market offeror, or a person associated with the on-market offerer, shall not give, offer to give or agree to give to a person		
	whose shares may be acquired pursuant to the take-over announcement,	
or to a person		
	associated with such a person	
any benefit		
	(whether by payment of cash or otherwise) not provided for under the terms of the take-over announcement or,	
		if those terms have been varied under section 17,
	under the terms so varied.	

which the offers constituted by the announcement remain open. The second example is a very long prepositional phrase/circumstance. Note how post-modification separates *offers* from its verb *remain*, making the meaning hard to follow. Furthermore, both the phrase with *associated* and the phrase with *constituted* consist of sentences that have been reduced to modifying phrases from a longer and more explicit form with 'which' (i.e. *which is associated/constituted*). In linguistics this may be referred to as **whiz deletion** or **rank shifting**. It is a common characteristic of legal documents (Charrow and Charrow 1979).

At the level of sentence structure, the pursuit of precision has also led to extreme caution among legal drafters in placing modifiers next to the element they are modifying, even when this produces an odd, or even marginally ungrammatical sentence structure, breaking up the natural sentence structure and producing structures that sound awkward and unlike everyday language, as in the examples mentioned in the previous paragraph. So in the sentence 'commits – (a) if the principal offence is an indictable offence, the indictable offence' the verb *commits* is separated from its object *the indictable offence*, which is placed at the end. Similarly, in table 2.1 the verb *give* is widely separated from its object *any benefit*. Crystal and Davy (1969) give the example 'We are proposing to effect with the society an assurance' instead of 'We are proposing to effect an assurance with the society'. Police language reveals the same phenomenon, for example 'I was not aware at that time of the nature of that substance that I now know to be sugar'. Here again the elements 'at that time' and 'now' are oddly positioned so as to be near the element that they modify.

A related issue is that of linguistic 'scope' for example deciding what is made negative when *not* is used. In the following case described in Cunningham et al. (1994) the issue was what actions are covered by the adverb *knowingly*. Interestingly, it became clear in the discussions reported in *Washington University Law Quarterly* (73, 3) that the lawyers believed that the scope of *knowingly* in legal register is different from its scope in normal English. The section of the statute in question reads:

(a) Any person who –
(1) knowingly transports or ships in interstate or foreign commerce by any means including by computer or mails, and visual depiction, if –
    (A) the producing of such visual depiction involves the use of a minor engaging in sexually explicit conduct: and
    (B) such visual depiction is of such conduct: ... shall be punished

The Supreme Court of the USA rejected what it acknowledged to be 'the most natural grammatical reading' that 'knowingly' modifies only 'transports or ships', to interpret the provision so that 'knowingly' also modifies 'involves the use of a minor'. Moore (in the *Washington University Law Quarterly* 73, 3: 866–7) states that there is a convention of interpretation of **mens rea** or *knowingly* type words, such that 'The law is to ignore the ordinary English syntax, to replace *if* with *and*, if that is necessary to applying the mens rea requirement of the statute to all material elements of the actus reus for that crime. That's how we do it in our culture, *i.e.*, we lawyers.' Moore is explicitly stating that legal grammar operates somewhat differently from 'ordinary' grammar.

Another characteristic feature of the text in table 2.1 is that it is a single sentence of 115 words, of extreme syntactic complexity (see also chapter 5). Hiltunen's (1984) analysis of the British Road Traffic Act of 1972 found a mean sentence length of 79.25. This compares with an average length for sentences in scientific text of 27.6 found by Barber (1962). There is then a tendency for sentences in legal documents to be very long. Indeed there is a tradition in legal culture whereby sections of documents are expressed in single sentences. Most writers (for example Tiersma, 1999: 56) believe that this is an attempt to ensure that single large blocks of information are all syntactically related, rather than being broken up, thereby avoiding challenges based on the coherence and connection of the constituent meanings.

Another characteristic of this type of text is revealed by the presentation in columns in table 2.1. Crystal and Davey (1969: 203) propose that sections of operative documents tend to have a logical structure of the following kind: if X, then Z shall (not) do/be Y. The 'if X' element is the conditions under which the main action takes place. In the section quoted above, it can be seen that the 'core' section prohibits Z from giving a benefit to people. Standing alone this would be universal in its application, and absurdly restrictive – it is only intended to apply in a strictly delimited set of circumstances. These conditions, and conditions on conditions, are laid out in the two right-hand columns. Bhatia (1994) refers to this as 'cognitive structuring'. He believes that this two-part structuring of core and conditions is a particular feature of operative documents that distinguishes them from other types of text.

Various grammatical means are used to construct the long and complex sentence in table 2.1, with its condition-based cognitive structure. In fact most of the resources for constructing complex sentences in English appear. Crystal and Davey's formulation uses the *if* form (concessive subordination) and in this extract we find *if*, *whether* and *subject to*. Secondly, note the relative clause with *whose*. Finally there is substantial coordination with *and* and *or*. Similarly, Section 33, of the Drugs Act, Western Australia 1981, quoted earlier, shares both the use of coordination with *or* and subordination with *if.*

The semantico-grammatical issue of conjunction or disjunction (and/or) is a long term problem for lawyers. Crystal and Davey (1969: 214) remark that 'No other section of the community can ever have been concerned so agonisingly about the possibilities raised by the form *and/or*' One motivation for the development of the canons of interpretation mentioned previously was to resolve such issues. The issue is both what is joined to what (words, phrases or clauses), and the exact meaning of *and* and *or* in context. For instance does 'charitable and benevolent institutions' mean 'both charitable institutions and benevolent institutions' or 'institutions that are both charitable and benevolent'? Obviously a regulation governing them would need to be clear on this issue. Crystal and Davey (1969: 217) note that the latter interpretation (perhaps an unlikely one) was taken in one case, while in another case 'it was decided that 'religious, charitable and philanthropic objects' could refer to (a) religious object only, or (b) charitable objects only, or (c) philanthropic objects only, or (d) objects that are religious and charitable and philanthropic'.

There is a canon of construction that applies in many jurisdictions which says that *and* and *or* mean the same thing. Solan (1993b: 45) gives the New York version:

> Generally, the words 'or' and 'and' in a statute may be construed as interchangeable when necessary to effectuate legislative intent.

Later in the same chapter Solan (1993b: 54) notes that 'logicians interpret *or* to mean and/or while in common usage *or* generally is thought to mean either, but not both. In essence, the court in *Siebel* held that *or* is to be construed as *and* whenever possible, and as *or* otherwise, an interpretation somewhat different from both the logical and everyday meanings of *or* ' – more evidence of the slightly different grammar of the law. Solan (1993b: 45–55) gives a range of court cases and judgments involving *and/or* which reveal judges using their understanding of the intention of the law, rather than strict grammatical interpretations of legislation, contracts and jury instructions, even though these judgments are often couched as grammatical arguments.

The structural complexity we have observed, particularly the frequent use of coordination, is characteristic of legal language. In general, written language tends to use such structures less than spoken language, however in legal written language they are very common. This is probably not a carry over from the original oral codes of the Germanic tribes, but is more likely a result of the attempt to achieve unambiguous precision by packaging all the circumstances together.

Presaging chapter 5, it is reasonable to ask whether this degree of complexity is necessary to meet the need for precision in meaning. We shall see in that chapter that the Law Reform Commission of Victoria offers a substantial simplification of this text.

Speech Acts

When I buy my train ticket to work, I say 'A return to Redfern, please'. (Because I am at the railway ticket office, the words *ticket* and *station* are redundant – a fuller form would be 'a return ticket to Redfern station, please'.) Like most sentences, this one has a conceptual content – the return ticket, and a speech act element, manifested in *please* – it is a request. (The politeness of this is also negotiating a social relationship with the ticket clerk.) The sentence has two parts to its meaning, a proposition, since it is referring to a physical object, a ticket, and a speech act, since it performs the interpersonal act of requesting something. There is a famous example from the father of the study of speech acts, Austin (1963) 'There's a bull in that field'. On the conceptual level it refers to the existence of a beefy animal in a certain place. At the speech act level, it could be a warning if uttered when someone was about to open the gate of the relevant field, or it could be a simple observation if we were enjoying the view from a jet aeroplane. So the same sentence can perform different speech acts – in this case, a warning or an observation. Speech acts are sometimes referred to as 'functions', and there is a branch of semantics devoted to the (sometimes controversial) study of them. Lyons (1977) gives a rigorous account of the interaction of these two types of meaning.

'Performatives' are a special class of speech act which 'do' whatever it is that they say they do. So, given the right circumstances, saying 'I name this ship the White Shoe' really does name the ship. However, this works only with social acts – saying 'I hereby make this bed' sadly does not produce a change in the physical world. Usually we perform speech acts without specifically using a performative expression, for example 'I'll bring it tomorrow' is a commitment to bring something, it performs the speech act of committing oneself, without using an explicit performative (as in 'I commit myself to bringing it tomorrow' or 'I promise to bring it tomorrow').

The notion of performatives has a role to play in understanding operative documents. We noted in chapter 1 that the modern will in figure 1.5 marks various expressions as performatives by both underlining and capitalization. The speech acts made explicit in this way are *revoking*, *leaving* (property), *appointing*, *declaring* and *witnessing*. Sometimes we have to sign at each speech act performed in a legal document. The first speech act contains the wording 'I hereby revoke'. *Hereby* is used in legal language to make it explicit that a (usually binding) speech act is being performed. See also Trosborg (1995) on this topic. Legal language is full of open performatives of this type, such as 'I hereby promise to pay . . .', 'I object', 'I authorize the bearer of . . . ', 'I hereby renounce all rights in . . .' and so on.

The explicit marking of a speech act is particularly noticeable in the enacting formulae at the beginning of legislation. The following are examples, some taken from Kurzon (1986).

England

> Be it enacted by the Queen's most Excellent Majesty, by and with the advice and consent of the Lords Spiritual and Temporal, and Commons, in this present Parliament assembled, and by the authority of the same, as follows
> . . .

USA

> Be it enacted by the Senate and House of Representatives of the United States of America in Congress assembled, That . . .

Germany

> Der Bundestag hat mit Zustimmung des Bundestages das folgende Gesetz beschlossen
>
> (The Bundestag has decided with the agreement of the members the following law)

Italy

> La Camera dei Deputati ed il Senato della Repubblica hanno approvato;
> Il Presidente della Repubblica
> Promulga la seguente legge
>
> (The House of Deputies and the Senate of the Republic have approved;

The President of the Republic
Promulgates the following law)

Egypt

ينشر هذا القانون في الجريدة الرسمية ويعمل به اعتباراً من اليوم التالي لتاريخ نشره يبصم هذا القانون بخاتم الدولة وينفذ كقانون من قوانينها ؟

(This Act shall be published in the official gazette and shall become effective from the day following the publication date [. T]his Act shall be stamped with the State seal and be implemented as an Act of State.)

In both the US and English formulae, the expression 'be it enacted' is used. This is an example of a direct 'performative' that is the words themselves do the enacting directly. Notice the use of 'as follows' in the English formula, which gives the power to enact to all the following text. The US 'that' syntactically constrains severely the text that follows, mostly demanding that things be given the form 'shall (be/do)'.

The German formula is not explicitly performative in the same way, using the verbs 'decide'. The Italian verb *promulga* 'promulgate' ('publish as coming into force' *OED*) is directly performative. The Egyptian law does not use a performative verb, but does none the less state that the Act 'shall become effective'.

Jackson (1997) uses a careful analysis of the processes of the enactment of English laws to challenge the notion that these are in fact enactment speech acts. However even if the intended meaning of the words (their illocutionary force) does not in reality apply (their perlocutionary force), this does not change the meaning and intent of the performative act.

Discourse

A major discourse feature of the language of the law is the genres that are used. These are addressed in chapter 4. However, reference will be discussed here – that is the way a participant or entity is referred to in a text. There are two issues – first how to establish who or what is being referred to in the real world outside the text (which is dealt with above in the section on 'Words'); and second how to refer back to the earlier mentions of a participant within the text.

Pronouns

In everyday speech and writing, we tend to introduce reference to a participant for the first time by clear reference to the outside world such as *Linda Javanovic, The Bell Telephone Company*, or *Macintosh PowerBook 1400c* but thereafter, so long as it is clear, we will refer back using pronouns such as *she* and *it*. However, in operative documents pronouns are mostly avoided. Once more, this is due to the pursuit of precision, avoiding any possible ambiguity that might arise if a pronoun is used – for instance in 'Henry asked Max if he could come back tomorrow', it is unclear whether 'he' refers to Henry or Max. However, the complete avoidance of pronouns is probably not justified on this basis – there are many occasions when only one possible referent can be found. However legal drafters find it safer to avoid pronouns, since lawyers are notoriously expert at exploiting any possible ambiguity or alternative interpretation. In figures 2.1 and 2.2 it can be seen that true pronouns are not used: in a non-legal text this would be unlikely.

Sometimes pronouns are used however, and Solan (1993b: 38–45) gives a number of cases where possible ambiguity in pronoun reference leads to litigation, or forms a basis for judgments. Solan also points out that the judgments are inconsistent, and that a textual argument based on pronoun reference is masking other agendas, particularly social justice, as in the sad cases he recounts of Mr Bass and Mr Eddings.

One way that pronouns are avoided is that the full name or a noun phrase is used. For example in table 2.1 *the take-over announcement* is simply repeated towards the end of the text. However, sometimes alternative approaches are used to reduce the length and repetitiveness of using a full form each time (see the sections that follow).

This phenomenon is not limited to English, and it can take an interesting form in Spanish, a language in which subject pronouns are mostly not used since person and number are carried in verb endings. However, if we examine the following interaction (from Gibbons 2001) between a Chilean court official (a *relator*) to a witness, we can see that this normal Spanish pattern is broken.

Relator: *En este tema del relato . . . tiene que decirme de la forma más clara*
y precisa todo lo que sepa o recuerde de los hechos que yo voy a
preguntar. Importante que ese relato sea en forma clara y precisa . . .
y un poco lento . . porque yo tengo que ir escribiendo todo lo que
usted *me dice.*

[Concerning the statement . . . you have to tell me in the
clearest and most precise form all that you know or remember of
the facts that I am going to ask you about. It is important that
this statement is clear and precise . . . and a little slow . . . because I have to write down everything you say.]

Witness: *Muy bien.*
[OK]

Relator: *Mm . . . No puede hablar con las partes que están acá presente ni*
con el abogado. Las preguntas siempre las hago yo.

[Mm . . . You may not speak with the parties present here . . .
nor with the lawyer. It's always me that asks the questions.]

Witness: *Bien.*
[Right]

Relator: *Para que yo se las reformule para contestarlas ¿ya? Y en respecto de*
los hechos constitutivos de la terminación de los servicios del señor
Oro [apellido cambiado] en servicios alimenticios limitados. Con este
constitutivo a que nos referimos . . . primero . . . si fué o no fué
despedido . . . si recuerda **usted** *la fecha en que fué despedido . . . por*
qué persona fué despedido . . . y qué . . . y qué razones se . . . eh . . .
argumentaron para . . . para . . . proceder a depedir al señor Oro
¿ya?

[So that I can formulate the questions for you to answer them
– Ok? In respect of the constitutive facts of the termination of
the services of Mr Oro [name changed] in limited catering services. The constitutive facts to which we refer are . . . first . . . if
he was or was not dismissed . . . if you can remember the date
when he was dismissed . . . by what person he was dismissed . . .
and what . . . what reasons . . . were given for . . . for . . . proceeding with the dismissal of Mr Oro – Ok?]

In this interview the first use of *yo* is redundant because the information is
carried in the verb form, and this is even more the case in the three subsequent repetitions. The use of *usted* is justifiable on the first reference, but
not on the second use, nor indeed in many other subsequent uses in this
interview. This is a form of hyper-precision similar to that found in English.

Defined pro-forms

One way to establish unambiguous reference while avoiding redundancy, is to set up special meanings for words or expressions by means of definitions, so that these words can be used throughout the body of the text. For instance in table 2.1 'the principal offence' is established as a defined term to be used throughout the subsection. It acts like a precise pronoun, avoiding the long and complex noun phrase, so I shall refer to it as a 'defined pro-form'. Such forms are used to copy a concept through a text. They are sometimes known in legalese as **referential indices**.

These definitions can be part of the main text, or they can be given in a glossary at the end. The text in figure 2.1 contains another example of the establishing of a defined pro-form in the body of the text, in the section labelled 'definitions'.

This type of document has been developed to cover many possible clients. Rather than changing names all the way through, names are established at the beginning and are copied through the document by the word *client* or *party*, as are the *consultancy services*. Other words that are commonly used in

---

Consultancy Agreement

Dated 15 March 2001
BETWEEN
Dr Justin Thyme, Department of Languages, University of Sydney
(**"Dr Thyme"**)
AND
Tyde Investments Company, George St, Sydney (**"the Client"**)

WHEREAS:
The Client has requested that Dr Thyme carry out the activity described in **Schedule 1** (**"Consultancy Services"**)

IT IS AGREED AS FOLLOWS:

1. DEFINITIONS
"Parties" means Dr Thyme and the Client and **"Party"** means either one of them as the context requires
...

Figure 2.1   University of Sydney consultancy agreement

---

18. Definitions

In this policy, some words have special meanings:

- "accident"
  includes a series of accidents arising out of the one event
- "car"
  means a motor vehicle with 4 or more wheels either registered for use on a public street or capable of such registration and includes the car's equipment
- "you"
  means any one of the persons who are named as the insured in the current schedule, or them all.

Figure 2.2   NRMA car insurance 'Plain English Policy' (1986)

this way are *owner, offence, agent* and *life insured*. A more old fashioned usage is *the party of the first part, the party of the second part,* etc. (lampooned by the Marx Brothers in *A Day at the Races*).

An example of defined pro-forms established in a glossary is found in figure 2.2. It is interesting to note that in figure 2.2 even a pronoun *you* is established as a specialized and defined pro-form. Sometimes defined proforms are printed with an initial capital letter to show that they have been defined and are being used in that defined way (see Tiersma 1999: 117). This use of defined pro-forms also means that essentially the same document can be used for different transactions, with the reference of the proform redefined for each use. Tiersma points to a future in which texts are routinely stored and accessed upon computers; then defined terms could be given in hypertext, so that the reader can, at will, be led to a definition of the term as used in that text.

Core noun with deictic

Another way of attempting to ensure certainty of reference within a text is to repeat the core noun, along with a deictic, which points fairly clearly to the place where the full form is used. For instance in table 2.1 *the terms so varied* is used to refer back to *those terms have been varied under section 17* – *terms* is the core noun, and *so varied* is used as a deictic expression to copy *varied under section 17*. Similarly in the same text *such a person* is used to refer back to *a person whose shares may be acquired pursuant to the takeover announcement*. In this example, *person* is the core noun, and *such a* is used to refer to all the material after *person*. Obviously repetition of this noun phrase would be unnecessarily clumsy and long. While *such a person* is general in meaning, apparently opening its reference to misinterpretation, this is countered by the interpretation principle **noscitur sociis** mentioned previously which says that words should be interpreted according to the textual context in which they appear.

Interpretation

While the meaning of individual words or expressions is one way in which the meaning of an operative text may be examined, another angle is to see a text, or section of a text as an entity with a global meaning and intent. In most cases interpretation of whole texts is reasonably clear and unambiguous. It is over so-called 'hard cases' that debate concerning principles of interpretation arises. Solan (1993b: 177) describes such cases as ones where the legal 'doctrine says nothing about how a particular dispute should be resolved, or when what it says cannot be clearly applied to the facts in dispute, or when it says something that will lead the judge to commit what he considers an injustice.' It may be worth reminding readers that judicial decisions impact not only on individual cases, but also enter future decisions through 'precedent' – the system of checking to see how other judges have ruled on a particular piece of legislation, other operative document, or the use of a word in speech.

To give some idea how these varied linguistic systems can operate in tandem, let us examine a judgment from Malaysia *Malaysia Tobacco Co Bhd v. The Roadrailer Service Bhd* [1995] MLJ 847. The undisputed facts of the case were that The Roadrailer Service Bhd, a transport company, agreed to deliver certain goods (presumably tobacco products) worth RM359 558.34 to Northern Malaysia. However the haulier was robbed of the goods *en route*. The issue was whether the haulier was liable to make good the losses of the tobacco company, on the basis of the following clause in their agreement.

Indemnity

15.1   The hired haulier shall be fully responsible for the safe receipt and delivery of the goods. The hired haulier undertakes to indemnify the company in full for all losses, shortages/damaged goods, arising from whatever cause including misdelivery and mishandling by person with the hired haulier's control, theft, burglary, pilferage, fraud, dishonesty and criminal breach of trust.

15.2   ...

The haulier denied liability on two linguistic bases: (1) that 'theft' does not include 'robbery'; (2) that 'cause ... within the hired haulier's control' does not include robbery, since robbery is not within the control of the haulier. The judge in this case, Judge Mokhtar Sidin, rejected these arguments and found the haulier liable.

In the case of (1) it could be argued that 'theft' is taking by stealth, while 'robbery' is taking by the use of violence or by the threat of violence. The judge however followed a precedent from *Wong Kon Poh v. New India Assurance Co Ltd* [1970] 2 MLJ 287 which found that 'robbery is an aggravated form of theft ... on any reasonable construction'. This in essence an argument based on word semantics. However the precedent also used a constructed scenario.

> where a thief attempted to sneak off on the appellant's motorcycle and managed to do so, it was of course a case of theft which was covered by the policy; but, if the thief, while interrupted in the act, drew a dagger and warned the appellant not to prevent his getaway, how in the name of commonsense can it be argued that the taking the latter case, was not as much a risk insured against as the taking by stealth?

This scenario uses two bases for argument – shared world knowledge of the act of stealing (notice the appeal to common sense), and, I would argue, in the last part, an attempt to reconstruct the intention of the person who wrote the clause.

Turning to (2), it was rejected by the judge on the basis that

> the interpretation submitted by the defendant is absurd. It is clear to me that the words 'by person within the haulier's control' were only applicable to wrongdoings stated in the first part of the clause, ...

Here the judge is making a grammatical judgment concerning the constituent structure of the complex sentence. The judge does not provide any evidence or support for his statement (it is likely that he is using the 'last antecedent rule' however). Linguistic descriptive tools could provide a systematic analysis of the issue. In my view, the judge's decisions were linguistically well founded.

The importance of linguistic factors in this decision is not unique. As noted earlier, in some jurisdictions it is common for the initial summary of judgments to have a section on 'Words and Phrases' where, for example, definition issues are highlighted. The question raised by Solan (1995) is whether linguists might make a positive contribution to the interpretation process. In the case of 'theft' the judge was able to use a precedent – however in the precedent case itself, it is clear that a linguist might use a range of techniques to address the semantic scope of 'theft' – some of which we mentioned above – such as analysis through concordancing and language corpora (Coulthard, 1994a). World knowledge-based understandings might be examined by a questionnaire of the type documented in Labov and Harris (1994), perhaps by asking people whether they felt that robbery was covered by the word 'theft' in this context. The judge's scenario also has the potential to form part of a research instrument – see for example the scenario questions in chapter 5. The grammatical basis for resolving (2) could be made far more explicit by a linguist. Whatever the technique used, the linguist would clarify and make more concrete and explicit the basis for deciding, and in some cases might provide useful additional information. The question that remains unanswered is – would this really help? While such a process would open up further challenges (linguists after all often disagree), for true accountability to be achieved in legal interpretation, the interpretation process requires the maximum level of clarity and explicitness, and needs to be as fully informed as possible.

My understanding of this complex and contentious issue is that legal interpretation draws on three sources, which are described below. These understandings are drawn mainly from Solan (1993b), Tiersma (1999) and the special edition of *Washington University Law Quarterly* (73, 3). This journal was also the source of the following legal problem (originally drawn from the legal philosopher H. L. A. Hart) which is used as illustration:

> if there is a statute which bans vehicles from a park – is a person riding a bicycle along a cycle track in the park violating the statute?

(1) *Textual semantics.* This involves examining the wording of an operative document, at word, phrase, sentence or complex sentence level, within the context of the text as a whole (see the telephone directory and tobacco company cases discussed previously). There are two less obvious qualifications to this however. It is clear that judges do their interpretation within the parameters of legal register – words and grammar are not given their everyday construction, but one based on legal traditions in their use (see the previous discussion of *knowingly*). Those who call this the **plain**

meaning rule are using a misleading description, since legal register is not plain language and legal meanings are not plain everyday meanings. Second, the study of the psychology of reading has demonstrated un-equivocally that readers must use their **schemas** or world knowledge to make sense of text (Anderson and Pearson 1988; Kintsch 1988), and many of these schemas are culturally influenced (Baynham 1995). Judges of necessity use their schemas, but do not always recognize or acknowledge that they are doing so. They are in effect making judgments based on their understanding of the world and society, which means that this basis of interpretation (1) cannot in reality be deployed in isolation from basis of interpretation (3) below.

The bicycle scenario: On the basis of the textual meaning alone, bicycles are vehicles, and therefore the bicycle rider has committed an offence.

(2) *The legislators' intentions.* Rather than looking at the surface meaning of the words, the notion here is that the role of the judicial system is to achieve the legislators' intentions. This is likely to be the view of the role of the legal system held in the wider community particularly by legislators, but it is probably the one to which lawyers least adhere, although in *Mian Bashir Ahmad & Ors v. State of Jammu & Kashmir & Ors* AIR J&K Section 2.6 Acting Chief Justice Mufti Baha-Ud-Siddin states that it is 'a settled principle in India, that in order to determine the true nature and character of a legislative enactment it is permissible to take into consideration the history behind the enactment, the evils it was intended to eradicate and the circumstances under which it was enacted'. A similar view operates in the UK. The problem raised by American textualists is that it is difficult to determine the legislators' intent to the extent that it is not made explicit in the wording of the statute. Although poorly drafted legislation is common, the only means that judges have of determining the legislators' intent is by asking the legislators, undermining the separation of powers, or by examining records of the debate surrounding the legislation, which is costly in time, difficult in practice, and not necessarily reliable or effective as a means of determining intent.

The bicycle scenario. If the statute is an old one, it is likely that the legislators intended to exclude bicycles, which were much disliked in the early years of their history. If the statute is more recent, it may be hard to determine the intentions of the legislators.

(3) *Applying societal standards.* Much legislation and many other operative documents were produced in previous centuries when the world and society were different from their modern descendants. The adjudicator's role may then often be one of translating a text into the modern context, and in the process perhaps changing the application of the law. For instance, what was regarded as punishably indecent clothing in the nineteenth century is worn by judges nowadays, and they would not be party to attempts to impose these nineteenth century standards on twenty-first-century citizens. Similarly the element of the former British Lord's Day Observance legislation which used to make it necessary for a person buying an ice-cream on Sunday to eat the wrapper, was simply not applied by the police or courts. Similarly, when legislation is adopted from other cultures without sufficient modification, it is not applied literally by the legal system. This happened frequently in British colonies, and one suspects in the importation of continental legal systems into Asia. What all this can mean in practice is that judges apply their own moral standards when reaching their decisions, even though these may be masked (see Philips, 1998, for many examples). Solan (1993b) provides evidence that judges prefer to write their judgments as emerging inevitably from the wording of the legislation, using basis of interpretation (1), when they are in reality often making moral judgments, using basis (3).

The bicycle scenario. If current standards and understandings are applied, the cyclist is clearly not committing an offence in cycling along a designated cycle track. In this particular case this is clearly the basis for a sensible interpretation.

There is a continuing debate among lawyers: as to whether all three of these bases are valid; as to the weight to be attached to each of them in the interpretation process; and as to whether the first of them is to be used as the normal basis for interpretation and the other two are only 'fall back' bases, to be used when the first does not provide a clear resolution (this is the position of some 'textualists'). To many linguists it is clear from modern semantics and pragmatics that the notion that (1) can stand alone is untenable. As we observed in the discussion of (1), schemas enter into understanding, and schemas are to some degree socially and culturally constructed. I will venture to say that while all three clearly need to be used, the balance between them is an issue for lawyers and legislators. The main area where linguists could make their contribution is (1), although they are able to provide input to (2) and (3), for example in (2) the understanding of intent falls into pragmatics.

Knowledge Issues

Knowledge or discourse?

The notion of knowledge schemas will recur in this book, since it is self-evident that there are knowledge differences between lawyers and non-lawyers. Some legal jargon refers to legal concepts that require technical language since they are not part of everyday knowledge. However this issue extends well beyond the understanding of single words. Stygall (1994: 203 and elsewhere) makes a convincing case that lawyers are operating within a different conceptual and discoursal 'frame' – they construct, discuss and present events in way that differs from and may be unintelligible to non-lawyers. Like all specialist professions, lawyers have a unique subculture. Stygall also shows that, despite the lawyers' best efforts, in the courtroom that she observed this led to a failure of communication with jurors and a verdict that those operating within a legal frame might well regard as inappropriate – Stygall writes (1994: 202) 'the participants in this trial had consistently different understandings of the same experience'. Howe (1990: 215) notes 'Through the centuries lawyers have evolved their own way of reasoning.'

This different legal frame will manifest itself in several subsequent chapters.

The challenge for educators

The complexity and technicality of legal English is a considerable challenge for those charged with educating lawyers. Philips (1982) makes the point that much legal education is concerned with learning technical language, or as she puts it 'acquiring the cant'. The challenge is even greater when the language of the law is a second language, as it is for the majority of people subject to Common Law administered in English, taking into account the sub-continent, Malaysia and Singapore, anglophone Africa and the Pacific Islands. This issue is further addressed in Howe (1990) and Feak, Reinhart and Sinsheimer (2000).

Conclusion

As we have seen, the pursuit of precision is a significant driving force in the drafting and interpretation of legal documents. Their complexity and technicality is not simply a sinister plot to baffle and deceive, but is to a significant extent a reflection of the purpose of such documents – to define and control human behaviour in an unambiguous manner. This is a demanding task which places great responsibility on drafters. Furthermore, where every slip or possibility of misinterpretation may be exploited in the adversarial system, extreme caution and care in their production is required. The need for precision in such circumstances is undeniable, and it is hardly surprising that sometimes extreme linguistic measures have been deployed. However, when the pursuit of precision combines with extreme conservatism, archaisms and the planning and processing possibilities of the written language, the result may be language that is at best complex, and at worst arcane and unintelligible to non-lawyers. As I noted in Gibbons (1994) 'the pursuit of precision has produced obfuscation'. However, as we shall see in chapter 5, this problem may not be entirely intractable.

3

Interaction and Power

Detritus was particularly good when it came to asking questions. He had three basic ones. They were the direct ('Did you do it?'), the persistent ('Are you sure it wasn't you what done it?') and the subtle ('It was you what done it, wasn't it?'). Although they were not the most cunning questions ever devised, Detritus's talent was to go on patiently asking them for hours on end, until he got the right answer, which was generally something like: 'Yes! Yes! I did it! I did it! Now please tell me what it was I did!'

Terry Pratchett (1996)

Introduction

Power and solidarity

While the preceding chapters were largely concerned with written language, this chapter is mostly about spoken language. It examines interaction among lawyers, police and prison officers, and between these representatives of the justice system and the public. In such interaction the human relationship between the participants is mostly negotiated and manifested in language. Such relationships have been found to have two major axes: power and solidarity. This has been noted by linguists, social psychologists and anthropologists (Brown and Levinson 1978; Brown and Gilman 1960; Giles and Coupland 1991; Giles and Powesland 1975). The terms power and solidarity are used here in the broadest of senses. Solidarity includes group membership and interpersonal affect. Power includes both an individual's power over other individuals gained in day-to-day interaction, and social power, manifested typically in social hierarchy and organizational structures.

One aspect of interpersonal relations that we have already touched upon is group membership – there is a long and rigorous history of investigation of this in the field of social psychology, among others beginning with Henri Tajfel, and carried on by Howard Giles, who has also helped elucidate the relationship between group membership and language. In chapter 2 we noted that knowledge and use of specialist language is a powerful marker of membership of a specialist group, and such markers act both to support in-group solidarity and to exclude others. Specialist language carries important interpersonal information, even when that is not the primary motive for its use.

Concerning power, the justice system is arguably the most directly powerful institution in societies subject to 'the rule of law' (a telling expression). Politicians may enact laws, but it is the justice system that interprets and does or does not enforce them. In daily life a police officer is probably the most powerful person that an ordinary person encounters. In democratic societies this power is not necessarily a sinister conspiracy by dominant groups. Although the balance between control and freedom is by definition uneasy and continually negotiated, if we accept the democratic system, power is conceded by elected representatives to the justice system in order to enable the orderly working of society. If we accept that a system for applying the law is necessary, then authority will be ceded to law officers. To do their work, judges, police and prison officers must have their authority recognized, and their decisions and orders acted upon – maintaining that authority is a legitimate preoccupation (for judges see Philips 1998: ch. 5). An important manifestation of power relations is language behaviour. The manner in which power and authority are exercised through language is a significant issue in the study of language and the law.

The power of the legal system is beyond question. Goodrich (1988) gave the following description of the situation in England

> those who 'come before' the system of justice are rarely if ever successful in their pleas. The conviction rates in 1978 were 84 per cent of English Crown Court cases, 93 per cent of indictable offences, 95 per cent of non-indictable cases in the Magistrates' courts. It is the bureaucracy in the form of the police, administrative agencies and large corporate enterprises that are overwhelmingly the victors in the adversarial process of trial. In criminal cases for example the majority of defendants are unrepresented and statistically the vast bulk of them plead guilty as charged. . . . The defendant's day in court is seldom a voluble one, their hearing is brief and their processing swift.'

The literature on courtroom language tends to assume an elaborate ritual contest between skilled opposing lawyers – in reality this is rarely the case. As Goodrich notes, the law is a bureaucracy, and much of the power is a manifestation of organizational hierarchy.

The police too have considerable power. They often have a major role in deciding who comes to court, and in local courts their account of events carries great weight. Furthermore in the 'who polices the police?' dilemma, if they overreach the limitations on their powers, it may be difficult to check them. The words of Indian Dalit or untouchable Chunni Lal Jatav sum it up: 'All the judges of the Supreme Court do not have the power of a single police constable.' A constable, he says 'makes or breaks us' (*The Hindu*, 11 July 1999).

However the workings of the legal system, while wielding power, also purport to be **impersonal**. In principle the decisions reached by the law are unaffected by the personalities or personal feelings of those involved. Metaphors frequently used to characterize the law are a machine, or a disembodied system. This means that people in the courtroom are often referred to only by the name of their role in the courtroom, for example 'the witness may step down' said to a person at the end of their testimony. This may also partly explain the frequent use of passive voice in legal contexts (see chapter 1).

As a consequence of the above, Goodrich (1987: 3) observes that legal register is a 'hierarchical, authoritarian, monologic and alien use of language'. This chapter examines how that hierarchy and authority are manifested in legal language. It briefly indicates some of the externally imposed rules of interaction in the Common Law system. It then goes on to establish a distinction between primary and secondary realities that is needed as part of the conceptual framework that is used throughout the remainder of this book. Once more the model of communication frames the body of the chapter, looking at many aspects of communication where power asymmetry is manifested, beginning with non-verbal communication then moving on to the grapho-phonic level, address forms, the over-elaboration of 'copspeak', the speech of witnesses, turn taking in courtrooms, the much debated topic of coercion in questioning, and finishing with the many pragmatic strategies used by lawyers to control witnesses and their testimony.

Rules of interaction

To understand human interaction, one must understand the frames within which it operates, the assumptions and external regulations that hedge it around and impart much of its meaning. The strategic point of a deliberate violation of rules cannot be understood if one is not aware of them. This section outlines some of the externally imposed rules that operate within the Common Law system.

Lawyer–client

There are a range of constraints upon lawyer–client interaction governed by lawyers' ethics. In the Common Law, there is a norm which produces constraints upon what the defence lawyer will allow the client to say, what the lawyer will allow her/himself to hear from a client, and the advice that the lawyer can offer. This norm is that if clients say they are innocent the lawyer must act as if that is true, despite any personal convictions to the contrary. One interpretation of this is that lawyers' convictions are for sale. A more charitable but still disturbing interpretation is that lawyers are engaged in a ritual game, in which some detachment from reality is required.

Trials

In principle the norms of interaction in all courts involve politeness and formality. A formula used by judges to express the meaning 'come here' is 'you may approach the bench' – polite in the construction of the command, and formal in the use of the words *approach* for *come*, and *the bench* for *here*.

As noted earlier, in Roman Law systems the judges' role is to seek out the truth by examining evidence, to place that 'truth' within a legal construction, and to reach a verdict. The evidence is often written, witnesses are frequently not called – rather their written statements are used, as are written statements from police officers. Non-controversial evidence is rarely given in oral form. Only when the evidence is in conflict will the judge normally examine witnesses, to seek out the truth.

In a Common Law trial the legal process is 'adversarial', the prosecution and defence take up opposing positions and attempt to 'win' the case. There is no attempt (as in mediation or family courts) to try to find any middle ground or a compromise solution. As Evans (1983) notes 'It is, after all, a kind of miniaturised warfare, is the trial, conducted with all manner of rules of decency and honesty; but a kind of warfare it is.' These rules of decency and honesty include linguistic rules concerning counsels' questions and witnesses' answers, discussed in the section on questioning. Stone (1984: 299) notes 'Cross examination is a process of communication between two minds which often involves overt or concealed conflict. The advocate initiates and controls the process.' This raises the question how does the advocate maintain such control linguistically?

Police

Police treatment of prisoners is constrained by legislation and by rules of procedure that are contained in printed guidelines and are imparted by training and senior officers. In particular in Common Law countries the police have responsibilities for the health and well-being of witnesses and suspects, and there are strict regulations governing the time people may be deprived of their liberty before appearing before a judge. The norms of interaction include the right to silence – that is the right not to say anything, although this right has been weakened in Britain (see the section on silence). Furthermore, current guidelines normally include the notion that police interviews should be as open and non-coercive as possible. These regulations, and adherence to them, is discussed in the section on questioning.

Primary and secondary realities

Hale and Gibbons (1999) show that two intersecting planes of reality are manifested in courtroom discourse: the **primary** courtroom reality, consisting of the courtroom itself and the people present; and the **secondary** reality, the events that are the subject of the litigation. As we have noted already, the primary courtroom reality is a unique cultural and physical context. Police investigation and questioning likewise has these two layers, the current reality of the interview room (in a prison or police station), and the reality under investigation. There will be reference to both realities in the language of the courtroom or interview room. In chapter 1 we saw how the primary reality can be manifested linguistically, through the changes in language produced by the immediate context. The other plane of reality, the world outside the immediate context of courtroom or interview room, (most importantly the particular context and events that are the subject of investigation) is also manifested linguistically. For instance, if the subject of litigation is a robbery, then in court (the primary reality) witnesses will present linguistic accounts of the robbery – the secondary reality. The two layers are in constant interaction.

The use of the term realities is based on Bennett and Feldman (1981), but it should be noted that Clark (1996: 16–17) discusses this area in terms of 'layers of action'. He writes: 'Layer 1 is the primary layer of any conversation, where the participants speak and are addressed then and there as themselves. Layer 2 is built on top of layer 1 . . . Each layer is specified by its domain or world – by who and what are in it' (Clark 1996: 16). The secondary reality or realities are in Halliday's terms 'projected' through the primary reality. This chapter is concerned mainly with the manner in which relationships are managed within the primary reality of courtroom, police station or prison. The construction of the secondary reality is mainly addressed in the next chapter.

Non-Verbal Communication

Although this book is concerned primarily with language, the communication of power by non-verbal means is so marked in legal contexts that it would be remiss not to mention it.

Goodrich eloquently describes the non-verbal aspects of the courtroom as follows:

> On the portals of the court buildings will be inscribed the royal motto, '*Dieu et mon Droit*', while in other regimes it would be '*Fiat Iustitia*' or some variant thereon. The windows to the building are likely either to be barred or to be somewhat higher and narrower than is usually the case. Access to the rear of the building be likewise barred and the entrance to the courts will be in some varying measure imposing not simply by virtue of their size but also by dint of their elevation from the street. Whatever the form it takes, . . ., the threshold to the court building will be marked and physical access to the seats of justice will involve both a visual and conceptual ascension from the quotidian street to ritualized space. That the situation and external structure of the courts signify a degree of distance from the everyday and from the mundane concerns of public space gains further emphasis upon entry into the ritualized internal spacing of the courts, of the judicial world secreted in the heart of the city and wrapped in an archaic and sacral atmosphere of special functions and the silent unravelling of other times.
>
> The strategic organizing principle of the courtroom is a didactic one. It is that of the visibility of justice rather than of its audibility. The ritual character of proceedings in court have, first, an obvious material character in the higher courts in the form of the ceremonial dress of legal participants, in judicial robes and wigs, barristerial gowns and wigs, the use of royal red and emblazoned royal arms on and frequently also above the judicial seat or throne. To the aged pomp of the furniture and scale of the courtroom can be added the not altogether incidental features of procedure and address. . . .
>
> (Goodrich 1988: 148–9)

In similar vein, Oddie (1988: 49) describes English lawyers as people who 'are dressed in the clothes of the eighteenth century and are prone to use language of the nineteenth'. Recently some courtrooms have lost some of their external character, particularly when occupying levels of high rise buildings. In many cases separation from the everyday world is maintained by security checks rather than raised entrances. However the internal character of Common Law courtrooms remains consistently and deliberately imposing, with the judge's social elevation reflected in her/his physical position on a dais. (As well as Common Law courts, some of these trappings are found in other legal systems, for example in superior courts in China.) In the well of the court only court officials and lawyers are allowed, and they may move around during proceedings. Another non-verbal marker of power is that in the Common Law courtroom all must be on their feet when the judge is, so those in the courtroom are told 'be upstanding' or 'all rise' (or another formula) when the judge (and jury) enter or leave, and may not resume their seats until the judge (and jury) are seated or departed. Similarly lawyers usually remain on their feet while speaking. People leaving and entering the court will usually bow to the judge. All these are non-verbal markers of the authority of a person who has power over liberty, and in some countries, life.

In some jurisdictions, however, it is the legal system as bureaucracy that is most clearly marked non-verbally. Compare the pomp and circumstance of some Common Law courts with the following description of the Roman Law Juzgado 6° Penal, Oaxaca Centro, Mexico, taken from my field notes of 14 December 2000:

> A big room crowded with desks and word processors. Soft background muzak. A large Christmas tree with flashing lights. Christmas decorations, including large plastic reliefs of Santa and reindeer, a snowman, and a Christmas stocking. People wander in and out in an uncontrolled way, sometimes chatting loudly to staff. Other people are dictating statements to staff, who type them up on a word processor. The judge's area is enclosed, but has a large window so that everything going on inside is visible. The judge wears an ordinary suit, and emerges and mixes with the staff. No dais, no flags, no crests, no judicial garb. Essentially a modern open plan office with an area for the 'boss'.

Grapho-phonic Level

At this level, there is little doubt that legal English spellings and pronunciation are social markers, rather than a necessary means of communication – interpersonal rather than technical in their orientation. Looking first at pronunciation, as Tiermsa (1999) notes, the Latin and Norman French terms and expressions that are still used by the legal profession may have either a traditional English pronunciation, or a pronunciation based on the way in which learners are now taught to pronounce Latin and modern French, or even a mixture of the two. The English pronunciation includes stressed syllables (in bold in table 3.1): Norman French and Latin almost certainly did not have this stress pattern. While some of these 'English' pronunciations seem to be partly based on how their written form would be pronounced in English, it is perhaps worth noting that English church Latin (still occasionally used in Anglican churches) shares many of these pronunciation features, so this may also be a product of the impact of church Latin on the language of the law, and part of the survival of medieval pronunciation. Some examples (based on the alternative pronunciation given in the *Chambers English Dictionary*) are shown in table 3.1.

Table 3.1 'English' pronunciations of law Latin

Written form	*'English' pronunciation (stress in bold)*	*IPA*
amicus curiae	ah **my** kus **ku** riay	æˈmɑikəs ˈkuriei
bona fides	**bone**-uh **fie**-deez	ˈbəunə ˈfɑidiː z
res judicata	**race** ju dee **kay** tah	reis dʒudiˈkeitə
tort	**taught**	tɔːt
voir dire	vwah **dear**	vwaː diə(r)

Note: the pronunciations are presented in regular spelling in the second column, and in the International Phonetic Alphabet in the third

Tiersma (1999: 55) explains the coexistence of two pronunciations as follows 'the pronunciation of foreign terms presents lawyers with a difficult dilemma: they must choose between 'talking like a lawyer,' which requires using pronunciations that sound odd and uneducated to the modern ear, or imitating the more prestigious accents of classical Latin and modern Parisian French, which are taught by the schools as the correct standard. Usually talking like a lawyer is automatically the prestigious choice, making the decision an easy one. Here, however, lawyers are torn between the traditions of their own profession and what is regarded as prestigious by the rest of society. The result is that inconsistency reigns.' It should also be noted that as far as writing is concerned, there is also some inconsistency in spelling between Norman French and modern French spelling.

The other noticeable peculiarity of legal English spelling is archaicisms. 'Judgment' (rather than 'judgement') is always used by lawyers: use of judgement with an 'e' is a marker of non-membership in the legal profession. Some lawyers also use the spellings 'lodgment' 'abridgment' and 'acknowledgment' without an 'e'. This spelling is not consistent across words – lawyers do not always omit the 'e' in 'judgeship', and never do so in 'management'. It is worth noting that the prestige and influence of the law is such that *judgment* has penetrated everyday spelling – it is Basil Blackwell House Style! Another example is 'persuant' rather than the modern 'pursuant'.

In what follows I have not distinguished vocabulary, grammar and discourse since they interact in ways that make them difficult to separate, for instance coercive questioning is a lexical, grammatical and discoursal phenomenon.

Address Forms

Lawyers

Among lawyers perhaps the most interesting markers of power and prestige (as well as the impersonal nature of the justice system) are the address forms used in court.

This is particularly marked among judges and magistrates, who are rarely referred to by name in court. The form of address used to the judge (the second person) is *Your Honour*, *Your Lordship* or *Your Worship* depending on her/his rank. These address forms are followed by the third person of the verb 'If Your Honour pleases' 'Does Your Worship believe . . .'. In Spanish the judge may be addressed as *Usía Su Señoría Sr Juez* (Your Excellence Your Lordship Sir Judge). Even more tellingly in the first person judges may refer to themselves as *the court* or *the bench*. The judge, then, is not treated as an everyday interactant, but as an impartial third party, as the embodiment of the judicial system itself, thereby imparting authority to the judge's statements and decisions. In less formal US courtrooms, some lawyers may call judges *Judge* + *surname* (e.g. *Judge Freeman*) or *Judge* to their face.

In the second person, counsel may address or refer to each other as *my friend* or *my learned friend* and may also refer to each other in the third person as *the Crown, Counsel for the Prosecution* or *Counsel for the Defence*. Once more names are rarely used in Britain or Australia, since the person's courtroom role is seen as their primary identity. In my many appearances as expert witness, when I have heard the name of counsel used in court, it was often when they were being admonished by the judge. In the USA, however, the use of names is more common. The Clerk of the Court and the Usher tend also to be addressed by the title of their office. The forms of address represent a hierarchical social structure, in which all the 'inner' members, the lawyers and officials, have a defined status and role which is primary in interaction. Similarly, Michael Walsh (personal correspondence) reports that in Aboriginal Land Commission hearings, Aboriginal witnesses are often called by their first name (e.g. *Topsy, Billy*), while expert witnesses and lawyers receive title + last name (*Dr Walsh, Mr Charlton*), and the judge is called *Your Honour*.

Even when judges are named in the third person their powerful honorifics are maintained as in *His Honour Judge Gobbo*, or *Her Honour*. In legal documents judges' names are usually followed by a capital J, for example *Siti Norma Yaakob J*, or by a series of capital letters if the judge holds a special position, for example *V. C. George JCA* (Judge of the Court of Appeal), *Eusoff Chin CJ* (Chief Justice). Judges and other lawyers are also often referred to in both speech and writing as *learned*, for example *learned counsel for the appellant, the learned judge*. To gain perspective on this, one might ask about the impact of academics in meetings referring to each other as *the learned Associate Professor*. This phenomenon is not limited to English. Duarte i Montserrat and Martínez (1995) say that, as a legacy of the sixteenth century, in Spanish courts lawyers refer to each other as *ilustrísimo, excelentísimo, honorable* or *magnífico* (most illustrious, most excellent, honourable or magnificent). In Australian courtroom transcripts, while judges are referred to as above, it is common for lawyers to be referred to by their title + last name (*Mr Javanovic*), while witnesses are referred to by their first and last names only (*Wong Kit*). A clear social hierarchy is marked in this way.

Tiersma (1999: 169–70) presents interesting examples from brief 'sidebar' discussions in American courts. This is where a judge and counsel come together informally across the side-bar rather than the front of the judge's dais, operating outside the hearing of the jury and the usual rigid procedural framework of the court. In these examples one judge uses surnames and another given names when addressing counsel, although this usage is still not reciprocal. Tiersma also gives examples of the use of slang over the side-bar, and comment that this 'subtly reminds the participants that they are members of the same profession and need to maintain a certain level of collegiality' (Tiersma, 1999: 170): in other words, in-group solidarity comes into play as well as courtroom hierarchy. In Australian and British courts I have not come across evidence of counsel being addressed by their given name in court. O'Barr (1982) says that in the USA there is a tendency for witnesses to be addressed more by their given names when the offence is less serious, and by their surnames when the offence is serious.

Police

The police service is organized along essentially military lines, with 'ranks' such as *senior constable, sergeant, inspector* and, in the USA, *captain*. These ranks are a direct manifestation of hierarchical power relations. As in the armed forces, ranks can be used as forms of address face-to-face 'Yes, sergeant' or even 'Yes, sarge', and to talk about third parties, although given names may be used informally. In Chile, the carabinero hierarchy includes the full range of military ranks including colonels and generals. In Records of Interview participants may be referred to by their role in the proceedings , for example 'witness indicates stick', possibly a marker of the formality and impersonality of the interview.

Prisons

While some research on language has been performed in prisons (for example O'Connor 1994), I have found little about the language of prisons. However, like the police service, state prison services are usually organized along military lines with 'ranks', and therefore these ranks, for instance 'Governor', can be used both as forms of address, and to talk about third parties.

Over-elaboration

An interesting aspect of the language of the law is the use of formal rather than informal vocabulary – the use of *solicit* rather than *ask*, *proceed* rather than *go*, *effect* rather than *make*, and so on. This is not limited to English – Duarte i Montserrat and Martínez (1995: 96) mention the exact parallel tendency of legal Spanish to use *solicitar* rather than *pedir*, *proceder a* rather than *ir a*, and *efectuar* rather than *hacer*. It can also be associated with archaic language – for instance a barrister may *crave leave* from a judge, rather than *ask for permission*.

This phenomenon is particularly marked in the case of the police – it is sometimes stereotyped as the police officer saying 'I was proceeding down the highway in a south easterly direction' rather than 'I was walking down the road'. This is sometimes referred to as 'copspeak'. There is often no propositional reason for using this language, since it is not required for precise expression of ideas. Rather it seems to be an attempt to be formal that goes beyond what is needed. It may sometimes be an attempt to adjust speech to a higher register (see the conclusion to this chapter), and to make claims to power and authority. Maley and Fahey (1991: 8) give the following example from a police sergeant's courtroom testimony.

PO: I was unable to maintain the light being illuminated
C: To keep the torch on?
PO: To keep the torch on.

A common manifestation is the use of *male/female* to describe adults, rather than *man/woman*, as in this description of wanted persons given by a senior police officer on Australian radio.

One male in a white T-shirt. The other male is not further described.

Sometimes this goes so far as to refer to men and women as *male person* or *female person* (the suspect is of course unlikely to be a male duck). A written example (humour unintended) from the previous New South Wales Police Service Instructions to Police is:

If you are required to attend premises used for prostitution in the course of your duty, avoid allegations of impropriety by making an entry in your notebook, diary or duty book showing the purpose of the visit.

Notice the complex vocabulary particularly grammatical metaphor (not saying for example 'write down why you went there'), and the even more complex syntax.

In the following short extract from an interview, Olivia Lau (a student at Sydney University) is talking to Michael, a young New South Wales police constable about this phenomenon. He says openly that the reason for the use of over-elaboration (despite strictures against it during his training at the NSW Police Academy) is to be appropriately formal.

Olivia Lau: Basically, I'm investigating 'copspeak' and the use of 'Plain English' instead
Michael: Oh, 'Copspeak' is things like 'decamped' . . .
Olivia Lau: I haven't heard of that one.
              . . .
Olivia Lau: There was a good one . . . oh, what was it? Something about some guy got shot and he was dead
Michael: Oh. He was hit by a projectile from a high powered weapon, numerous times until his bodily functions ceased.
Olivia Lau: That's pretty good 'copspeak' (*laughter*)
Michael: (*laughs*) Something like that
Olivia Lau: So, do you actually use that type of language?
Michael: Well . . . they've told us not to . . . and just to use normal English . . . so we try our best, but it always pops its head up.
Olivia Lau: But, where do you get it from? Like, do you know what I mean.
Michael: yeah . . . its just, umm . . . when you're doing a police statement, you think it's gotta be formal

Later in the same interview Michael gives the same 'formality' explanation for his asking a second language English speaking shop-lifter how she 'removed the items' rather than 'took the clothes' in the following extract from a police record of interview:

Q.   10   How did you remove the items?
A.   I took the clothes and put them inside my body, underneath my clothes.

I have also found examples in police interviews where there is a blending of casual language with formulaic copspeak. In the following example the casual language is in *italics*, while the over-elaboration is in **bold**.

Is there anything **further** that you would like to tell me **in relation to this matter** *that we are talking about?*

Examples of copspeak vocabulary

Word	Everyday equivalent
affirmative	yes
decamp	leave the scene
disturbance	fight
en route	on the way
exit	get out (eg. *exit the vehicle* = get out of the car)
male/female	man/woman
negative	no
party	person
vehicle	(usually) car

The copspeak phenomenon has been noted in Britain, Australia, the USA and Canada, but is not limited to the English speaking world. Chilean informants state that it is also common in the speech of their police. One provided the following example of language used by a policeman when she left her car to plead about a speeding ticket.

Vuelva y retorne al vehículo, y permanezca en él
(Go back and return to the vehicle, and remain in it)

Rather than:

Vuelva al auto y quédese ahí
(Go back to the car and stay there)

Note in particular the exact parallel in the use of the word *vehicle*, the use of a doublet *vuelva y retorne*, and the formal written vocabulary of *retorne* and *permanezca*.

Linguistic Indicators of Power

Emerging in part from early work on language and gender, particularly Lakoff (1975), a number of researchers (e.g. Scherer 1979) isolated speech attributes that appear to make speakers seem more (or less) influential or powerful to hearers. Powerful attributes include:

- **loudness** and variation in loudness
- a larger **pitch** range (i.e. varied intonation)
- **repetition**
- **silent pauses** rather than filled pauses (*um*, *er*)
- **interrupting**
- **not using expressions of agreement**
- **fluency**
- **coherence**

Speech attributes that may make speakers seem less powerful are:

- **hedges** – 'sort of', 'kind of', 'you know'
- **hesitation** – um, er, oh well, let's see
- **uncertainty** – often asking questions
- **use of** '*sir/ma'am*'
- **intensifiers** – 'very', 'definitely', 'surely' (note the effect of using an intensifier rather than an unqualified statement; e.g. 'I definitely saw him' vs. 'I saw him')
- **time taken** – powerless take longer to say the same things
- **mitigation** – 'would you mind if', 'sorry to trouble you'

This is important for both the courts and police interrogation, because powerful speakers are more likely to be able to dominate discourse, and because less powerful speakers may be less convincing as witnesses. A large and important study was performed at Duke University to investigate the effects of such speech attributes in legal contexts. This was reported initially in Conley, O'Barr, and Lind (1978), and then extended and expanded in Lind and O'Barr (1979) and O'Barr (1982). I will attempt to summarize its major findings here.

Their methodology was derived from research into the social psychology of language. Lengthy recordings of courtroom discourse were made in Durham, North Carolina, and analysed to detect linguistic features of interest. Fifteen minute segments of courtroom discourse were re-recorded after careful 'doctoring' to enhance various of the characteristics mentioned above that were of interest to the team. There were two actors, one male, one female, who made powerful and powerless versions of the testimony (a total of 4 tapes).

In the first study, the tapes were played to university students, and in a standard social-psychological framework, they were asked to complete rating scales about the voices. The rating scales were:

- competent, intelligent, qualified (= competence)
- likeable (= social attractiveness)
- trustworthy
- powerful, strong, active (= social dynamism)
- 'how much do you believe . . .', how convincing . . . (= convincingness)

The results are shown in table 3.2.

Table 3.2   Mean ratings of witnesses using powerful and powerless speech

Evaluation dimension	Power testimony	Powerless testimony
Female witness:		
Competence	2.38	0.72
Social attractiveness	2.48	0.54
Trustworthiness	3.04	1.65
Social dynamism	0.67	−0.67
Convincingness	3.35	1.77
Male witness:		
Competence	1.77	0.11
Social attractivness	2.52	1.23
Trustworthiness	3.48	2.00
Social dynamism	0.83	−0.98
Convincingness	3.89	2.48

Source: Lind and O'Barr 1979: 73

The difference between the male and female voices is not large, and on most variables is insignificant. However, the difference between the 'power testimony' and the 'powerless testimony' is significant ($p < .05$) for both sexes on all the evaluation dimensions. While all the dimensions might affect the way testimony is evaluated by jurors, the dimensions that have the strongest implications are 'trustworthiness' and 'convincingness'. In terms of the model presented earlier, the behaviour of witnesses in the primary courtroom reality affects perceptions of the secondary reality, the events under litigation.

O'Barr later played the taped voices to another 96 students (46 male, 50 female), but this time the rating scales were changed to enhance their relevance to jurors' judgments of witnesses. The scales were:

- convincing
- truthful
- competent
- intelligent
- trustworthy

The introduction of the 'truthful' dimension is particularly important. The results were equally strong.

Table 3.3   Average ratings of witnesses using powerful language

	Female witness		Male witness	
	Powerful	Powerless	Powerful	Powerless
Convincingness	3.00[a]	1.65	3.52	2.09
Truthfulness	3.70	1.88	4.24	2.86
Competence	2.61	0.85	2.44	0.18
Intelligence	2.57	0.23	1.80	0.18
Trustworthiness	3.04	1.65	3.48	2.00

Source: O'Barr 1982: 74

All differences between the 'power testimony' and the 'powerless testimony' are statistically significant ($p < .05$) for both sexes. O'Barr (1982: 75) notes 'this experiment demonstrates that the style in which testimony is delivered strongly affects how favourably the witness is perceived, and by implication suggests that these sort of differences may play a consequential role in the legal process itself.' In other words, behaviour in the primary reality may affect the portrayal and the perception of the secondary reality.

Coherence and cohesion

We noted above that testimony is often presented in the form of a narrative account of the events that are the subject of the court's deliberations. They are 'stories' (Bennett and Feldman 1981): see chapter 4. It is a common courtroom practice for counsel to fragment such narratives by eliciting them point by point by means of questions. This is once more a power issue, since in the fragmented 'question heavy' narrative, it is the lawyer who is overtly in control of the discourse, constraining what the witness can say (see also 'Coercion in questioning' below), and deciding the organization and ordering of the account. O'Barr and his colleagues felt that if a story was presented in this fragmented way, it might be less convincing, and jurors might associate the witness's lack of control with a lack of competence and power (this is based on psychological 'attribution theory').

The method used to investigate the issue was the same as the previous studies. This time the tapes had the same content, but in the 'narrative style' tape recordings thirty questions were used to elicit the narrative, while in the 'fragmented' tapes, 131 questions were used. Once again, male and female speakers were used, so there were four tapes. The subjects were 82 undergraduates (42 male and 40 female), some of whom were law students, and some psychology students.

The results (O'Barr 1982: 80) were not so clear as in the previous studies, but indicated that students generally gave a lower rating to the witness's competence and social dynamism (equivalent to interpersonal power) in the 'fragmented' testimony, and also perceived the lawyer to have a lower impression of the witness's competence and social dynamism.

Over-elaboration

O'Barr (1982) refers to over-elaboration as 'hypercorrect register'. It probably occurs in the speech of witnesses when they attempt to adjust their speech to legal register, and perhaps also to make claims to the power and authority of that register. Unfortunately there is a tendency to overshoot and use an excessively elevated style. The phenomenon was also noted by Labov (1969). O'Barr (1982: 86–7) gives the following wonderful real example from courtroom discourse (elements in italics are formal, those in bold are over-elaborate).

Counsel: Immediately after the collision, what happened to you?
Witness: Well, *directly* after the **implosion**, I *vaguely* remember being
          hurled *in some direction*. **I know not where**, but I went, I
          hurtled through the air *some distance*. I must have been uncon-
          scious at the time. I did **awake** *briefly*, and during that **in-
          terim**, Mr Norris was standing over me, uh, **perhaps more
          than likely** getting ready to *administer* first aid. But, I, I **re-
          lapsed** into a **comatose state**, and I, I can't remember any-
          thing after that for the next **72 hours** or so.

Once more O'Barr and his colleagues used a guise voice study to examine
the impression that such a style gives to listeners. This time only two male
voices were used. They spoke either in a formal or an over-elaborate style.
The judges this time were asked to score the voices on the following scales:

- convincingness
- competence
- qualified
- intelligence

They were also asked whether they would award compensation to the
plaintiff. The results are shown in tables in figure 3.3 and 3.5.

Table 3.4   Rating of witnesses speaking in formal and hypercorrect styles

Dimension	Formal	Hypercorrect
Convincingness	3.2[a]	2.1
Competence	2.2	−0.1
Qualified	−0.6	−3.2
Intelligence	0.4	−1.3

[a] All differences are significant at $p \leq .05$.
Source: O'Barr 1982: 86

    Tables 3.4 and 3.5 show that the over-elaborate speaker is judged more
negatively on all the rating scales, and worryingly, is much less likely to
receive compensation for injuries. We must then ask who is likely not to
control formal register, and to overcompensate in this way. The answer in
all probability is the less educated.

Table 3.5 Compensation awarded against defendant speaking in formal and hypercorrect styles[a]

	Formal	*Hypercorrect*
No compensation	14	8
Compensation award to plaintiff	7	13

[a] Chi square = 3.46; $p < .1$.
Source: O'Barr 1982: 87

In general this set of studies shows how behaviour in the primary reality can affect the portrayal of the secondary reality. The studies demonstrate how interpersonal variables in language behaviour in the primary reality affect credibility, in other words the hearer's willingness to accept the speaker's account of the secondary reality. Another way to view this is that the communication of the speaker's social identity affects the communication of the propositional content, or ideas.

The implications of this set of studies for the justice system is disturbing. It appears that people who are less powerful in society may reflect their status in their speech behaviour, and thereby be less convincing as witnesses. Particularly when they are the accused, or when they are plaintiffs in injury cases, this effect could be damaging, and they may be less likely to receive justice. A criticism sometimes directed against this type of study is that they use an experimental context with a simulated jury, while the reality of the courts is more nuanced and complex. Like most research work, we can only examine parts of the whole picture. Although there have not been studies like those of O'Barr and his colleagues on the interaction between police and the public, it appears likely that there will be similarities in the way linguistic factors operate.

Turn Taking

Turn taking is an interesting manifestation of power relations. In the courtroom the most powerful person, the judge or magistrate can speak and interrupt at will, so judges can take a turn almost whenever they wish. The least powerful people, observers, can be punished, imprisoned even, for contempt of court if they speak at all or even laugh. Witnesses are given a 'turn' at talking, but they have little control over when they speak, and over what they say. Witnesses may spend hours or even days awaiting their turn. Furthermore, counsel frequently interrupt witnesses, but witnesses are not expected to interrupt counsel. Counsel are given many more turns at talk, but these are constrained: during questioning of witnesses, the counsel who called the witness asks questions (examination-in-chief), then the opposing counsel may ask questions (cross-examination), then the counsel who called the witness is given an opportunity to ask follow up questions (re-examination) – see the section on jury trials in chapter 4. Counsel may interrupt each other according to strict rules of procedure, for instance to raise an objection, but they do not usually interrupt the judge. Jurors may rarely ask for assistance during proceedings through their foreman, but they are generally not allowed to speak until they deliver their decision through their representative. Court officials rarely speak publicly inside the courtroom. Once more these turn taking conventions reveal a hierarchical social structure. However, in a context where two sides are attempting to present competing or conflicting views, control of turn taking may be needed to prevent a verbal brawl. The assumption underlying courtroom turn taking is that it is the best means of maintaining order in court. For a more detailed discussion, see Philips (1998: ch. 5).

In police interviews control of the interview rests with the interviewing officer – s/he has control of topic and turns. This can result in topics and turns being decided against the wishes of the interviewee. Fairclough (1989: 18) gives the following powerful example.

This text is part of an interview in a police station, involving the witness to an armed robbery (W) and a policeman (P) in which basic information elicitation is going on. W, who is rather shaken by the experience, is being asked what happened, P is recording the information elicited in writing.

(1)   P: Did you get a look at the one in the car?
(2)   W: I saw his face, yeah.
(3)   P: What sort of age was he?
(4)   W: About 45. He was wearing a . . .
(5)   P: And how tall?
(6)   W: Six foot one.
(7)   P: Six foot one. Hair?
(8)   W: Dark and curly. Is this going to take long? I've got to collect the kids from school.
(9)   P: Not much longer, no. What about his clothes?
(10) W: He was a bit scruffy-long, blue trousers, black . . .

(11) P: Jeans?
(12) W: Yeah

How would you characterize the relationship between the police interviewer and W in this case, and how is it expressed in what is said?

The relationship is an unequal one, with the police interviewer firmly in control of the way the interview develops and of W's contribution to it, and taking no trouble to mitigate the demands he makes of her. Thus questions might be quite painful for someone who has just witnessed a violent crime are never mitigated; P's question in turn 1, for example, might have been in a mitigated form such as *did you by any chance manage to get a good look at the one in the* instead of the bald form in which it actually occurs. In some cases, questions are reduced to words or minimal phrases – *how tall* in turn 5, and *hair* in turn 7. Such reduced questions are typical when one person is filling in a form 'for' another, as P is here: what is interesting is that the sensitive nature of the situation does not override the norms of form-filling. It is also noticeable that there is no acknowledgement of, still less thanks for, the information W supplies. Another feature is the way in which the interviewer checks what W has said in 7. Notice finally how control is exercised over W's contributions: P interrupts W's turn in 5 and 11, and in 9 P gives a minimal answer to W's question about how much longer the interview will take, not acknowledging her problem, and immediately asks another question thus closing off W's interpellation.

(Fairclough 1989: 18)

Questioning

In the quotation given at the beginning of this chapter, Terry Pratchett offers an unkind but amusing characterization of police questioning in his description of the technique of Sergeant Detritus of the Guard. It introduces several significant issues concerning questioning – the notion of questioning technique; gradation in the directness of questioning; and coerciveness.

Two objectives of questioning

There may be two objectives of legal questioning. Onc is a genuine process of elicitation of information. Another is to obtain confirmation of a particular version of events that the questioner has in mind. The first type –

real information gathering – is in a sense 'unmarked', it is what we normally assume when the topic of questioning is raised. However, there can be many other agendas when questions are put: for instance in classrooms, teachers often ask questions to check whether students have mastered information, rather than to learn from them. In a trial, counsel usually already have extensive documentation of the events under litigation (indeed the Prosecution is obliged to reveal its information to the Defence in some Common Law trials). Lawyers often hope that no new information will emerge during a trial to disrupt their prepared case. In this context questioning is mostly not intended to elicit new information, but to supply a particular prepared account of events to the judge (and jury). Bülow-Møller (1991) even goes so far as to say that in a Common Law trial the real participants in court are counsel and the judge (and jury), communication is primarily from counsel to judge (and jury), and that witnesses are the means used to communicate counsels' portrayal of events. Jacquemet (1996: 9) similarly writes 'courtroom questioning techniques are primarily used to win, not to help the courts to discover facts' in the context not only of the Common Law, but also of the Italian justice system. In Roman Law trials the situation may be rather different. While the prosecution can use the full range of questioning techniques, the defence may have to ask its questions through the judge, who may reject or reformulate the questions. Certainly intense cross-examination, involving challenging and pursuing, is impossible in this context (Jacquemet 1996: 160–1).

Police questioning may also have (at least) two similar purposes. First the police may need to gather information about the object of their investigation, usually a crime. Secondly, however, they are attempting to obtain evidence that will lead to a successful conclusion of the investigation, usually a conviction. Baldwin (1993) refers to this as the pursuit of truth versus the pursuit of proof. While the first purpose is probably best served by open and non-coercive questioning, to elicit the witness's version of event, many police officers still believe that the second purpose is best achieved by coercive interrogation, to obtain confirmation of the police version of events, sometimes in the form of a 'confession' – in the words of Auburn, Drake, and Willig (1995: 355) 'Overwhelmingly, research conducted in many contexts has shown that police officers see the main purpose of the interview as one of obtaining a confession'. The problem with the second approach is that it has been subject to increasing challenge in court, discrediting both the police and their cases and, where vulnerable and persuadable witnesses are involved, has led to a number of proven miscarriages of justice. In turn this has brought about strong challenges to coercive interrogation from criminologists and human rights activists.

Shuy (1998b: Chs 1–2) provides a lengthy account of the interactive difference between 'questioning' which is a genuine search for the truth, and 'interrogation', and provides a particularly clear and forceful description of the difference, beginning 'Interviewers make use of less of their power than do interrogators. An interview probes but does not cross-examine. It inquires but does not challenge. It suggests rather than demands. It uncovers rather than traps' (Shuy 1998b: 12–13). He suggests that among the interactive language resources that characterize interviews (as opposed to interrogations) are question types, the organization of these question types into questioning genres, supportive feedback and clarification requests that are direct but not strongly coercive such as 'Could you explain that a bit more?' (these are also a form of question).

Coercion in questioning

Both police interviews and courtroom testimony mostly take a question and answer format, and it is the powerful parties – lawyers and police – who mostly ask the questions. In her classic book on testimony, Loftus (1979: 90–1) writes 'The form in which a question is put to a witness exerts a strong influence on the quality of the answer'. She also exposes the frailty of memory, and the ease with which a witness's memory and testimony can be influenced by a questioner (see particularly Loftus, 1979: 77–9; 90–9). When counsel and police, rather than gathering information, are attempting to have someone assent to a particular version of events, this involves both the construction of a particular version of events, in other words control of the information; and obtaining the compliance of the person being questioned, perhaps in part by not allowing the questioner's version to be denied. As Stygall (1994: 146) puts it 'For lawyers, the focus of attention to question forms is on how to control witnesses. Their assumption is that by controlling what the witnesses say, they will also control what the jurors think.' Cooke (1995a: 73) describes the questioning in a trial as follows: 'It became evident, in the course of numerous cross-examinations by counsel of those perceived as hostile witnesses, that a common strategy was to attempt to upset, unsettle, confuse, confound or otherwise intimidate such witnesses through an aggressive barrage of questions, in order to negate or discredit their testimony or to bring into question their personal credibility.' The attack on 'testimony' is an attack on the content of what they say, while the attack on 'credibility' is an attack on the person. This distinction will be expanded upon in what follows.

One way of constructing a particular version of events during questioning is to include elements of this desired version of events in the questions. The more information there is in the question, the less control the answerer has over the information, or the loading in the language used to describe it. Furthermore, information embedded in a question tends to be accepted by the answerer – Loftus (1979: 78) shows that information in the form of a question is 'a powerful way to introduce it'. Another aspect is the pressure exerted upon the answerer, both to reply, and to agree with the questioner. A related issue is the extent to which the information contained within the question is deniable – the question may contain presuppositions in a form that makes them difficult for the answerer to disagree with or challenge. This distinction between control of the person and control of the information is useful, although in practice the two will combine in a single question. This means that both aspects will need to be examined for their appearance in any individual instance of a question.

Questioning is one area where institutional talk can differ substantially from everyday conversation. Where there is an imbalance in the power relationship between the speakers, there is a tendency for the more powerful speaker not only to give more directives (which is predictable from the power relationship: see Mumby, 1988) but also to ask more of the questions, and for the less powerful speaker to be expected to provide more answers. This has been observed in doctor–patient interaction (Heller and Freeman (1987) and classrooms (Phillips 1985) as well as legal settings. For instance Harris (1984: 5) gives the following explicit exchange from a British magistrate's court.

J: I'm putting it to you again – are you going to make an offer – uh – uh to discharge this debt
Defendant: Would you in my position . . . .
J: I'm not here to answer questions – you answer *my* question

Harris (1984) also points out that in her data there are a number of examples of defendants requesting permission to ask questions of the magistrate, because they realize that this is a violation of the normal discourse rules of the court.

These power asymmetries do not only affect the right to ask questions, and the obligation to answer them. Power asymmetries can also affect the content of the less powerful person's answers. Loftus (1979: 98) points out that powerful people (including lawyers and police) 'can manipulate others more readily. They can persuade others, they can change attitudes, and they can influence the behaviour of others in countless ways'.

An element that commands and questions have in common is that they are both demands. Broadly speaking, a command is a demand for action, while a question is a demand for information. However, words such as 'demand' do not fit comfortably with the everyday experience of questioning or commands. In reality there is an interaction between modality and the demand feature. So commands may be ranked for their modality, from a hint, through a request, a simple command ('put the kettle on'), to a military order; in other words, from a very weak command to a very strong one (Searle 1976: 5, noted this, and there is supporting data in Gibbons 1981, and Trosborg 1997: 61).

Questions, too, have a modality range in the degree to which they expect compliance from the answerer. At one end of the scale, a question may be indirect, a subtle hint that some information would be welcome ('I wonder if . . .'), at the other end of the scale lies the military 'name, rank and number'. The strength with which the demand for information is made may depend on two variables in the power relationship. First there is individual power, which may simply be the power of the personality, but there is also social pressure since human relationships are a network of rights and responsibilities, sometimes including the responsibility to provide information: Grice's maxims (Grice 1975: 46), for instance, are based on this assumption. The second source of power may be the institutional relationship between participants: by definition, those in more powerful positions expect compliance from the less powerful – they expect their questions to be answered, and for answerers to agree with them, so a boss will probably expect compliance from an employee.

However, a second competing variable, politeness, is also at play (Brown and Levinson, 1978). There is widespread concern across human societies to avoid encroaching upon the autonomy of others. This means that even when the power relationship is such that one party expects compliance, her/his question may be expressed in a less demanding way 'could you tell me if . . .'. In this case the pressure on the answerer to provide information is masked, or perhaps mitigated, by politeness in the language.

The previous sample of police questioning from Fairclough (1989: 18) is a clear illustration of a situation where institutional power overrides normal politeness and the avoidance of imposition upon others. The power relationship in this case meant that the police officer assumed that only he had the right to ask questions, the right to expect answers, and therefore gave short shrift to the woman's questions and problems.

Another aspect of politeness is that in normal discourse there are 'preferred responses', extensively documented in Conversational Analysis (Heritage 1984: 265–9; Nofsinger 1991: 71–5). It has been shown that there is often a preferred (more polite) response to a particular conversational move. For example the preferred response to an invitation is an acceptance rather than a refusal. Responses in the courtroom or in police interviews may be influenced by this – for instance the preferred response to an evaluation is agreement rather than disagreement (Pomerantz 1984), exerting some pressure for agreement. A dispreferred response might affect a judge's and jury's opinion of a witness. In this case, politeness can serve as a mechanism for coercion.

Examining questions

A methodological tool to examine the nature of coercion is to look at the grammatical structure of questions from the powerful parties – lawyers and police – to see what kind of answer they license. While it is possible to answer a question in a way that is not expected by the question, or to challenge the question itself, particularly its assumptions, there is usually an **unmarked** response – for example a polar or 'yes–no' question such as 'Is this your shoe?' expects either 'yes' or 'no' as a reply, in other words 'yes' or 'no' is the answer licensed by the question. Although other replies are certainly possible, there is a strong tendency in courtroom discourse for lawyers to insist upon a 'yes' or 'no' response to polar questions. In a recent case in which I was an expert witness, the judge required me to give a 'yes' or 'no' answer to a lawyer's question, when I believed that such an answer was misleading.

Modality in questioning is managed in various ways. One is the level of directness or indirectness. One linguistic resource used is interpersonal metaphor, in which one speech act takes the linguistic form of another. So a question 'Has he arrived yet?' can be framed indirectly in the linguistic form of a statement 'I wonder if he's arrived yet'. In this example notice too that the other person's autonomy is preserved by not mentioning them, the question taking the form of an enquiry addressed inwards to the speaker rather than the addressee, thereby reducing overt pressure to answer. The examples in table 3.7 contain both direct and indirect forms, since they vary on the modality parameter, but not on the information parameter – for example 'Can you tell me what colour that nightdress was?' contains and demands the same information as 'What colour was that nightdress?', but the first is less coercive than the second, giving slightly more scope for non-compliance with the demand for information.

While indirectness could be seen as a 'weakening' device, there are also a number of 'strengthening' devices, which make the demand for compliance greater than that of a simple question. One is the use of 'tag' questions, which take the form of a statement, followed by a tag which places a degree of pressure for agreement upon the interlocutor. There are several tags that are common in legal questioning. In every case, if one constructs a simple polar question from the examples, the tag form is clearly more coercive. These are outlined in table 3.6.

The parameter discussed above is that of the questioner's power over the interlocutor, and concerns the latter's obligation to comply. A second type of control can also be exercised however, control over the information in the reply. This is in part a consequence of the amount of information embedded in the question itself. Sometimes questions contain all the information, and are put only for confirmation ('so you arrived at 4:30, eh?'). The more information included in the question, the greater the questioner's control of the information, so the answerer can contribute less new information. In legal terms, a question that includes the information is a 'leading' question.

Concerning information control, some main forms of question are laid out and exemplified in table 3.7. They include types of information elicitation that have the function, but not strictly speaking the interrogative form, of questions. Questions make the assumption that the answerer has the information. They are roughly ranked on a spectrum from less controlling to more controlling.

Another interpersonal metaphor and frequently observed question type is the 'requestion'. This is when a command has as its demanded action a verb of speaking, or perhaps more accurately, a verbal process. The example from table 3.7, Mr Gomez, could you please give your name' (Hale and Gibbons 1999: 211), has the characteristics of a request for action (e.g. 'could you please give a donation'), but the action required is the provision of information. Danet and Kermish (1978) call this a 'requestion' and Harris (1984) an 'interrogative request'. It may be worth repeating at this point that the control exerted by a question is not simply a matter of grammatical form. The form of the question interacts with other linguistic resources such as intonation and tone of voice, and various elements of the existing situation, particularly the structural power relationship, to create the degree of coerciveness of the question (see Eades 2000).

A technique for controlling information that is particularly clever or

Table 3.6 Questions formed with tags

Question type	Examples	Comment
Statements with reverse polarity modal verb tag	*Court* C: Well you see, you were saying to your wife, let me go, I want to hit this son of a bitch, weren't you? C: You're making this all up, aren't you?	*In examples like these, where the tag is combined with strong content and rise–fall intonation, this form places strong pressure for agreement*
Statements with same polarity modal verb tag	*Police* (P: What's his name? W: Micko) P: Micko, is it? *Court* C: He just volunteered that information, did he?	*Can be used to throw doubt on the credibility of a previous statement*
Statements with positive agreement tag	*Police* P: I have received information that you removed 1 pair of track pants, 2 pairs of ladies black pants, 1 ladies track top, 1 pair of ladies track pants from Target Store today without paying for them. Is that correct? P: You went to see him in Glenelg, is that right? *Court* C: It is the name of a disease. Would you accept that?	
Statements with negative agreement tag	*Court* C: . . . you saw the defendant and he came up to you and he held his fists up to you and	*Highly coercive – it seems to challenge the answerer*

	said things that weren't very nice and you said things back to him and did exactly what he did. Isn't that right?	
Questions with 'or not' tag	*Police* Was the car going or not?	*Possibly patronizing*
	Court C: Do you remember the infection or not?	

Table 3.7 Information control in questions

Question type	Examples	Information control (assumed and demanded)
Broad request for narrative	*Court* C: Do you remember the events of the 18th of January 1993?	*The topic is assumed, but the information on the topic is not constrained*
Limited request for narrative	*Police* P: Is there anything that you would like like to tell me in relation to this matter that we are talking about?	*Here only additional limited information is requested*
'Why' or 'how' questions	*Police* P: Would you care to tell me how the heroin came to be in your house tonight?	*Substantial information can be assumed, but there is some freedom in the information to be given*
Statement with rising intonation	(Written transcripts do not contain information about intonation)	*Neutral – can be information for confirmation, and/or an opening for comment by the witness*

Polar (yes/no) questions	*Police* P: Did you or did you not hit the big man with the wood? P: Did you actually see him hit the ground?	*The information is given in the question, but it is made overtly open to challenge*
'What' question without embedded information	*Court* C: Mr Gomez, could you please give your name (Hale and Gibbons 1999: 211)	*The nature of the information is specified – this information may be broad or narrow in scope.*
Wh- questions with embedded information	*Police* P: Can you tell me what colour that nightdress was? P: Who owned or took weapons to the hotel? *Court* C: What did she yell?	*There is pre-supposed information (that there was a nightdress; that weapons were owned/ taken: that she yelled). The response is restricted to a specified item of information.*
Either/or questions with a vacant slot	*Police* P: Did they tell you at that particular meeting or at some other time? W: About three months later. *Court* C: Did you close the door, do you remember, or did someone close the door? W: . . . I didn't close it. Could have been the doctor.	*There is given material, but the open slot usually provides the opportunity to supply new specified information*
Either/or questions	*Police* P: Was it a large club or a small club?	*Provides only two predetermined alternatives*
Rising intonation question	*Police* P: You were waiting for a train to go back to L? P: You pushed the little man?	

Statements with tags	(see table 3.6 above)	
Statement	*Court* C: You wanted to get into a fight. W: That's untrue	
Projected statement (questioner)	*Court* C: I presume that within that side of your book there were some conclusions?	*Similar to a statement, but more difficult to deny*
Projected statement (witness)	*Police* You were saying the big man hit F with the axe?	*'Quoting' back the witness's meaning – difficult to deny convincingly*
Agreement statements	*Police* P: Do you agree that when Police went to your home earlier tonight they found 20 bags containing heroin inside a leather bag in the loungeroom of your house? P: Do you agree that you told us that about that time you were at C railway station?	
Memory statements	*Court* C: Are you aware that your daughter says that she saw the doctor four times . . . in 1993?	

insidious (depending on one's view) is to use presupposition in such a way that the information content included by the questioner is made difficult to challenge. This can use a range of lexico-grammatical resources. These comments are based on linguistic analysis (my thanks to Jim Martin for his suggestions). Each category first has an invented sentence about a burglary to show the permutations, and then real examples. There are many grada-

Table 3.8   Deniability of information in lexico-grammatical forms

Lexico-grammar	Example	Response licensed by the form (using the burglary example)
Polar question	Did you burgle a house last night?	*"No I didn't"*
Information in a relative or subordinate clause	Police P: Do you own a watch? (What can you) tell me about the house **that you burgled last night**	*Perhaps "I didn't burgle a house".* *("No" is no longer licensed)*
	Police P: Could you identify **the woman who you shot?**	
	P: How far away from her were you **when you fired the first shot?**	
	P: What did you do **once you were inside the house?**	
Information in a whiz deletion/rank shifted	(What can you) tell me about the house **burgled by you last night?**	*Perhaps 'Not by me'.* *(Left open to follow up 'So you know about the burglary'?)*
	Police P: How many times did you hit **the man on the ground?**	
	Court C: Did you notice **the person near the library?**	

Information projected (reported speech of witness)	(How come) you told us earlier **that you had burgled the house?**	*Addressee cannot deny the information, only the projection e.g. 'I said nothing of the sort'*
	Court C: Well wasn't the evidence that you gave the court a minute ago **that he never touched the fence?**	
	Police P: You're saying **that he appeared to have been drinking?**	
Information as a memory or mental process	Do you remember **burgling the house /** You are aware **that you burgled the house?**	*Addressee cannot deny the information, only memory/thinking, etc.*
	Police P: Did you think **the girl wanted you to do this?**	
Information nominalized	P: You thought **he was alive at that stage?** Did you return to the scene of your latest **burglary?**	*Addressee cannot deny the information at all*
	Police P: Was anyone else hurt as a result of that first **fight?**	

tions and other possibilities: table 3.8 illustrates only some of them. In these cases the information is progressively 'buried' grammatically as we work our way down the table, and therefore more difficult to challenge.

Hale and Gibbons (1999: 215) give the following example of a lawyer's question to a witness in court.

C: You say when the you saw the defendant walking up the lane way,
you gave him a nasty look, didn't you?

The counsel states that the witness had admitted giving the nasty look. In
fact the witness had never at any stage either before going to court or in
court said any such thing. The tag gives the defendant the opportunity to
deny the act. Unfortunately, however, this question was posed through a
translator who did not translate the tag!

Official regulation of questioning procedures

Given the issues raised in the previous section, it is not surprising that
there have been attempts to regulate questioning in order to reduce coercive or abusive questioning, both in the courts and among police.

Courts

In the courtroom, there are in principle clear rules about 'leading questions'. A leading question is one where information is included in the
question, rather than elicited from the witness. Leading questions are not
normally permitted during examination-in-chief, when counsel is questioning a 'friendly' witness about the events under litigation. When counsels attempt to adhere rigidly to this rule, there can be agonizing exchanges
where the witness misses the point of the questioning, because if the
lawyer made the question more precise or pointed, this would involve
leading the witness. Sometimes judges intervene to resolve the dilemma.
However, in my experience leading questions are in reality common during examination of friendly witnesses.

Leading questions are, however, common in cross examination of 'hostile' witnesses. Certain types of leading question may use specific formulaic language forms such as 'I put it to you that . . .' and 'Is it not the case
that . . .' which marks their special status.

C: I'm putting to you that this defendant did not take any knife out of
his bag.

C: And I put it to you again that the defendant did not push you in the
back.

These formulas too tend to be coercive. Such leading questions are generally used to present a version of events that contradicts in some way that of the witness, attempting to push a change in testimony, or at least to present an alternative version of events to judge and/or jury.

Another rule is that opposing counsel can object to a question that contains an unproven supposition. Finally there is a rule that both counsel and witnesses should observe at least minimal courtesy – in principle abuse or facetiousness are not allowed.

Answers from witnesses are similarly constrained by rules. The first frame is that provided during the swearing in – to tell 'the truth the whole truth and nothing but the truth'. In essence, a witness should not give a partial reply, nor one that contains irrelevant information. Another rule of answering is that witnesses must answer – a refusal to reply may be contempt of court (unless they are defendants who take their 'right to silence').

Police

Senior police officers are well aware of the problems of interrogation described earlier, and in many police forces efforts have been made to address them. As a consequence, in Australia, Britain and the USA there has been a major effort to persuade police to use 'cognitive' interviewing techniques, which are much less coercive than the traditional police interrogation. In the USA this is exemplified, for example, in the work of Inbau, Reid, and Buckley (1986). In Britain, the introduction of a new Evidence Act (PACE) in the 1980s (after some notorious failures of police interrogation) led to large scale retraining of police officers in interview techniques. However, Baldwin (1994: 67) is cynical about the efficacy of changing police culture – he writes that, despite the PACE reforms in the UK, in police interviews 'officers are in many cases hell-bent on securing a confession'.

Among some police officers in New South Wales, pressure for less interrogation led initially to a rather strange interview technique, where the information was still controlled by the police officer, but after each question the officer said something like 'Do you want to say anything about that', for example:

P: I have been told by A that you made threats to her so she would pay the money. Do you wish to say anything about that?

P: During that telephone call you demanded $1000 from her. Do you want to say anything about that?

The intention of this technique would appear to be that of masking an interrogation as an interview in order to enhance its acceptability in court.

More recently the NSW Police Service have established programmes to help police officers to obtain narrative accounts from an interviewee, rather than attempting to extract an account they have pre-determined. In 1996–7 I was given an opportunity by the New South Wales Police Service to work with them on revising language aspects of the procedures laid out in their *Code of Practice*. This was done by a lengthy process of negotiation, and I was not involved in drafting the final version of the revised *Code of Practice*. What emerged contained improvements, and inevitably compromises and errors. The previous guideline for police officers concerning questioning (given below) states:

- do not assume that the person understands even simple questions
- phrase questions in a way that avoids a simple 'yes' or 'no' answer. This will ensure the person has some understanding of the question.

Its common failure can be seen in the fact that I have appeared in a number of cases to testify to the satisfaction of the court that people had not understood questioning. Furthermore, despite the stricture concerning the avoidance of yes/no polar questions, in Gibbons (1996: 293) a NSW police interview is documented in which 145 questions out of 449, that is 31 per cent, were answered with 'yes' or 'no'. The problem with this guideline may lie in its lack of explicitness. It does not supply concrete procedures for checking comprehension, and some police officers with limited language awareness may not be clear about the alternatives to 'yes/no' polar interrogatives.

One issue negotiated during meetings, was that the revisions include explicit information about alternatives to 'yes/no' questions, and encouragement to obtain a narrative account.

The final version which was negotiated for the *Code of Practice* (Commissioner of Police 1998: 23) was:

> Do not presume people understand even the most simple questions. If you believe suspects do not understand any other question ask them what they understand by them *(sic)*. Ensure each question is clearly understood by the suspect.

> Where possible, phrase questions to avoid simple 'yes' or 'no' answers. Ask open questions which require narrative answers. These generally start with either what, where, when, why, who or how.

Listen to what people say and don't interrupt.

There are problems with the wording of this, but it is nevertheless considerably more explicit than its predecessor, and provides more concrete procedural guidelines. I have yet to obtain police interviews made since the *Code of Practice* was introduced to see whether it has had any concrete outcomes.

Another means of encouraging the use of open questioning is the use of electronic recording of police interviews. This exposes the real questioning process to external examination and challenge in court. In Britain and in most of Australia, before the introduction of the electronic recording of police interviews, two types of document would often emerge from police interviews, a Record of Interview, which purported to be a transcript of the interview (although we saw in chapter 1 that these transcripts were at best heavily edited), and a Statement, which was a summary of the evidence presented by the interviewee. In principle, Statements were written by the interviewee; in practice they were almost always written by police officers to be signed by the interviewee. Before they became corrupted by ingrained bad practices, these two documents served the two purposes discussed above. The Record of Interview recorded the elicitation of the Witness's version of events, and the Statement served as a confirmation of the police understanding.

The introduction of video recordings of police questioning was intended to serve as a vehicle to obtain an unchallengeable record of the witness's version of events. The intention was that all substantive interviews would be recorded, once police officers had checked that the interviewee had useful information to offer, and had some idea of what questions to ask. However, in reality, I have observed that in many video recorded interviews police officers go in with a clear version of events established from thorough previous (unrecorded) interviews, which they wish the witness to confirm 'on camera'. In other words the video interview is being pushed in the direction of an oral Statement. A clear linguistic indicator of this is the high use of 'projection', or forms of reported speech. In the following transcripts from a video recorded interview, question 211 makes explicit reference to an earlier interview. In the other sequence the police officer is attempting to get the suspect to admit approaching some men with the intention of robbing them, as the officer believes he had stated in a previous unrecorded interview. When the direct line of questioning fails, the officer makes progressively greater use of the earlier interview, using many projections in his third attempt, question 135.

Q. 211   P: Do you agree that prior to this interview, you told me that the big man had an axe?

Q. 133   P: Why did you approach the men and ask them for a cigarette?
A.   W: Because I – because have no cigarette nothings and we can't have enough money with me
Q. 134   P: Do you agree that earlier tonight you told us that it was your idea to rob these men?
A.   W: What you want to say?
Q. 135   P: I'm asking you, do you agree that earlier tonight, when we spoke to you, you said that it was your idea to rob these men, take some money from them. Do you remember telling us that?
A.   W: Yes.

Question 135 is very insistent, demanding compliance, using several of the coercive features discussed earlier, and one may wonder about the value of the 'yes' response.

Pragmatic Strategies

Question form is not by any means the only technique used by lawyers or police officers to construct and affirm their version of events. A range of other devices can be used in such a way that one particular interpretation emerges more powerfully. This may not be based purely on grammar and intonation, like questioning, but instead may use the whole range of link-ages between elements of the communication process and the social con-text – the phenomenon often referred to in linguistics as pragmatics. Like questioning, pragmatic strategies fall into two distinct categories. One cat-egory consists of tactics that influence or discredit testimony by shaping perceptions of the person giving the testimony, often by enhancing or diminishing their credibility ('person targeted'). The other category is tar-geted at the portrayal of events itself ('idea targeted'). The boundary be-tween these two categories can be fuzzy, and there are times when they are entwined, but it can still be useful to ask whether it is the message or the messenger that is being supported or undermined. The listing of strategies here is not exhaustive, but it illustrates the range of linguistic devices used in questioning.

Person targeted strategies

Status manipulation

One category of person-targeted strategies used by lawyers is of the type referred to by Garfinkel (1967) as a 'social degradation ceremony', and he also refers to the court as 'the perfect stage for acting out society's ceremonies of status degradation'. Rather than attacking the content of the witness's testimony, this strategy attacks the witness's character. This can have a dual purpose. It may serve to portray the witness as in some way unreliable: it is an attack on credibility. Alternatively, particularly if the person subjected to this strategy is the plaintiff or defendant, it may render them more worthy of their plight or punishment, thereby changing the portrayal of events. A disturbing example of the latter is in rape cases, where women or child victims are sometimes portrayed as in some way having invited the rape, or being in some way worthy of rape or being responsible for the rape (Liebes-Plesner 1984).

The reverse of this process is **status support** often afforded by friendly counsel, particularly to expert witnesses. A rather embarrassing introduction in the courtroom by a zealous barrister will serve as an example.

C: Coming back to your interest in bilingualism you have familiarised yourself with the literature in relation to bilingualism?
W: Yes, I teach courses in that area.
C: You have done your own practical research in relation to bilingualism?
W: I have.
C: You have expertise in relation to assessment of English language proficiency of persons, is that correct?

Notice the rhetorical wording to emphasize the knowledge and capacity of the witness: *familiarized yourself*, the loaded term *practical* in *practical research,* and *expertise.*

Later in the same case, the opposing counsel attempted the reverse process of **status reduction**.

C: The bottom line is you cannot say how much he did or did not understand during the interview he had?
W: We cannot gauge the exact amount.
C: Again it would be impossible for you in your sphere of expertise to determine whether or not at any part of the interview, since you cannot get into his mind, whether he was coy?

W: I am not a psychologist.
C: Therefore you are not able to say whether he is being smart, cunning or just deliberately misleading?
W: I am not a psychologist.

The questions labour the issue, and their wording is confrontational. They overtly challenge the capability of the witness by using *you* linked to a negative concerning ability 'you cannot' (twice), 'it would be impossible for you', 'you are not able'. This is in direct contradiction of normal rules of politeness which would attempt to preserve the face of the speaker (Brown and Levinson, 1978). The questions are also made more emphatic by the use of rhetorical effects: the first question begins with the rhetorical flourish 'the bottom line is', and the third question uses a three part rhetorical structure in 'smart, cunning or just deliberately misleading' (see 'Three part structures' below). Most expert witnesses have experienced similar deliberate attempts by hostile counsel to reduce their credibility and to coerce them (and the jury) by the use of rhetoric, indeed many lawyers regard these as standard adversarial tactics to 'test' witnesses. Bülow-Møller (1991: 50, 55) provides more examples.

Another way in which witnesses may be humiliated is by sarcasm, although this is not always permitted by judges, for example

C: You'd seen a knife before?
     . . .
C: They've all got shiny blades, haven't they?

Various of the interpersonal features we have discussed can be used tactically to manipulate status, for instance address forms may serve to depress or elevate the status or 'persona' of witnesses. These will be addressed in what follows.

Address forms
Bülow-Møller (1991: 43) discusses the tactical use of address forms. She mentions that a photography expert is addressed as *Mr Kirk* by the prosecution, but as *Sergeant Kirk* by the defence, in order to highlight his status as part of the 'system'. A pathologist is addressed appropriately by the defence as *Doctor* but by the prosecution, which regards him as a hostile witness, by his given name *Cyril*. This is actually contested by the lawyers in the following example.

DC: Your Honour, I don't mean to be picky, but somehow it seems to me that during the course of this trial we have tried to show respect for people, and wouldn't it be proper for a doctor to be called Doctor?

J: I agree

PC: I'm sorry, it's coming on a downward path, Cyril, I mean **Doctor**, **Doctor** . . .

Bülow-Møller remarks that this intervention gives the impression that the prosecution counsel 'is merely tactless in seeking to demean an expert witness'. However this defence counsel uses given names to friendly witnesses, showing that he has done his homework in coming to know his witnesses, and that he is human. O'Barr (1982: 6), in similar vein, shows that lawyers in his recordings use forms of address to personalize friendly witnesses, and to depersonalize opposition witnesses, for example calling a friendly witness 'the accused Joseph Smith' then 'Joe Smith' then 'Joe', but a hostile witness 'the prosecution witness Jones' or 'Jones'.

Personal pronouns
O'Barr (1982: 37) suggests that 'we' can be used to a jury to appeal to common values; that 'you' can be ambiguous between collective jury and individual members, so they may feel personally addressed; and that 'they' can be used to refer to an unknown or external group, marking them as social outsiders. He gives this example of the repeated tactical use of 'you'.

> Ladies and gentlemen, in **your** examination before **you** were selected as jurors, **I** asked whether **you** could put aside feelings of prejudice, passion, revulsion and pity, and decide this case on the evidence. Each of **you** swore **you** would do just that . . . **You** made that pledge.

A fundamental means of closing or increasing social distance (see 'accommodation' below) in most European languages is the choice of pronouns for 'you' – a more intimate and informal T-form, or a more formal and distant V-form (see Brown & Gilman 1960). The use of the informal T-form (which is used to children in most contexts, and traditionally to servants) in a formal context can be patronizing and insulting. Likewise asymmetrical use, where the powerful party expects V, but addresses the less powerful party as T, can be deliberately status reducing. Jacquemet (1996) documents the use of varying levels of formality in pronoun use in court, and the manner in which interpersonal power is negotiated by this means, including an incident in which a judge silences a particularly recalcitrant witness by saying (in Italian) 'shut up, T'.

Contrast

Drew (1990) describes a tactic by which a lawyer attempts to establish contrasts between statements by the witness that seem to make them contradictory and undermine their credibility. In the following example, the lawyer sets up the existence of phone calls, and an unlisted number, and the witness's denial of having given the caller the number. The underlying question, never addressed or resolved during this examination, is 'how did the caller get the number, if the witness did not give it to him', thereby setting up a question about the witness's reliability.

C: Now subsequent to this you say you received a number of phone calls?
W: Yes
C: From the defendant?
W: Yes
C: And isn't it a fact Miss that you have an unlisted telephone number?
W: Yes
C: And you gave the defendant your telephone number didn't you?
W: No, I didn't

Distorting modality and the infallibility trap

There are various ways that Counsel or police may attempt to exploit modality in a witness's statements. It may involve attempting to force a witness to express certainty about something that is best left modalized (e.g. 'Please answer yes or no'), or else the witness's modalizations may be distorted as vagueness or full uncertainty. Maley and Fahey (1991) give a number of examples. Bülow-Møller (1991: 55) says 'the witness can be made to appear evasive, unsure, or . . . ludicrously over-confident'. She gives the following example of the latter – the 'infallibility trap'.

C: You make room for the possibility that the CIA or the KGB could fool you?
W: No.
C: You don't think they could?
W: No.
C: . . . Thank you!

In one case my testimony contained a translation of some passages in a 'secret language', a kind of pig Latin (see chapter 8). The defending counsel questioned me repeatedly concerning the translation, attempting to secure a statement of absolute confidence in the translation. If any flaw emerged subsequently, the translation would have been entirely discredited. Maintaining the appropriate level of modality – of confidence but not claiming perfection – is difficult under aggressive rapid questioning involving frequent interruptions (see below).

Accommodation

Giles (in Giles and Powesland, 1975 and elsewhere) developed 'accommodation theory', according to which people make their language more like that of an interlocutor in order to reduce social distance, or make their language less similar in order to increase social distance. This may involve a change in style or accent, or a switch to another language. Jacquemet (1996: 118–22) shows judges using this strategy in order to help *pentiti* witnesses to answer. It often involved a switch to street language, or to southern Italian dialects such as Sicilian or Neapolitan. Sometimes judges also mix standard with dialect in a strategy of neutrality (Scotton 1976), to lay claim to the associations of both varieties.

Turn taking

Turn taking may also be used strategically by lawyers. O'Barr (1982) on the basis of recordings of courtroom discourse, suggests that a nervous witness can be intimidated by looking at her/him in silence, violating normal turn taking rules concerning the length of silence in interaction (Hutchby and Wooffitt, 1998), until the atmosphere in the courtroom becomes tense, then shooting a question. Interruption and overlapping can also be used strategically.

Exploiting bias

Although I have been unsuccessful in finding documentation of this tactic, I have observed counsel deliberately exploiting the cultural and ethnic biases of jurors.

Idea targeted tactics

Vocabulary choice

Loftus (1979) showed that even small differences in wording can influence the content of answers, and even the memory of events. Loftus (1979: 94) writes 'the precise questions asked during the interrogatory are crucial, for small changes in their wording can result in dramatically different answers'. She gave as an example (Loftus 1979: 77–8) a study in which subjects saw a film of a traffic accident which did not involve any broken glass. Some were asked the question 'About how fast were the cars going when they smashed into each other?' while the rest of the subjects were asked 'About how fast were the cars going when they hit each other?' The only difference between the questions is the words *smashed into* versus *hit*. The *smashed* question elicited a much higher estimate of speed. Furthermore when subjects were interviewed later they were asked 'Did you see any broken glass?' Again far more of the subjects who had been asked the *smashed* question had a false memory of broken glass. This study vividly illustrates how the wording of questions could affect a jury's understanding and mental picture of an event.

Danet (1980), talking of the construction of alternative versions of the same reality, showed how in a manslaughter trial, an unborn child was referred to as a *fetus* by the defence, and as a *baby boy* by the prosecution. This was based on the notion that the death of a fetus is less likely to merit a verdict of manslaughter than the death of a baby, so by the use of vocabulary the same act was constructed or not as a punishable offence by a word choice. This is part of a more general pattern of vocabulary choice where connotations can be positive, neutral or negative, for example *slim–thin–skinny–emaciated*. There are also sets of vocabulary with similar conceptual content, but different ideological loading. A notorious set is *freedom fighter–guerrilla–terrorist*, where different constructions of the same person are given, and different motives implied. (This linguistic resource is also exploited by propagandists and politicians.) The intense political debate in the USA concerning abortion introduces a similar ideological construction into the use of the terms *fetus* and *baby*, and in more recent times *unborn child*.

Hedging

O'Barr (1982) suggests, in accord with the work of feminist linguists that hedging is a mark of lack of power. While this is true on some occasions, Jacquemet (1996: 113–18) gives a convincing example of its use as a witness strategy, when mafiosi deliberately hedge every statement so that what is said is so vague as to be virtually useless as testimony. He refers to this type of behaviour as 'smoke screen strategies'.

Repetition

Sometimes lawyers repeat their own questions. Maley and Fahey (1991) give a number of examples of hostile counsel repeating questions, and they suggest that the objective is to produce some inconsistency between replies to the same question which can then be used to discredit the witness. It can also serve to put pressure on the witness and underline the counsel's disbelief of the answer. Maley and Fahey (1991: 12) provide the following example. The repeated questions are in bold.

C: **What were they [the police officers] doing there?**
P: I don't know
C: Well, you are the one who was there Mr M?
P: They were standing there. What would you be doing there?
C: Don't you worry about what I was doing. **What did you say they were doing?**
P: Standing.
C: **Standing, three officers, do I understand you to say?**
P: Yes.
C: **Standing there?**
  . . .

The last turn above consists of a repetition of the witness's statement which is another common practice of lawyers or police, used to highlight a particular element of the testimony. Often the quotation is subjected to an intonation contour (as in the questioning intonation in the above example), or a framing such as 'you claim that . . .' which throws doubt on the content of the repeated element. Jacquemet (1996: 167) gives an example of counsel repeating lines of testimony that contain a factual inconsistency. This defendant has just stated that a person had been affiliated into the mafia in **Pianosa**. Counsel then reads from a previous statement by the defendant, which said that that person had been reaffiliated in **Novara**, repeating and emphasising the inconsistency, in lines 30 and 31.

	Original	*English translation*
26	imputato.	defendant:
27	'fu rilegalizzato,	'he was reaffiliated
28	al carcere do novara	in the prison of Novara
29	da Leonardo Francesco,'	by Leonardo Francesco'
30	al carcere di NOVARA/	in the prison of NOVARA
31	da Leonardo Francesco	by Leonardo Francesco

Repetition can also serve a positive idea targeted role. Although the Gricean maxim of quantity would appear to preclude repetition, it is common in conversation as a form of emphasis. O'Barr (1982) found that used sparingly, it can reinforce elements of testimony.

Reformulation
This is where the lawyer does a form of summing up, giving a 'gist' or 'upshot' of what was said. Sometimes the reformulation is flagged by the use of linguistic signals such as: *in other words*; *so it is true to say that*; *so you're saying that*, for example

C: In other words, you feel that, .. you believe that the shots came from beHIND the President, is that corréct?

Bülow-Møller (1991: 45)

P: Can you remember making a complaint to me that . . . concerning your brother?

Hall (1998: 49)

There are a number of other examples from police interviews in figure 4.6 under projected and agreement statements. Bülow-Møller (1991: 52) gives the following devastating reformulation.

C: Did you imply to him by your total utter silence that Dr. Fink or whatever his name is was an incompetent?

The attorney, Lerm, gives the following example of his own use of reformulation (Lerm 1997: 172).

C: Good, but I am also . . .
W: (interrupts) I did not tell them everything.
C: Yes we shall get to that. You did not tell them everything, did you, so you **concealed** certain things did you not?
W: I know I only told them, I don't know, I did not . . . I don't know.

Notice that the counsel, by using 'conceal' in the reformulation, adds an element of intention that the witness did not express, and finds difficult to refute.

In the Grand Jury trial of former President Clinton of the USA, lawyers also distorted the content of his utterances during reformulation, attempting (unsuccessfully in this case) to lull him into thinking that the lawyer was only seeking confirmation of what Mr Clinton had already said.

In the following example the Clerk of the Court (C) reformulates against the defendant (D)'s expressed wishes (Carlen 1976: 115–16).

C: Do you plead guilty or not guilty?
D: Well, yes and no
C: Do you plead guilty or not guilty?
D: Yes, I was guilty of trespassing, and no, I wasn't intending to steal
C: So you plead not guilty?
D: That's not what I said
C: **Not guilty**.

But Drew (1990) shows that when a lawyer's wording attempts to construct a different version from that of the witness, the witness may resist. In the following example, the witness repeatedly resists the lawyer's reformulation of her evidence and replaces it with her own.

C: And you went to a bar in Boston, is that correct?
W: It's a club
C: It's where girls and fellas meet isn't it?
W: People go there
C: And during that evening didn't Mr X come over to sit with you?
W: Sat at our table

Compare the witness's resistance to the lawyer's formulation in this extract from Atkinson and Drew (1979: 111; italics in the original)

C: Were they in fact *a Protestant mob* that was attempting to burst out into Divis Street?
W: Prior to sending this message I must have known that there was *a crowd of people* there.

There is the possibility of using reformulation to assist a witness by improving his/her expression, or by producing a wording that would have a better fit to the legal framework. In Common Law courts this would probably be disallowed, but Jacquemet (1996: 129) gives a number of examples of this phenomenon in the Camorra trials in Naples. The reformulation often involved a shift to the standard language, or a shift to a higher register (this contrasts with the reformulations into everyday register to make things more intelligible for witnesses, for instance interpreting for the deaf, as discussed in chapter 6).

Reformulation as a speech act label
In the examples above from Hall (1998) and Lerm (1997) it can be seen that the witness's statement is reformulated by means of a speech act label: 'complaint' and 'conceal'. This may have the effect simply of summarizing, but it is also possible by choosing a speech act word to impart a particular 'spin' in the reformulation. Atkinson and Drew (1979) give numerous examples including: 'Are you suggesting that the expert witness lied to the court?' where a witness had queried the accuracy of an expert testimony. Here the reformulation with 'lied' puts the witness in a difficult spot. Bülow-Møller (1991: 52) gives the following example:

> [a series of questions follows that aims to bring Dr. Fink's knowledge of high velocity rifle wounds to the jury's attention. And then the second, crushing reformulation:]

C: So don't keep secrets, OK?

Naming the speech act here is, as Bülow-Møller states, a crushing tactic, which also casts doubt on the credibility of the witness's testimony.

Presuppositions
Presuppositions are a well described topic in semantics. The best known example is 'When did you stop beating your wife' which presupposes wife-beating by the addressee. We have already introduced this topic in the section on questioning. This tactic has the potential to confuse witnesses and mislead hearers by inserting as given content something that is new or disputed. This makes it a favourite tactic of lawyers, even though there are rules of procedure concerning the 'leading' of witnesses that should in principle preclude its misuse. (Bülow-Møller 1991) gives the following example.

C: It is perfectly understandable that the witnesses were confused as to the origin of fire

It had not been established that the witnesses were confused. Similarly in the following example the witness had **not** said anything about people **speaking** to the little girl.

C: You, erh, made something of a little girl that was turning her head, do you remember that?

W: Yes sir I do

C: Do you know what was being said to the little girl when she turned her head?

W: No

C: Do you make room for the possibility that her name was, let's say, Mary . . . and that her mother said, Mary?

In experiments, Loftus (1979) found that questions presupposing the presence of items or events, for example 'Did you see **the** broken glass' elicited different responses from those which did not make the presupposition for example 'Did you see **any** broken glass'. (The first question presupposes the existence of broken glass, while the second does not.) In this case the linguistic difference is a subtle choice of determiner, and as such is hard to recognize and challenge.

Natural narrative structure
In chapter 4 we will see that lawyers follow natural narrative structure to help the jury follow the 'story' – in other words they use a story-like structure, particularly in summing up after testimony, in order to naturalize their version of events. O'Barr (1982) found that one strategy is to use unnatural narrative orders to elicit inconsistent answers from hostile witnesses by disrupting their schemas and prepared stories. The lawyer may also use a series of questions which limit the response (usually yes–no questions) to accumulate a portrayal of events that is not that of the witness, yet which the witness is not given the opportunity to challenge.

Jacquemet (1996) documents extensive use of narratives by witnesses, once more partly with the aim of naturalizing their testimony.

Negative suggestions
O'Barr (1982: 6) suggests that if a witness is strongly hostile, lawyers ask the reverse of what they wish to discover: for example if they want to establish it was dark, they ask 'Is it not a fact that it was light' and hostile witness may say 'No, it was dark'.

Three-part structures
Drew (1990) discusses the rhetorical emphasis that can be gained by grouping concepts into threes. (This rhetorical device is found in the language of

politicians as well as lawyers – see Hutchby and Wooffitt, 1998). Drew gives the following example.

C: Mr R. had the audacity to stand up here and tell you about the most serious crime **in Florida, in the United States, and in the Bible,** the Bible which says THOU SHALT NOT KILL!

This device is also used to throw doubt on exactness in following example.

C: All right, what speed did your speedometer register?
W: It was thirty five
C: Exactly 35?
W: That's right
C: Not 36 or 34?

Evaluative third parts
Sinclair and Coulthard (1975) point out that questioning need not consist only of a two part structure 'question–reply', but that there is frequently a third part in which the questioner evaluates the reply. The evaluation can be speaker targeted ('good girl') or idea targeted ('that's right'). Their data are from classrooms, but Berry (1981) has also pointed out that such third parts are frequently found in other situations of unequal power such as doctor–patient consultations and business meetings. In such contexts evaluation is usually idea targeted, since the evaluation of adults (rather than what they say) is face-threatening.

Evaluative third parts may be used in legal settings to support or challenge answers to questions, for example:

C: Would you agree with me that to be able to complete that process the Defendant needs to read or understand English?
P: The Defendant didn't read the record of Interview.
C: **No that wasn't my question with respect.** Questions at large . . .

Mendoza-Denton (1995: 59–60) proposes that positive evaluative third parts can provide strong support during questioning, and that an unequal distribution of supportive evaluative third parts ('acknowledgments') can influence the impression given by evidence.

Rhythm and pace
The next three strategies are all related to the timing of speech. O'Barr

(1982) found that the rhythm and the speed or pace of speaking can be manipulated for effect – sometimes a fast pace is used to signal that things can be taken for granted, while a slow pace is used for emphasis, but it must not be over-used as this can cause jurors to lose attention.

Bülow-Møller (1991) found that the two counsel in the trial she analysed made different use of pace and rhythm. The prosecution lawyer used dismissive short questions with a falling intonation pattern to give the impression that the content could be taken for granted, and that it was a waste of time asking the question. He also use a rapid pace to give an impression of anger at injured innocence. By contrast the defence lawyer was slow, patient and courteous, giving the impression of sweet reason and restraint, while being ironic about the prosecution's apparent emotionality.

Interruption

In hostile cross-examination it is common for counsel to not permit the witness to finish what s/he is saying, particularly if it contradicts some element of the 'story' that counsel is trying to construct. In principle interruptions should occur only when an answer is not relevant, and in other circumstances the judge should intervene to allow witnesses to finish, but in my experience as an expert witness this happens much less than unwarranted interruptions.

In an experimental study by O'Barr (1982), subjects judged recordings which varied according to the amount of interruption by counsel and the witness's reaction to the interruption. There were four simulated recordings of a lawyer questioning a witness which had the following characteristics:

1. no interruption/overlapping;
2. some overlapping, but lawyer and witness equally persistent in resisting interruption;
3. the lawyer dominates by persevering in three-quarters of the instances of simultaneous speech;
4. the reverse of (3), where the witness perseveres.

The results are shown in table 3.9.

Note that the lawyer's control is rated lower in **all** situations involving simultaneous speech. This means that the use of interruption as a strategy is likely to backfire on the lawyer. Note also that the lawyer is rated as less fair, less intelligent, and not giving the witness the opportunity to present his/her evidence.

Table 3.9   Ratings of interruption

	Witness dominates	Lawyer dominates
Witness given opportunity to present evidence	1.5[a]	−.1
Fairness of lawyer to witness	2.0	.4
Intelligence of lawyer	2.8	1.7

[a] Higher values indicate more positive ratings. For all reported differences $p \leq .05$.
Source: O'Barr (1982: 90)

Silence

Mendoza-Denton (1995) argues that the length of time left after a statement by a witness can affect the impact of that statement. She notes that a longer silent pause after someone has spoken may give an impression of greater respect for the speaker (this is then an interpersonal strategy), and may 'underscore the import of [the speaker's] words, and allow the weight of [the speaker's] responses to 'sink in' with the audience' (Mendoza-Denton 1995: 55). This tactic can also be used to make a statement more telling, whether for a positive or negative effect – lawyers will often repeat loudly a response from a witness which they believe to be particularly significant, then leave a period of silence in which the response reverberates in the courtroom: Mendoza-Denton (1995: 16) writes of 'pregnant pauses and poignant silences', indicating that silence itself can be meaningful. A shorter silence, for example when the next question comes almost immediately, may obscure answers by distracting attention, particularly if there is a sudden change of topic. Witnesses can also use silence as a strategy to avoid answering questions, although this can be taken as contempt of court unless they are the accused, in which case no conclusions may be drawn from this in most Common Law jurisdictions (see 'The Right to Silence' in chapter 8).

Adversarial versus scholarly techniques

The terminology and ideas in this section are drawn from Stratman (1994). He distinguishes two types of brief that could be used when making an appeal. One type, the **adversarial**, uses an entirely one-sided approach that makes no concession to the opposing opinion. The alternative is to take what he calls a more **scholarly** approach, which attempts some degree of balance and takes the opposing opinion seriously. He summarizes the difference between the two techniques in 3.10.

Table 3.10   Comparison of rhetorical recommendations in scholarly and adversarial theories of brief writing

Part of brief	Scholarly theory	Adversarial theory
Argument	● Make overall argument structure at least generally parallel to opponent's argument structure. ● Provide explicit concessions to opponent's arguments, to demonstrate candor. ● Provide explicit refutations of opponent's arguments, and separate them from affirmative arguments, to inoculate judges against opponent's claims. ● Avoid using insinuation, feints. ● Always cite adverse precedents; distinguish those you can, make limited concessions to those you cannot.	● Avoid making the argument parallel in structure to the opponent's argument. ● Make no concessions to opponent's arguments, since concessions imply weakness. ● Do not provide explicit refutations, since these will give greater exposure to opponent's claims; if refutations must be used, make them implicit by mixing them with affirmative arguments. ● Use frequent insinuation, feints. ● Cite only those adverse precedents that you know your opponent will discuss, and try to distinguish or qualify them.

Source: Stratman (1994: 9)

Since the appeal court clerks and judges must weigh both sides of a case, Stratman produces talk-aloud protocol data to show that the adversarial approach is less convincing than a scholarly approach. There are interesting parallels with the difference between Common Law and Roman Law approaches, and to a lesser extent with the two types of questioning discussed earlier in this chapter.

Conclusions

This section on 'Pragmatic Strategies' has illustrated how language can be used in the courtroom to press for a particular version of events, and to influence perceptions of witnesses. There are ethical issues involved here which lie outside the scope of a book such as this, but it is important to recognize that these strategies are not accidental, since there are books, for example Mauet (1996) designed to teach such strategies to lawyers in training.

Conclusion

Over the last three chapters we have examined the decontextualized, formal, specialist and power laden language of the legal system. Such language is distant on all four of those parameters from everyday conversational language, which tends to be contextualized, informal, non-specialist and low in power differences. The extreme variants used in the legal system are not within the register range of most ordinary people, but everything except the specialist aspects can be acquired through high levels of education, and experience of institutional contexts. Following the sociolinguistic literature on diglossia (Ferguson 1964; Fishman 1967) hereafter this type of register will hereafter be referred to as **high register**. Knowledge of the genres of the law is another component of high register, and this will be examined in the next chapter.

This chapter has attempted to explore the way relationships between people in legal contexts are constructed through language. As we have seen, the relationship in this formal and hierarchical context is overwhelmingly one of power, to some degree enmeshed with issues of differential control of knowledge and expertise. As I noted in the introduction, in democratic societies, power is given by elected representatives of the populace to the legal system to implement policies enacted by those same representatives. Power is necessary for action. The issue that arises is how far it is appropriate to use this power linguistically in the pursuit of proof rather than truth, of a desired verdict rather than balanced justice. Language is probably the most powerful interpersonal weapon other than force itself.

The use of powerful language and high register generally in legal processes becomes particularly problematic when one of the parties comes from a group that has less power in society, and is unlikely to command high register, and therefore may be less competent to cope with the legal process – for instance children and ethnic minorities. This issue will be examined in chapter 6.

4

Telling the Story

Current reality is the only movie . . . everything else is shadows
                                        Paul J. McCauley (1991)

Stories are a parasitical life form, warping lives in the service only of
the story itself.
                                        Terry Pratchett (1988)

Introduction

This chapter examines the notion that there are genre structures that
underlie both the realities that are in constant interaction in the legal
process, the present and current reality of the police station, cell, courtroom or lawyer's chambers, and the secondary reality that is the reason for
the legal process, including crimes and disputed events. A third plane that
comes into play is the law itself. First the notion of genre is examined in
this introduction. Then the major genres of the primary reality are given,
and three of them are described in more detail as illustrations. The next
part of the chapter is concerned with the use of the narrative genre to
reconstruct the secondary reality. Finally the interaction of the primary
and secondary realities is examined, along with their 'fit' to the legal framework.

Genre

The notion of genre, introduced in chapter 1, needs to be expanded for the
purposes of the next two chapters. The distinction established in the previous chapter between the primary and secondary reality is important here,
since procedures in the primary reality of courtrooms, lawyers chambers,
prisons and police stations may be staged processes, and therefore describ-
able as genres. However, the secondary reality outside the courtroom may
also be reconstructed through genres. There is a large literature on the use

of narrative genres by witnesses in court, and this theme will be explored in the second part.

The importance of describing legal genres can be illustrated by the interaction between the eminent linguist Charles Fillmore, and a number of eminent legal authorities reported in *Washington University Law Quarterly*, vol. 73 (1995: 922–31), particularly the discussion of the following sentence

> After this marriage in the absence of any agreement to the contrary the legal relations and powers as regards to property might, by reason of some change in our domicile or otherwise, be other than those of our present domiciles or other than those which we desire to apply to our relationship powers and capacities.

Charles Fillmore (like other non-lawyers, including myself) finds this 'incompetent' and unintelligible. The lawyers, however, were able to draw on their knowledge of the genre of contracts of this type, to say that such a clause is inserted at the beginning of many such contracts to cover the contingency of the parties moving to another state where the law is different. Despite the chronically poor drafting of this language, their knowledge of the genre enabled the lawyers to apply an appropriate interpretive framework, and thereby understand it and be in agreement over its meaning. Genre, as researchers into literacy have found, is critical both to the construction and the comprehension of discourse (Perkins 1987; Wallace 1990).

The flexibility of genres

Swales (1990: 33) attacks one version of the genre concept as 'a disreputably formulaic way of constructing (or aiding the construction of) particular texts – a kind of writing or speaking by numbers.' Kintsch's (1988) critique of schema theory similarly notes that 'such fixed structures are too inflexible and cannot adapt readily enough to the demands imposed by the ever-changing context of the environment'. Swales (1990: 51–2) makes the important point that most attempts to rigidly impose genre models will fail because genres are 'prototypes' (rather like the prototypes of word meanings in Rosch, 1973), that they are underlying models that are sometimes not followed or are intentionally modified. Indeed if we accept Martin's definition of genre given in chapter 1 'a staged goal oriented social process', it is clear that individuals and societies modify and adapt social processes (other than rigid rituals) to fit changing circumstances, so genre structures are constantly evolving and it would be unrealistic to expect unfailing consistency in genre structures any more than in other aspects of human behaviour. Individuals will manipulate, merge and vary generic structures in the attempt to make them maximally functional for their purposes, or because of less deliberate factors such as poor planning or lapses of attention. This does not invalidate the attempt to find underlying structures, indeed a long-term objective is to understand variable and creative areas of usage. In essence, genre based models need not be reductionist, but rather an attempt to understand underlying generalities. Another useful way of understanding this is to recognize that more general flexible 'deeper' genre patterns may underlie more formalized and rigid 'surface' genres that are used for specific social purposes.

Genres within genres

There can be several layers of genre type discourse structure. For instance a trial is organized into a predictable sequence of stages, given in table 4.1 so it is a form of macro-genre. Within a trial, examination-in-chief or a judge's summing up will also reveal distinct stages. Finally the conclusion of examination-in-chief may consist of a staged reconstruction of the evidence, for confirmation by the witness. There are then three possible layers within which generic structure can be found: a macro-genre such as the trial, a genre such as examination-in-chief, and a genre stage such as a conclusion. Another example of a three-layered structure is a police interrogation, which will often consist of a sequence of interviews, each of which has a different purpose, such as an early exploratory interview, followed by in-depth interviews, concluding with a confirmatory interview which is usually done 'for the record'. This series of interviews is therefore a staged, organized and purposeful process. Each of these interviews will in turn have its own structure, as we shall see later. Finally, within an interview, an early stage may be a narrative account by a witness (narratives have a well established genre structure – see Hasan in Halliday and Hasan 1985: 52–69). Linguists sometimes refer to the occurrence of genres within genres as 'nesting'. The last example of narrative appearing within testimony is in fact over simple. The courtroom process, as we shall see, can be viewed partly as a process of constructing and testing master narratives. If the courtroom processes themselves are also genres, we have narratives of the secondary external reality being constructed through genre processes in the primary courtroom reality, interweaving secondary genres into primary genres in a complex way.

Genres of the Primary Reality

Legal genres

Maley (1994: 16) provides a useful chart of legal genres, which is presented in a modified and expanded form here (table 4.1). In this chart, genres are in **bold**, major stages of the genres are given in regular type beneath, and participants in the construction of the genres are given in *italics*. The second (underlined) line of the table represents macro-genre stages, in left to right chronological order. Within each column, the stages are roughly sequenced from top to bottom. The bottom line in SMALL CAPITALS is the mode used. This chart is inevitably a simplification of the nuanced complexity of legal processes mentioned previously.

Concerning table 4.1, it is worth noting that consultation can take place throughout a trial (it is iterative), and some of the elements listed as dynamic are standardized in their wording, namely subpoenas, jury summons and swearing in. What emerges from this chart is the extensive range of legal genres involved in the court system, each with particular characteristics that enable it to perform its role. The chart does not attempt to cover ancillary genres, such as the written reports from probation officers sometimes used by judges before sentencing.

Concerning the nesting of genres within other structures, an individual witness's *appearance* has a distinct generic structure containing several of

Table 4.1   Legal genres

Codified	Dynamic		Codified
Pre-existing	Pre-trial	Trial	Reording and law-making
legislation *legislature, drafters*	**police interview** *police, witnesses, suspects*	**procedural genres** calling and swearing in of witnesses, etc. clerk, officers	**case report** *judge and reporter*

reglation, by-law	**subpoena, jury**		
authority, drafters	**summons**		
	clerk, witness,		
	sheriff, jurors	**opening statements**	
		prosecution/plaintiff	
will contract		*counsel^*	
lawyers, parties	**consultation and**	*defence counsel*	
	instruction		
	lawyer–lawyer;		
	lawyer–client		
		prosecution/plaintiff	
precedent/		**case** (consists of	
judgment		**appearances** – see	
	commital	text)	
	hearing, pleading	*counsel, witnesses*	
	and voir dire		
	judge, lawyers,		
	witnesses, jurors	**defence case**	
		consists of **appearances**	
		– see text)	
	swearing in of	*counsel, witnesses*	
	jury and		
	instructions		
	court officials, jury,	**closing statements**	
	judge	*prosecution/plaintiff*	
		*counsel^*	
		*defence counsel^*	
		prosecution/plaintiff	
		counsel	
		jury summation and	
		instructions	
		judge to jurors	
		judgment	
		verdict, sentencing	
		conclusions	
		jurors, judge	

WRITTEN	SPOKEN AND WRITTEN	PRIMARILY SPOKEN	WRITTEN

the elements mentioned above, as is shown in the following outline. (This outline uses a convention presented on p. vii, namely: ( ) = an optional element. The person with whom the witness interacts is *italicized*.)

APPEARANCE

Opening
calling in *court officer*
swearing in *court officer*

Examination-in-chief *friendly counsel*
Cross-examination *opposing counsel*
(**Re-examination** *friendly counsel*)
Dismissal *judge*

In lower courts there may be a single examination performed by the judge. The opening and dismissal are concerned with the primary reality of the courtroom, while the examinations are mainly oriented to the secondary reality of the events under litigation.

As we have already seen, while the court system is perhaps the most important context for the use of legal language, there are many others. Particularly important are the contacts that lawyers have with clients outside the courtroom, often in lawyers' officers or chambers; police interaction with witnesses and suspects and with other police officers; and the interaction of prison officers with other officers and with prisoners. Each of these contexts has its own particular genre, which are in many cases little studied.

It is not possible at present to give genre descriptions of all the varied genres used in the law. Stygall (1994: ch. 2) provides a detailed account of the genres used in a single trial. The illustrative genre descriptions which follow are based on those available in the literature and on my analyses.

The case report genre

At the end of a court case the judge presents an oral judgment. After the case is over, this is written up and may become the subject of a Case Report. In cases where more than one judge is involved, typically appeals, more than one judge may contribute judgments. These judgments have been the object of considerable attention from linguists, notably Solan (1993b), and their genre structure has also been analysed (Maley 1985; Bhatia 1987, 1993). The genre structure of the judgment presented here is based on that of Maley, but is somewhat modified and extended.

Reports play a vital role in the Common Law system as records of judgments which can be used as a basis for subsequent judgments – they constitute 'judge made law'. Not all judgments are reported – only those which may have some significance for the future. This analysis is based on several hundred Malaysian reports from the *Malayan Law Journal* for the 1980s and 1990s. There is slight variation in the structure of law reports over time, among jurisdictions and among reporting journals.

The Report falls into two main sections, the prefatory material, and the judgment itself. The judgment is authored by the judge; some of the prefatory material is added by the reporter for the relevant law journal. The following list illustrates how the report is structured:

CASE REPORT GENRE

PREFATORY MATERIAL
Heading
Name of case
Court name
Reference number
Name(s) of Judge(s)
Date(s)

Keyword summary
Law & Procedure
(Evidence)
(Words and Phrases)

Summary of judgment
In English
   Summary (Obiter) (Per curiam)
In Bahasa Malaysia
   Summary (Obiter) (Per curiam)

(*Appeal*)
From/To

References
(Notes)
(Cases)
(Legislation/Regulation)
(Previous lower court)
Names of counsel
(Date)

JUDGMENT
Orientation
Participants
Previous litigation

(*'Facts'*)
[narrative genre]

Issues
Counsels' argument
Judge's interpretation/reasoning

Decision
(Legal issues)
Finding
Verdict
(Penalty/Award)
Costs

(*Obiter*)

Figure 4.1 consists of the Heading and Keyword summary sections of Report *Malaysia Tobacco Co. Bhd v. The Roadrailer Service Bhd* [1994] MLJ 847.

The Keyword summary of the type shown in figure 4.1 will usually contain summaries of civil or criminal procedure. There may also be sections on tort, contracts, evidence, and the meaning of words and phrases. The headings used in the Keyword summary are not fully standardized in the reports I have examined – they vary across reporters and over time.

The Summary of the judgment reproduces the structure of the full Judgment to a large extent (see below). It may be followed by an Obiter, which is some kind of moral to be drawn from the case, for example in one

Malaysian Tobacco Co. Bhd v. The Roadrailer Service Bhd

HIGH COURT (KUALA LUMPUR) – CIVIL SUIT NO. S2-22-12-93
MOKHTAR SIDIN J
23 SEPTEMBER 1994

Contract – *Indemnity* – *Indemnity against theft in haulage contract* – *Non-delivery of good due to robbery* – *Whether robbery is theft within context of indemnity clause*

Words and Phrases – *'Theft'* – *Whether includes robbery*

Figure 4.1

case report the judge gave a warning to lower courts to be moderate in the wording of their discussion of cases referred from other courts. The Per Curiam section is a conclusion that is drawn as to how the court system should operate. If either the case is an appeal from another court, or if the case is going to be appealed to another court, this may be stated after the Summary.

The references commonly include references to other cases, since reference is usually made to other cases in the Judgment. These are made following the rigid and compact format which is used for most purposes in legal references. Notes are quite common, while references to legislation or regulations are less frequent.

Moving now to the Judgment itself, this usually opens with a naming and description of the major participants in the events of the case. If there has been previous litigation this may also be mentioned at this point as a type of 'framing' of the subsequent discussion. Sometimes the judge also 'flags' the Decision at this point, giving a decision and then the basis for the decision, rather than the reverse order.

Next the so-called 'Facts' of the case are described. In many cases, particularly civil ones, these facts are not disputed. Where they are, the undisputed element is usually presented at this point, then the counsels' conflicting accounts and the judge's conclusions are presented. These follow a narrative structure, although the narrative may not be concluded. Sometimes the Facts are not discussed, and a simple reference is made to preceding judgments. This is the main point at which the events of the secondary reality are presented (through language).

Next legal (and sometimes fact) Issues are discussed. The discussion of each issue will typically consist of the arguments presented by counsel, and then the judge's interpretation. Maley (1985) splits these into two, issues and reasoning, however in the judgments I have studied the two interweave to such a degree that this division into two separate stages is difficult to sustain.

Finally the Decision concerning the case is presented. On rare occasions there is no Decision, and the judge instead may give Orders, for instance for a re-trial or a follow-up hearing. The Decision occasionally discusses legal issues, gives a short description of the finding, the verdict, and penalties or awards. Usually the judge at this point decides responsibility for costs. On rare occasions this may be followed by an Obiter, which is a type of Coda (see above).

The guilty plea genre

This section is based upon the significant contribution of Philips (1998) to our understanding. In chapter 3 of her book, Philips provides the following genre description of guilty pleas in Arizona (I have modified the format slightly to match that used for the other genre charts).

GUILTY PLEA GENRE

Opening
Call of the case
Self identification by lawyers
   (repair slot)

Substance of procedure
(Social background questions)

Nature of charge	Rule 17.2a
Plea agreement comprehension questions	Rule 17.4c
Conditions of plea agreement	Rule 17.2b
Sentencing possibilities	Rule 17.2b
Constitutional rights	Rule 17.2c, Rule 17.3
Coercion questions	Rule 17.3
Factual basis	Rule 17.3
(repair slot)	
Findings	

Closing
Sentencing arrangements
Probation investigation arrangements

Although Philips' terminology differs slightly from that used in this book, the parallels in the genre description are striking. Importantly, Philips also shows (on the right hand side) the textual source for various elements of the 'Substance of procedure' stage, which reveal extensive intertextuality between this oral genre used by judges, and sections of Rule 17 of the *Arizona Rules of Criminal Procedure*. Philips quotes all the relevant sections of Rule 17, and provides a transcript of a judge's realization of these within the oral genre. This example is part of a more general phenomenon of intertextuality between the spoken language of legal professionals and written legal texts.

The lawyer–client consultation genre

When clients consult lawyers concerning a legal issue, as with the other genres described here, the purpose of the interaction means that certain types of information will need to be exchanged. However, because of the less formal context, the generic structure is much less rigid than the Case Report. The description that follows should be seen as soft or fuzzy, rather than as strong and clear. Law schools may transmit an idealized lawyer–client consultation structure to their students, but this is not always followed.

The description given here is based on work by Körner (1992), although it is somewhat different in its conclusions. The examples are taken from Körner (1992).

LAWYER–CLIENT CONSULTATION GENRE
(Opening)

Orientation

Problem (secondary reality)
(Identification)
Recount/Explanation

(Legal explanation)
(Construction)
(Procedure)

Recommendation

(Closure)

In addition to the steps outlined above, at any stage there may be a side sequence in which the lawyer establishes or sustains rapport with the client, often by expressing sympathy. This occurs most commonly after the Problem stage, but may occur at any time. (In these examples L = lawyer; C = Client.)

L: It's outrageous

L: I've worked in these factories myself and I know how dangerous they are, and how you must do things by the book and nobody does them by the book because they fire you for being too slow. It's a terrible problem.

A typical Opening would be a greeting of some kind.

An Orientation will usually consist of the core issue at stake, often with some idea of the time frame. If the lawyer is familiar with the problem, s/he may provide the orientation. An example of an orientation follows.

L: Now Mr W what happened?
C: In February I have an accident on my thumb

The Problem stage usually involves a fuller account of the secondary reality, and (as is discussed in the next section) this typically takes the form either of a narrative recount, or of an explanation of a state of affairs. These are embedded genres. If this is not an initial consultation and both parties are familiar with the case, then this stage may be omitted.

The Legal explanation may consist of either or both of construction and procedure. The legal construction is an explanation to the client of the legal view of his/her situation. The legal procedure is a description of the legal process that might be followed. An example of the latter follows.

L: OK, when you get to court on the first of May alright the first thing that's going to happen is that the magistrate is going to ask if you're represented . . .

The Recommendation consists of the lawyer recommending a particular course of action, by the lawyer, by the client or by both. Körner (1992) notes that this often involves modalization, sometimes involving a modal verb such as 'we could . . .', or 'you should . . .'. Examples follow.

L: What I suggest you do is you commence a worker's compensation claim

L: You could also go to the Industrial Commission and pick up the documentation to use.

A Closure would be the type of exchange discussed by Schegloff (1973), perhaps involving a pre-closure and a farewell.

The central features of the consultation are likely to be iterative, perhaps involving several sequences of Problem^(Legal explanation^)Recommendation.

The police interview genre

The importance of police interviews is described by Gudjonsson as follows:

> in a majority of criminal cases powerful forensic evidence is lacking and information collected from interviews becomes the most important evidence. Furthermore, a certain type of evidence by its nature can generally only be obtained from interviews, such as that related to issues about intent, thoughts and feelings. In the light of the above, it is true to conclude that interviewing is often the most important fact-finding method available to the police.
>
> (Gudjonsson 1999: 7)

The following description of the police interview genre is based on a number of video tapes and transcripts of Australian police interviews that I have studied while working as an expert witness. Police interviews in other Common Law countries are similar. This type of interview is of the formal type, which mostly takes place in police stations or prisons. The structure of unrecorded informal interviews, which are common but officially frowned upon, is likely to be less pre-determined.

FORMAL POLICE INTERVIEW GENRE

Primary reality framing
(Place) (Date) Time of interview
Persons present
Interviewee's Name (Address) (Date of birth)
Cautions
   Right to silence
   Recording
(Interpreter present/(not) required)

Secondary reality core
Orientation
   Subject of interview
   (Date and time of incident)
Questioning
   Question-answer $^{1-n}$ [narrative structure usually underlying]
   (Introduction of evidence from Secondary Reality)
   (Invitation to give further evidence)

Primary reality framing
Recording issues
Cautions
   Uncoerced interview
(Invitation to sign)
(Further actions)
Closure (Time)

As the genre outline above reveals, the interview begins by referring to the circumstances of the interview itself – the primary reality. Any of the elements of the framing may be achieved in a single exchange, or may require a number of exchanges. The interview begins by putting on record the time, and often the place and date of the interview. Next reference is made to the people present in the room – this is partly to cover the police against claims that intimidation by third parties was taking place off camera. Next cautions are administered, which cover suspects' right to silence – in the traditional Common Law system suspects do not have to contribute material that may incriminate them. (This right has been weakened in Britain – see the section on 'The Right to Silence' in chapter 8.) Next the interviewee is warned that the interview is being recorded in some form –

in New South Wales usually on video tape, in UK often on audio tape, and in many jurisdictions it is either written or typed during the interview. The core of the interview is a reconstruction of the secondary reality of the type discussed in the second part of this chapter. It will often have an underlying narrative structure.

Table 4.2 shows the opening section of the official transcript of a recording of a NSW police interview, with the above elements indicated. (Identificatory material changed.)

Table 4.2 Transcript of the opening of a police interview

Genre elements	Speaker	Transcript
Primary reality framing		
Time	PO:	Okay, the time is 9.30–9.51 pm.
Persons present		My name is Detective Sergeant A and this is Detective B and your name is?
	W:	X
	PO:	What's your surname, X?
	W:	Y
	PO:	X Y?
	W:	Yeah.
	PO:	Can you spell that for me, please?
	W:	Y-Y-Y
	PO:	YYY, that's your surname?
	W:	Yeah.
Place	PO:	Okay. We're at the Cabramatta police station?
	W:	Yeah.
Date	PO:	And this is the – today's the 23rd of November, 1997.
Persons present		Okay? Do you agree that there's no other person in the room apart from the three people I've mentioned; myself, Detective B and you?
	W:	Yeah, only three.
	PO:	Only three, that's right.
Name		Okay. For the purpose of this interview can you tell me your full name? Can you tell me again?
	W:	X
	PO:	What's your surname?
	W:	Y, Y-Y-Y.
Date of birth	PO:	Okay. What's your date of birth?
	W:	9/7/78
Address	PO:	Right and whereabouts do you live, X?
	W:	Temporarily to 728 Pool Street.

Secondary reality
core
Orientation   PO: Okay, all right. As I've already explained to you
  Subject   Detective B and I are making inquiries in relation to
  Date   the murder of a person named P Q on the 16th of
                         November, 1997. Do you understand that?
                  W: Yeah.

Primary reality
framing
Cautions   PO: Okay. I'm going to be asking you some questions
  Right to silence   about this matter and I want you to understand that
  Recording   you need not say anything unless you wish
                       but whatever you do say will later – will be recorded
                       and may later be used in evidence. Do you understand
                       that?
                  W: Yes.

                      . . . .

                  PO: Okay. Do you also agree that I told you that my
                       questions and your answers would be recorded on this
                       video machine as our conversation took place?
                  W: Yes.
                  PO: Okay and do you also agree that I told you at the
                       conclusion of the interview you will be given a tape of
                       our conversation?
                  W: Yeah.

Secondary reality
core
Orientation   PO: Okay. Okay. What I intend to ask you is some
  Subject   questions about the murder of P Q about 11 o'clock on
                       the 16th of November which is a week ago, last Friday
                       night. Do you understand that?
                  W: Yes.

Questioning   PO: Okay. Are you able to tell me anything about that
  Invitation to   matter?
  narrative   W: Yeah.
                  PO: What can you tell me about it? What I want you to do
                       is start right from the beginning, okay?
                  W: Yeah.

Of particular interest in the transcript is the manner in which the police officer repeats the elicitation of the interviewee's name in order to include both the 'persons present' and the 'interviewee's name' elements. The officer is also to some extent following the cognitive interview structure below, in that he makes a limited attempt to establish a rapport with the interviewee by saying 'okay' frequently, by using the interviewee's first name in the 'address' question, and by saying 'that's right'. He also attempts (with some success) to elicit a narrative from the interviewee.

The police cognitive interview
Cognitive interviews were introduced in chapter 2. This description is based on descriptions given by Shuy (1998b), on a presentation by Professor Ray Bull to senior officers of the New South Wales Police, based in part on the discussion of cognitive interviewing techniques in Bull and Carson (1995), and on Gudjonsson (1999: 8–10). The description here is of the 'target' genre for the secondary reality core (see the earlier description of the formal police interview genre) of police interviews – it is often not fully implemented in practice. The free narrative and questioning stages may repeat a number of times, individually or in sequence.

COGNITIVE INTERVIEW GENRE

Establishing of identity and rapport
The main objective of this stage is to get the interviewee as relaxed as possible, and to reduce the trauma of the police interview. Usually it involves topics not concerned with the case. This part of the interview can be used to elicit language and information that gives an idea of intellectual and linguistic development. (If rapport is not achieved with children or other disadvantaged groups, the interview may finish here.)

Free narrative
The objective of this stage is to elicit a narrative of the events under investigation in the interviewee's own words. This provides the basis for questioning later and often includes information that would not emerge through direct questioning. This stage can also be important because narrative accounts are more convincing as evidence in court (O'Barr and Conley 1990).

Questioning
In the following order – police will tend to use a lower question type if a higher one does not work
(a)   Open questions

(b)   Either/Or multiple choice questions
(c)   Specific but not leading questions
(d)   Leading questions (these are not always acceptable as evidence in court)

Closure
Using the interviewee's own language to summarize the account, and obtaining confirmation. If necessary the officer may recycle to Questioning. Ideally this stage is also used as debriefing to reduce the stress of the interview.

The effectiveness of cognitive interviewing has been assessed by psychologists. In the experiments described in Bull and Carson (1995), the interviewees see a film of an event. Half of the interviewees are given a cognitive interview, and half a structured interview, done by a skilled interviewer. Half of each of these groups are given a list of questions about the event **before** the interview, and half are given the same questions **after** the interview, to see whether the interviews improve recall. The questions used are of three types

1.   natural questions;
2.   misleading questions (designed to reinforce a wrong memory);
3.   leading questions (designed to reinforce a correct memory).

The results of the experiments are as follows.

1.   The recall from the cognitive interview is more accurate and more detailed (i.e. better in both quantity and quality).
2.   There is a slight increase in the number of errors as a result of the increase in information.
3.   Among children there is a slight increase in confabulation (invention).
4.   Among children with learning disabilities, there is **less** confabulation; in general they recall less, but their recall is equally accurate (around 80 per cent for all groups).
5.   Among adults leading questions have less influence after the cognitive interview.
6.   For all groups, resistance to misleading questions is much higher after the cognitive interview.

What these findings tend to show is that the opportunity to give one's own version of events produces memories that are more accurate, and that become more stable as a result of the interview itself. This is the reason why senior ranks in police forces in many English speaking countries support cognitive interviews. However, there may be resistance from ordinary police officers who see their role as obtaining proof in order to get a conviction, rather than seeking a more nuanced truth.

Representing the Secondary Reality

Introduction

Up to this point we have concentrated mainly on the primary reality and the legal framework. In this section I will look at how the secondary reality is presented in legal investigations.

Since the law is concerned with prescribing behaviour, legal frameworks attempt to divide the secondary reality into what should be and what should not be. As we saw in chapter 2, this conceptual frame is of necessity an abstraction from a general statement about classes of events. The legal process is one whereby an attempt is made to decide upon:

1. a **representation** of the secondary reality
2. the **'fit'** between the secondary reality and the legal representation (in a criminal case to see whether the secondary reality is legally permissible or not);
3. the **degree** of any difference between the secondary reality and legal theory, to determine punishment or reparation.

In a Common Law jury trial, all three stages are argued by the opposing sides – the nature of the secondary reality; the legal representation of such realities; and the degree of difference in any departure from the permitted reality that is the seriousness of the offence. In principle the jury arrives at a portrayal of the secondary reality on the basis of the material evidence, testimony from witnesses and the lawyers' presentations, then decides its 'fit' to the law on the basis of the lawyers' presentations, and more importantly the judges' summing up. As Solan (1995: 1072–3) writes 'One of the most frequent issues facing courts is the goodness of fit between a particular event that occurred in the world and a legally relevant concept'. It may be the judge or jury that decides on the 'seriousness' of any departure from

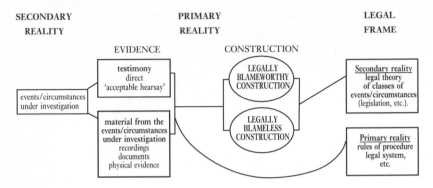

Figure 4.2   The interaction of the primary reality, secondary reality and the legal frame

the law and consequent reparations or punishment. In non-adversarial legal processes it is often the judge who decides all three issues on a similar basis. Police investigations will tend to be weighted more to the reconstruction of the secondary reality (while not ignoring the legal framework) while lawyer–client consultations will tend to concentrate on the legal construction of the events and circumstances.

Tensions and fits

Figure 4.2 attempts to present in a simple way the manner in which events or circumstances in the world are recreated in legal contexts, elaborating the three elements of the model somewhat more.

We noted earlier that the events or circumstances that lead to a legal examination do not usually take place during the legal process itself. The secondary reality (e.g. a crime) is removed in both time and space from the courtroom, lawyer's chambers, or police station, so it must be reconstructed in those places, and at the same time given a legal interpretation. The 'traces' that permit a portrayal of the secondary reality are two forms of evidence (Cross 1979): (1) what people say or write about the events and circumstances of the secondary reality – in legal terms, testimony (usually in Common Law systems greater weight is given to spoken testimony, while in Roman Law systems, greater weight is given to written testimony), and (2) things that are transferred from the primary reality to the secondary reality, for example a recording of a telephone conversation which took place during the events under investigation, a bloodstained knife or a fingerprint. On the basis of these two types of evidence particular constructions are made. In the Common Law system there are often two conflicting accounts of the secondary reality. These constructions, somewhat naively, are often referred to as the 'facts' of the case.

The legal process involves 'fitting' the reconstructed events to a legal notion of classes of such events in legislation, a process sometimes referred to as the application of the law. (In chapter 2 we saw the lengths to which the law goes, in attempting to define all and only the members of a particular class of events.) Sometimes the fit is clear, but on other occasions it is not. Figure 4.2 suggests that the competing reconstructions of the secondary reality are such that one party is legally blameworthy in one reconstruction but not in the other. Sometimes, when a person makes a confession to the police, or pleads guilty in court, there is a single construction. Even then, however, it may be that there are competing constructions which render the guilty party worthy of greater or lesser penalties, for instance involving background or mitigating circumstances for the guilty party, or statements of harm from the victim, which give a different slant to the construction of events. Finally it is worth noting that the process of construction of these accounts is hedged about by legal procedure. For example, in natural narratives of events the narrator often plays the role of one or more characters, speaking their words. However, in a courtroom this would be expressly forbidden by the rules involving 'hearsay' evidence, which is one of the 'rules of procedure' in figure 4.2.

Another challenge for the legal process is to establish the meaning of the legislation. This is done by reference to the legislation and precedent, and is discussed in chapter 1 as 'interpretation'.

Often (but not always) legal procedure genres such as the sequence of police interviews, or examination-in-chief can be seen as moving from left to right within the diagram, from an account that is overtly more interested in reconstructing the case, to an attempt to fit the account to the legal framework. In Common Law systems the police would not normally attempt to fit the events to a legal framework to the same degree as lawyers – this would be left to the public prosecutor. It is useful to remember that the legal framework and legal 'theory' is always present in the minds of the legal professionals, providing a legal construction through which the world is viewed and managed. This framework is contained to a large extent within what is known as 'sources of the law' such as legislation. It is worth mentioning the centrality of construction in legal decisions, as Maynard (1991: 127) states 'Abstract factors such as the law, the character of the defendant, and organizational roles do not influence decisions so much as the narrative structure . . . affects how participants bring these matters into play'.

The tensions within the judicial process have two main sources. One is that between competing versions of the same events, and the other is the 'fit' of the versions. Therefore, within the figure there are tensions between the two circled 'reconstructions' themselves, and between the constructions and the legal 'theory' presented in the top right hand box. These two tensions are the sources of most disagreement and disputation within the legal process. Although the Roman system is not so overtly confrontational in presenting two forms of the secondary reality, opposing parties in a dispute will often do so.

Means of representing the secondary reality

Since the events of the secondary reality are distanced in varying degrees from the court in time, place and culture, they are not present, they must be represented in some way. The representation of the second plane of reality can be done through real evidence such as photographs, diagrams and tape recordings, and by the introduction of physical entities such as weapons or clothing transferred from the other reality to the courtroom or police station (see below). By far the most common representation of this other reality is of course testimonial evidence which consists of descriptions of the events by witnesses – versions of the second reality presented through language – in Bennett and Feldman's (1981) telling metaphor 'stories'.

Non-linguistic means
The interaction between linguistic and non-linguistic means of referring to the secondary reality can be seen in the following examples from Hale and Gibbons (1999), where reference is being made in court to a diagram of a consulting room, which acts as a non-linguistic representation of the external reality. The extracts are from the official court transcript.

C: Can you . . . first of all, take the desk and the couch, do you agree with their positions?

C: All right . . . now . . . are you able to comment upon other things in the surgery, for example fridge. I put my finger where it says fridge, do you see that?

C: All right, what I want to ask you is about the screen . . . was the screen placed in the position where I'm putting my biro in the sketch. was the screen in an "L" shape, like that?

The external reality is being projected both through the courtroom language and the diagram.

In a similar vein, photographs are the representation in the following courtroom extract.

C: I approach Your Worship so I can have access to the photograph in the file if you don't mind . . . would you agree with me . . looking at ML5C which is the photographs, you agree that the door from the waiting-room. . the waiting-room to the Doctor's examination room is ad . . adjacent . . or beyond rather the end of the couch, do you agree with that?

The following extracts from official transcripts of New South Wales police interviews reveal similar phenomena. In the first, the account of the secondary reality is made in reference to a bank document, which is present in the primary reality of the interview room of the police station.

Q. 34 P: I now show you a bank draft drawn on the Dao Heng Bank of Hong Kong dated [. . .], for the sum of $20,000 made payable to [. . .].
shown bank draft
What can you tell me about this bank draft?

A. W: That is the one I received from Mr . . . and put into the bank account.

In the following extract from the official transcript of a police interview, reference is made to photographs, which introduce participants not present in the interview room from the external reality.

Q. 53 P: I am going to show you a folder of photographs. Would you show me the man you refer to as P.
shown folder of photographs

A. W: N wasn't there. D is dead, that's P, photo 12.

In the next extracts, the first from a record of interview, and the second from a statement, real objects from the secondary reality are introduced into the police station.

Q. 249 P: I would like to show you a portion of rope. Are you able to tell
me anything about that rope?
shown rope
A.   W: I don't know about that.

Detective A left the room for a short time and returned with a piece of
timber, which was part of a door jamb, with hinges and nails affixed. Detective A said, 'Have you ever seen this before?' He said 'That wood X find
and give to me'.

In the next extract from a police interview done in Goulburn Gaol, there
is an interesting interaction between the language representation, the surrounding context of the gaol, and the secondary context being reconstructed.

Q. 29 P: You said you were in the car, can you tell me how far away from
the car it was that S buried this bag.
A.   W: I don't know probably from here to that gate that's open, how
ever far that is.
(W. indicates a white gate a distance of about 15 metres away)

In this extract 'here' is where the two speakers are standing, 'that gate
that's open' is in the shared view of the surrounding context, and these
elements of the immediate context are referred to using language, in order
to reconstruct the secondary context.

Genres used in reconstruction of the secondary reality
The narrative genre is particularly important in the presentation of evidence, but Vargas (1984: 18) shows that some evidence is presented not as
'stories' or a sequence of events, but as a description of a state of affairs,
what I have termed Explanation previously. Narratives are appropriate
when the case concerns events which took place in a chronological sequence. When the case involves a state of affairs, for instance when the
coolant from a nuclear plant is polluting a lake with radioactivity, this is a
continuing state of affairs rather than a sequence of events. However, the
genre structure is similar, replacing events with elements of a situation,
and the *complication* element described below is still the core of the case.

The most widely used description of narrative structure is based on
Labov and Waletzky (1967). In recent versions it has the following stages.

NARRATIVE STRUCTURE

Orientation
Here a background is provided for the listener/reader, particularly information on the place, time and participants ('Once upon a time, a long time ago, in a small town in Hesse, there lived a tailor. . . . ').

Event $^{1-n}$
Here things happen, it may be one happening or it may be a number, but a pattern is often established.

Complication
Something unforeseen happens. Sometimes things go wrong.

Resolution
The complication is resolved in some way. Sometimes a new pattern emerges.

Coda
General conclusions are drawn. Sometimes it is the 'moral' of the story.

The orientation and the coda are **boundary units** (Sinclair and Coulthard 1975), which frame the story, but do not form part of the event sequence of the story itself. The other parts of the story are usually in chronological order, although for instance in modern novels this may be intentionally disrupted as a rhetorical device, and in court or police interrogation such disruptions may be used as a strategy to destabilize the witness by breaking up the narrative structure used as a memory framework (see chapter 3 'Strategies'). The place, time and participants established in the orientation run as threads through the narrative – they may change and participants may 'develop'. A typical linguistic characteristic of narrative is that the past tense is used in all stages except the coda, although sometimes narrators use the present tense to render the account more vivid. The sequencing of events is also typically rendered by beginning each event with a temporal expression such as 'next' or 'soon after'.

An important consideration in the construction of narratives is the audience. 'Audience design' (Bell 1997; Clark 1996) is based on the knowledge and beliefs, the 'schemas', of the audience. A good narrative uses such schemas, invoking them to make the narrative intelligible to the audience, linking itself to them in order to draw the audience in. Audience design also entails the use of rhetorical effects 'the story . . . must be told in ways that engage the audience through the use of powerful verbs, carefully chosen adjectives and the use of the active voice. Additionally, though, the marks of an engaging story are the use of repetition, imagery and metaphor' and I would add 'performance'. (One strategy that counsel use is to take the opposition story and strip it of such effects, in order to expose any weakness in the story structure.) In similar vein, Jackson (1988: 92) distinguishes 'the semantics of the stories told in court (their content) and that of the pragmatics of those stories (the process of persuading the court that the stories are true)'. In other words narratives have both ideational elements like those discussed in chapter 2, and interpersonal characteristics of the type discussed in chapter 3. Coulthard (2001) similarly describes the way police introduce narrative and dramatic effects into their written reconstructions of interviews.

What is this audience? It must be remembered that many trials are open to the public and are matters of public record. Snedaker (1991: 138) proposes a three tier audience: 'a primary audience of the judge and jury, a secondary audience made up of the press [nowadays 'media'] and courtroom spectators, and a universal audience consisting of all reasonable people'. Courtroom rhetoric is targeted mostly at the primary audience, but the secondary and universal audience also play their role, as does a possible appeal court. Interestingly, Stygall (1994: 179–82) documents the use of pronouns to refer to different audiences, some being deliberately deictic and referring to the participants in the trial, others being much more generic and containing Stygall (1994: 179) 'an abstract reference to the anonymous everyman or woman the law imagines and relies upon to decide cases', for example *we* could be used to refer to all members of the community.

The packaging of complex and multifaceted reality into a linear narrative carries obvious dangers of distorting the secondary reality. However, the need to make the secondary reality 'graspable' for a varied audience usually outweighs these concerns. Narratives are effective and useful as a presentation device, providing a framework on which an audience can hang many pieces of evidence, even if they sometimes distort or simplify. Jackson (1988: 76) writes 'Stories thus function not as some kind of optional, aesthetically-pleasing form, but as a response to the cognitive problems of abstraction and information overload.' However Jacquemet (1996: 131–2) notes that stories 'skip uninteresting (to the audience) details, and [. . .] indulge in likeable motives' at the same time as they 'provide a communicative frame for the allocation of truth-building legitimacy', and he ascribes these properties to the courtroom narratives he examines.

Legal narratives could be viewed as a registral sub-variety of narratives. Just as narratives for religious or medical purposes will differ somewhat from the archetypal literary narrative or children's story, so too legal narratives deploy the elements of narrative in a specific way. Of particular importance for the law is the issue of 'blame'. This entails assigning responsibility for events to particular participants. For instance the area of 'torts' includes issues of negligence and the duty of care. Therefore **responsibility for events is a central concern of legal narrative**. A related issue is the effects that events have upon participants. As a result the law's stories often explore the reactions of participants to events during the narrative reconstruction. The core of the narrative for legal purposes is frequently the **complication**, which may constitute the issue that is being adjudicated (the breach of contract, theft, etc.). Sometimes too the preceding 'events' play a minor role.

Narratives play various roles in the courtroom. First they are common in the testimony of witnesses, who usually present their account of some or all of the events that are the subject of litigation as narrative. Secondly, however, there are two 'master' narratives that counsel are trying to construct on the basis of elements from a range of witnesses and sometimes physical evidence, in which 'case characteristics and legal matters . . . are 'talked into being' by way of narrative and narrative structure' (Maynard 1991: 129). Snedaker (1991: 134) discusses the interaction between the master narrative and the witness's narratives, which she terms **satellite narratives** as follows: 'The [opening statement] kernel is the skeletal story, and satellite narratives fill out, elaborate, and extend the narrative through the information gathered during the examination of witnesses.' The genre structure of a Common Law trial reflects this in that the Prosecution/ Plaintiff case and witnesses are presented first, followed by the Defence case. However the master narratives permeate many other elements of the trial. It is important to note, however, that during testimony, jurors rarely experience a coherent narrative. The master narrative is built up piece by piece from a range of evidence: Stygall (1994: 120) writes 'Though as we shall see jurors make extensive use of a narrative structure through which to understand the events precipitating the trial, it is cognitive work that they must do on their own, lengthy narrative being absent in the trial's actual testimony' and also notes (Stygall 1994: 202) that lawyers have 'a concept of coherence that denies the importance of ordering'. It is normally only in the two counsels' closing statements or 'arguments' that all the satellite narratives are woven into the two master narratives, one for the Prosecution and one for the Defence.

Evaluations of narrative

The jury, according to research done by Bennett and Feldman (1981), make their decision on the basis of whose story is most convincing, in terms of its completeness, consistency and the credibility of supporting witnesses. In similar vein Jackson (1991: 175) discusses narrative as having three crucial elements, temporality/sequence, action/purpose, and intelligibility/experience (see also the descriptions above). A jury looks at the competing master narratives to see whether their elements fit together, whether the motives of the participants make sense and whether they can therefore reasonably be held responsible for the events, and whether the narratives correspond to their own experience and understanding of the world (their schemas) (Pennington and Hastie 1992, 1993). As Jackson (1991: 160 notes 'Credibility . . . is not a matter of individual witnesses or individual items of testimony, but a function of the evidence as a whole: does the overall story ring true?'

Concerning witness's stories (or satellite narratives), Jacquemet (1996: 184) notes that in reviewing the testimony of *pentiti* or informers, Italian judges 'followed three fundamental factors in deciding the credibility of the pentiti: consistency, good knowledge of details, and ability to provide contextual embedding for their testimony'. Bennett and Feldman (1981) argue that if witnesses come from a culture with a different narrative tradition from that of the judge (and jury), their story telling genre may produce confusion, and lead the hearers to assume that the story is confused or illogical: compare Michaels and Collins (1984). This may provide a partial explanation for the problems of Mrs Walsh described in Eades (2000: 182–5). Coates (1964) provides many anecdotal examples. This conflict in narrative conventions may impact on the weight given to the witness's testimony, and disadvantage people whose culture differs from that of those who sit in judgment. If the audience does not share with the narrator some of the schemas needed to understand the story, this too may render a story less convincing or less intelligible. The risk to witnesses from minority cultures is evident.

The Interweaving of the Primary and Secondary Reality: Master Narratives Interacting with Procedural Genres

Master narratives interact in a range of ways with the primary genre structures described previously. In this section the interactions between the narratives and the jury trial macro-genre and the judicial judgment are examined.

Jury trial proceedings

In a criminal trial the role of counsel is both to convince the judge (and jury) of the correctness of their master narrative, and to attack and undermine that of the opposing counsel. In the opening and closing statements this may be done on the level of the master narrative as a whole, but during examination of witnesses it is done at the level of satellite narratives and other pieces of evidence. Finally it is worth noting that the trial itself is a staged macro-genre (see table 4.1), which itself has some of the characteristics of a narrative. The three genre levels then are the trial, which is viewed here as a form of primary reality macro-genre, and the two types of secondary reality genres, the master narratives and the witness's narratives. Jackson (1991: 160) writes 'the law in practice cannot be reduced to a single narrative level, but rather should be conceived in terms of a multiplicity of narrative/discursive structures'. The following section looks at the interaction of these three narrative levels in various stages of the jury trial macro-genre. It also points out a major difference between legal narratives and everyday narratives: the fact that most legal narratives attempt to establish blame (Mather and Yngvesson 1982).

Opening statement
The initial introduction to the master narratives come in the *opening statement* by counsel. Maynard (1991) gives several examples of a short narrative (that he calls a 'synopsis') forming part of the opening statement in pre-trial hearings. Snedaker (1991) provides a detailed narrative analysis of the opening statements in the Chicago Anarchists Trial. The narrative in opening statements is intended to expose the judge (and jury) to a summary of the master narrative, which will thus provide a skeleton for the more detailed evidence that will emerge during the trial. Snedaker (1991: 134) writes 'the opening statement sets the theme by outlining the plot, describing the characters, depicting the setting, attributing the motives, and portraying the action of the story'. However, for counsel there can be a delicate balance between persuading the judge (and jury) to view the evidence in a particular way, and giving away too much to the opposing counsel ('signalling their punches'). As the trial is a macro-genre, the opening statement is in many ways a macro Orientation stage. Blame at

this stage can be openly assigned (or denied), or else it may be implied.

Appearance
In each witness's **appearance** (see table 4.1), during the (friendly) examination-in-chief, the counsel is trying to elicit all or part of the desired master story. The level of direction (see chapter 3 on coercion and control) from the counsel may depend on her/his faith that the witness will produce the desired story. If counsel believes that the witness will do so, there may be a fairly open invitation to narrative. The (hostile) cross-examination attempts to challenge and discredit this testimony in a variety of ways, most often by attacking elements of the story, by attempting to show that they are unsupported or contradicted by other evidence, either testimonial or real, that elements are open to other interpretations, or that the story is internally inconsistent. The whole story may be challenged on the basis of its content, particularly gaps and illogicalities, or there may be a person-oriented attack, attempting to discredit the evidence by discrediting the witness. Tactics used for the latter purpose are discussed in chapter 3. Since the witness is 'hostile', counsel will often use confirmation questions containing counsel's alternative version of events, attempting to get the witness's agreement. Witnesses who are aware of this process will often attempt to answer with more than the information requested in order to reaffirm their version, possibly in the discomfirmation sequence discussed by Atkinson and Drew (1979: 179–81). In re-examination, the counsel attempts to re-establish the friendly witness's story, and refute or defuse the attacks. An attempt is made to establish through questioning that harm has occurred, that there is a specific cause for the harm, and to establish responsibility for the harm. Appearances are the main basis for the competing constructions in figure 4.2. An appearance could be seen as a form of macro-event (Labov and Waletzky 1967) in the trial macro-genre.

Final argument
The final summing-up is where the defence and the prosecution attempt most fully to construct a master narrative which contains or explains all the evidence presented during the trial in a coherent way. These are the most complete of the satellite narratives, and constitute the final plank in the construction of the competing constructions in figure 4.2 There is, however, also a non-narrative element where counsel move to the right in figure 4.2, and present their view of how their master narrative reconstruction fits the framework of legislation, in particular to establish blame or blamelessness. The fit to legislation is particularly important where a jury

must decide among verdicts of greater or lesser severity, or where a range of offences must be judged.

Judge's summation and instructions
The judge's directions to the jury will often provide some form of summary of the master narratives, highlighting for the jurors the areas where the master narratives differ, instructing the jury as to the validity of the evidence within the rules of procedure (particularly certain evidence or statements that should be discounted), but principally discussing in detail the fit between the master narratives and the law. The judge therefore assesses both the constructions of the primary reality, and the fit of these to both elements of the legal framework. This could be seen as a type of macro complication stage.

Decision
The **verdict** is not given in narrative form, but as a simple statement of guilty/not guilty/uncertain, or in civil law, finding for one of the two parties or neither. Many jurors however express frustration at not being able to give an account of their reasons. This could be seen as a macro resolution stage.

Finally, in a criminal trial, if a guilty verdict is reached, the judge passes **sentence**, s/he awards costs and may speak to the parties, condemning or congratulating them. In a non-criminal jury trial, it is the jury that may decide damages. This could be seen as a macro coda, as society's final verdict on the principles involved. In the majority of court cases where no jury is involved, the judge also presents reasons for his/her verdict.

The macro-genre presented here is only one of several macro-genres of this type, for instance a coronial enquiry will differ in some structural respects from the pattern above.

The report summary

The written judgment which is produced after the case is a genre of its own, and was described previously. It contains a summary which may also have narrative characteristics. The following is an illustration from the summary stage of the judgment on *KFC Technical Services Sdn Bhd v. Industrial Court of Malaysia & Anor* [1992] 1 MLJ 564. In this case Kentucky Fried Chicken's Malaysian franchise was appealing an order to pay compensation to sacked workers, to the High Court of Malaysia.

The majority of the employees in the maintenance division of Fulcrum Sdn Bhd ('Fulcrum') joined a trade union, the second defendant ('the union'). The union then sought recognition from Fulcrum but Fulcrum issued retrenchment notices to all the employees who were members of the union. Upon a complaint by the retrenched employees to the Director General of Industrial Relations, Fulcrum reinstated them in December 1986. Fulcrum changed its name to KFC Technical Services Sdn Bhd ('KFC'). KFC accorded recognition to the union but this time terminated the employment of all its employees in the division on the ground that it was closing the maintenance division. Only those retrenched employees who were not members of the union continued to be employed by a related company. The union made representation to the Minister who referred it to the Industrial Court. The Industrial Court in its award held that KFC's employees were dismissed without just cause or excuse. The Industrial Court further decided that it was impossible to reinstate the dismissed employees and instead ordered KFC to pay compensation to its employees amounting to two month's salary for each year of service. KFC applied to the High Court to quash the Industrial Court award. It argued that there was in fact a genuine and bona fide closure of its business. It also contended that the amount of compensation normally ordered by the Industrial Court is one month's salary for each year of service.

[*Note*: KFC lost this appeal, and a subsequent appeal
to the Malaysian Supreme Court]

There are several interesting features of this text that identify it as a subtype of narrative. First, it is told in strict chronological order, as various connectives reveal, such as 'next' and 'upon'. Second, it is written in the past tense. Third, at the beginning it has an orientation to the participants. In the longer judgment of which this is a summary, the orientation also has additional information on the nature of the work done by the employees, and each of the events described above is dated. What is interesting is that the court's decisions also become part of the 'story'. The conclusion to the story on this occasion was the High Court's decision, which was given along with reasons in the next part of the summary. This text gives another example of the penetration of narrative into the judicial process.

It should be noted that it is these summaries (also called 'decisions' or 'opinions') that form the precedent for future decisions, in other words they are the basic building blocks of judge–made law. Not all decisions are reported in case reports, and where they are not there is little likelihood of their use as precedent.

Conclusion

Figure 4.2, which attempts to display the relationship between the primary reality, the secondary reality and the legal frame may help in the rather difficult task of understanding the major groups of variables that continually interact in the legal process. The genre framework, while not offering a complete understanding of legal process, can contribute to a broad understanding of legal processes and legal discourse. However, to speak of the law's 'stories' is to use a metaphor. The legal variety of narrative is different in important ways from the everyday story or anecdote, and there are elements that are not part of a narrative structure. Nevertheless, the use of a genre framework in combination with the concept of primary and secondary reality can take us some way along the path to a deeper understanding and conceptualization of these complex issues.

5

Communication Issues in the Legal System

[legal English is] wordy, unclear, pompous and dull

Mellinkoff (1963)

Introduction

Communication difficulties in the legal system can have two sources. It may be that non-lawyers cannot understand the language of the law. Or it may be that lawyers cannot understand the language of people who do not speak the standard language of the legal system. The second issue will mainly be addressed in chapter 7. Turning to the first issue, in previous chapters, particularly chapters 1 and 2, we have seen that the language of the law can be highly complex. Consequently there is widespread agreement that the language of the law is difficult to understand. Jackson (1990: 87) writes 'Although the English law is communicated largely in English, most speakers of the English language are excluded from the semiotic group of the law, since they cannot understand the particular register of the language which the law uses'. This chapter will present evidence that this is the case for a range of legal contexts, it will discuss why this is a problem, what the sources of difficulty are, and how these might be tackled (with evidence concerning successful changes). The communication model from the Introduction underlies the organization of the argument.

The most fundamental reason for making legal language intelligible is that the Common Law presumes that 'ignorance of the law is no defence'. If the law is presented in language that cannot be understood by the people to whom it applies, this presumption can lead to grave injustice as well as logical absurdity. This means that legal language should be intelligible to the audience for that language, including the people affected by it. More intelligible legal language would help non-lawyers to understand and appreciate the way the legal system works, to understand basic legal concepts (such as due process), to understand and protect their own legal and contract rights, and to understand and participate more meaningfully in legal proceedings. Perfect understanding of the law and the justice system may prove unachievable, but its pursuit is imperative. Indeed, perfect communication is rare, but the intelligibility of legal language can certainly be enhanced.

The Incomprehensibility of Legal Language

There is a long and robust tradition of criticism of the language of the law. It has been the object of much satire – see for instance Jonathan Swift's *Gulliver's Travels*, or the Marx Brothers films *Animal Crackers* and *A Day at the Races*. Among the many important social themes that he addresses, Charles Dickens attacks legal language in *Bleak House* (Dickens 1893: 8). Eagleson summarizes much of this criticism when he writes (Law Reform Commission of Victoria 1987: 11) 'Many legal documents are unnecessarily lengthy, overwritten, self-conscious and repetitious. . . . They are unintelligible to the ordinary reader, and barely intelligible to many lawyers.' Indeed many lawyers from around the world are critical of the language of the law. A doyen of British legal writing, Bentham (1838: 281) criticizes it unequivocally. The British Renton Report (Renton, 1975) notes that even lawyers and judges find that legal drafting is 'an impenetrable barrier to understanding it', and adds (Renton 1975: 37) 'To the ordinary citizen the provisions in the statute book might sometimes as well be written in a foreign language for the help he may expect to obtain there as to his rights and duties under the law. And this in an age . . . when the statute law has a growing effect on practically every sphere of daily life'. An American lawyer and founding father of the study of the language of the law, David Melinkoff provided the quotation at the beginning of this chapter, and devotes much of his classic book *Language of the Law* to a critique of the unnecessary complexities of legal English. Eagleson quotes the Chair of the Victoria Division Social Security Appeals Tribunal (Law Reform Commission of Victoria 1987: 10): 'It is unfortunate the Parliament of the Commonwealth of Australia allows legislation such as the Social Security Act of 1947 to remain on the statute books which is almost totally unintelligible to anyone. The fact that this Act directly touches the lives of every person belonging to this country gives the Tribunal even greater cause for concern. The current state of this most important Act can only be described as a national disgrace.' (Subsequently the first Australian

Commonwealth Act to be rewritten using plain language principles was the Commonwealth Social Security Act.) The High Court of Australia (in the *Hepples* Case) has condemned the convoluted drafting of taxation legislation. Figure 2.1 in chapter 2 is a good example of a not unusual legal text that is difficult to understand, particularly for non-lawyers.

It is not only the English of the law that is difficult. Duarte i Montserrat (1993) and Duarte i Montserrat and Martínez (1995) provide extensive documentation of the complexity of the Catalan and Spanish of the law. Cavagnoli and Wölk (1997) document this same problem for Italian. Gunnarsson (1984) discusses the difficulty of the Swedish of legislation. There are similar literatures for most other European languages. Okawara (forthcoming) describes the unintelligibility of legal codes to most Japanese, and the consequent attempts undertaken to make legal Japanese more intelligible, but she notes that even revised legal codes are still difficult for the ordinary Japanese to understand.

There are extensive psycholinguistic studies that demonstrate that legal language is not well understood by ordinary people (see for example Charrow and Charrow 1979, and the numerous references in Lieberman and Sales 1997). I will return to the testing of complexity later in this chapter. Other work and testing by plain language advocates has also found that even if the reader eventually comes to a full understanding of the text, reading legal register rather than plain language takes far more time and effort. This means that the use of such a register is inefficient and expensive. The cost of staff time and staff errors caused by unnecessary complexity runs into many millions of dollars in business and public service. For instance the Management and Personnel Office of the Cabinet Office in the UK estimates that the redesign of forms on plain language principles saved £4 million in 1984–5.

The language of the law is not only difficult to understand, it is also difficult if not impossible for non-lawyers to produce. The over-elaboration discussed in chapter 3 may be partly an unsuccessful attempt by non-lawyers to produce legal language.

Sources of Difficulty

This section will use the model of communication presented in the Introduction as a framework. As noted above, intelligibility means intelligibility for the relevant audience – in language produced by lawyers for lawyers, technicality and complexity can reasonably be greater and more shared knowledge can be assumed than in material for a lay audience.

Non-verbal communication

In chapter 1 we noted a range of consequences of the use of literate written language. The shift into written language originally happened at a time when modern formatting possibilities were not available to scribes. Traditional legal documents were largely unpunctuated and unformatted, failing to use subheadings and paragraph divisions.

The conservatism of the legal profession may explain why legal documents still tend not to utilize the full range of formatting possibilities offered by modern technologies. Modern printed texts can be laid out in a range of ways that assist understanding such as: highlighting with larger fonts, bold or underlining; the use of space on the page such as spacing between sections, indenting and margins; and other typographic resources such as symbols and bulleting. Felker et al. (1981) provide research evidence that all these means can enhance understanding. Given modern technologies, such as photocopying and digital storage, formatting can be retained when copies are made.

Penman (1992) makes a case that it is possible to focus too intensely on the vocabulary and grammar of the law, when formatting and other non-verbal resources such as diagrams can play a more important role in improving communication. One study she reports, looked at the NRMA Plain English Car Insurance Policy, which is regarded as a model of plain English. This policy had mainly been developed using a sentence simplification approach. Penman and her colleagues produced an alternative version, using a discourse level approach, looking at the structure of the whole document, lay-out and easy access to relevant information. They then tested the two documents, using a classic social psychology methodology of 18 'scenario questions': for example 'If your car is stolen, do you have to report it to the police?' and 'How much will the NRMA pay if your trailer is stolen?' Not surprisingly, their version was more comprehensible. There are important lessons here – first the importance of discourse level approaches, second the importance of testing out documents, and third a possible method for doing so. As technologies expand the range of resources in written modes of communication (for instance hypertext on computers) these will offer an even greater range of communicative possibilities.

Linguistic features

Turning to more linguistic issues, the problems caused by language are the particularities of legal language that we have examined in the previous chapters of this book – the effects of writing, particularly planning and distance from context; technical and specialized elements of legal language; and the use of interpersonal power. Looking first at the impact of writing, the **planning** time made available to writers (in contrast to the 'real time' production of language in spontaneous speech) has various linguistic consequences. One, 'increased explicitness in the logical structure' can boost understanding, when it involves careful 'signposting' of the structure of the text by use of numbers and headings as well as the formatting conventions, such as indentation as mentioned above. This type of discourse phenomenon is often referred to as part of good 'document design'. It also entails the use of initial abstracts, tables of contents and the logical sequencing of the information (Felker et al. 1981).

However the opportunity to plan the flow of information in a text is a double edged sword. At the discourse level it clearly aids comprehension, since it assists the logical organization of ideas. At the grammatical level, however, it may involve the use of elements of grammar that have been proven by psycholinguists to be more difficult to understand, particularly passives. In addition, passives without an agent (e.g. *the building was destroyed* where we are not told who or what destroyed the building) can be less clear because it is possible to lose track of the participants. (In legal language the use or abuse of this resource is particularly significant, given the prime concern within the law with agency and blame.) Sometimes this is desirable – the drafting manual that is part of Law Reform Commission of Victoria (1987: 38–9) notes 'There are many occasions, however, in which the passive is the proper voice to use, for example where the agent is unimportant and therefore does not have to be specified. The Infertility (Medical Procedures) Act 1984 has two clear illustrations.

1.   This Act may be cited as the Infertility (Medical Procedures) Act 1984.

10 (3). A procedure to which this section applies shall not be carried out unless . . .

In these cases it does not matter who does the 'citing' or the 'carrying out'. As with most guidelines for plain language writing, the proscribed form is one that should be used only when necessary, rather than totally avoided. Felker et al. (1981: 29) note that passives are more difficult to understand unless 'the intent is to focus on the object of the action', and they provide evidence from psycholinguistic research.

Another result of planning time is the potential to produce extremely long and complex sentence structures that would be impossible to produce or understand in the real time setting of normal speech, because of the cognitive processing involved. This is further discussed later in this chapter.

A further critical contributor to linguistic complexity is distance from context, realized as grammatical metaphor. Plain language advocates, who are not always aware of the full complexity of the phenomenon, address it by encouraging the use 'action verbs', and avoiding 'nouns created from verbs' (Felker et al. 1981: 35). Their prescriptions unfortunately tend to be limited to nominalisations that are morphologically derived from verbs – missing the other forms that grammatical metaphor can take (conjunctions to verbs, nouns to adjectives, etc. – see chapter 1). Charrow and Charrow (1979) present experimental evidence of the difficulty of nominalization. This difficulty emerges from several sources. First, grammatical metaphor involves a distortion of the relationship between the basic meaning of parts of speech such as verbs, adjectives and nouns (processes, attributes and things), and their meaning when used metaphorically: see for instance figure 3.1. This explains their lower frequency in spontaneous speech and child language, and in languages that do not have a literate tradition. Another source of difficulty is that they often have a complex morphological form, even in a comparatively common example such as *leadership* (lead+er+ship), as well as technical terms such as *unimpeachability* (un+im+peach+abil+ity). Additionally, in English we tend to construct our morphologically complex grammatical metaphors using words from Greek or Romance sources (*impeach* is from French – see also below), which are less familiar to people without a classical education, for instance *put in* is usually nominalized as *insertion* (although computer jargon tends to use everyday language as a source of nominalizations i.e. 'input'). Less literate people may be unfamiliar with the low frequency nominalizations found mainly in writing.

Another aspect of this process is that clauses with an overt grammatical structure which reveals the relationship between the elements are reduced to complex noun phrases. Charrow and Charrow (1979: 1321) state, concerning nominalization, that 'shortening a whole subordinate clause into a single nominal usually increases the complexity of the deeper grammatical and semantic structure. The meaning of the sentence becomes less clear, and the mind must work harder to decode it.' For example *drug abuse* is normally understood as misusing narcotics (abuse of drugs) – it could, however, also mean the bad language found in the drug culture (abusive language associated with drugs). Furthermore the packaging of information into complex noun phrases increases the 'density' of the information, and there is research evidence that this in turn increases comprehension difficulty (Felker et al., 1981: 43). The simple plain language recommendation is 'unstring noun strings' (Felker et al. 1981: 63).

However, grammatical metaphor is a two edged sword. Solomon (1996) points out that it is difficult to avoid, and attempts to do so can produce sentences that are more syntactically complex – one may be trading off complexity at the phrase level for complexity at the sentence level. Furthermore, grammatical metaphor can be a valuable resource in the construction of long texts, since it permits the 'packaging' (usually in a complex noun phrase) of concepts constructed or accumulated in the preceding text. In playing this role it aids communication for those who have mastered the linguistic resource, but as noted above such complex and heavy noun phrases can lead to comprehension difficulties for others.

Another consequence of the decontextualization of written language is greater explicitness concerning participants. This can be an aid to comprehension and disambiguation, but if it is done in the traditional legal way, for example *the party of the third part*, it can lead to comprehension difficulties (see the Marx Brothers film *A Day at the Races*). The plain language nostrum is 'use personal pronouns' (Felker et al. 1981: 31).

One problematic feature of the language of the law which was discussed in Chapter 2 and touched on above, is the use of archaisms and of words and expressions from other languages (in English, from Latin and French; in Spanish from Latin; in Japanese from Chinese). This can be attributed to the **standardizing** and conserving role of literacy, as well as the need for **technical** terms. Archaisms and foreign language elements are often unnecessary, and they can be replaced with modern native forms.

Chapter 2 also discusses other types of technical vocabulary. The case is made in that chapter for the usefulness, and sometimes necessity of technical language among lawyers. By definition, such technical vocabulary is not normally known to non-lawyers, yet the reality is that its use is not confined to an audience of all lawyers. To use it with a non-lawyer audience is therefore to guarantee incomprehension unless it is defined within the operational document in such a way that it can be understood. Alternatively the technical vocabulary can be used to communicate the status and exclusivity of lawyers and their knowledge (the interpersonal motive) rather than information. Felker et al. (1981: 59) provide a list of words where a high register term can be replaced with an everyday word, usually without loss of precision or information, for example *total* for *aggregate*, *show* for *indicate*, *begin* for *initiate*. The use of doublets and triplets may also introduce unnecessary complication. The communication problem becomes more severe when other languages such as Latin are used. As Duarte i Montserrat and Martínez (1995: 118) write: 'es preferible no usar este tipo de expresiones latinas en documentos que vayan destinado a un público general o que tengan un receptor no jurídico' (it is preferable not to use this type of Latin expression in documents intended for the general public or a non-legal audience). Perhaps the most worrying form of technical language is everyday words used with a specialist meaning (see, for example, *aggravation* below), which are most likely to lead to miscommunication with layfolk.

In Chapter 2 we saw that the pursuit of precision can lead to another potential source of communication difficulty – complexity in the grammatical structure (in contrast with semantic complexity such as grammatical metaphor or technicality). Structural complexity can be examined in terms of the notion of constituency. According to this model of language, morphemes constitute words; words constitute phrases (I use 'verb phrase' to refer to the verbal element only, not the verb and its object or prepositional phrase); phrases constitute simple sentences; and simple sentences constitute complex sentences.

This extract from a British Association of Removers contract, quoted in Davies (forthcoming), provides examples:

> The cost of any such arbitration shall be in the discretion of the arbitrator and the award of such arbitrator shall be a condition precedent to any legal proceedings in a court of law in respect of any matters hereby agreed to be the subject of arbitration.

Moving through the layers, the word *discretion* consists of two morphemes discret + ion. The verb phrase 'shall be' consists of the words *shall* and *be*, and the noun phrase 'any legal proceedings' consists of the words *any*, *legal* and *proceedings*, and the prepositional phrase 'in a court of law' consists of the words *in*, *a*, *court*, *of* and *law*. 'The cost of any such arbitration shall be in the discretion of the arbitrator' is a simple sentence which consists of a series of phrases, and the whole quotation is a complex sentence consisting of two simple sentences, although the element 'hereby agreed to be the subject of arbitration' is a reduced form of the simple sentence 'which are hereby agreed to be the subject of arbitration', which has been subjected to whiz deletion (see below).

There is potential for complexity at each level of constituency. This complexity may derive from the **number** of constituents and/or the complexity of the nature of the **relationship** between them. The possible types of structural complexity are:

- *syntactic complexity* (the relationships between and the number of simple sentences in a complex sentence);
- *inter-sentence complexity* (the relationships between and the number of phrases);
- *phrasal complexity* (the relationships between and the number of words in a phrase);
- *lexical complexity* (the relationships between and the number of morphemes in a word).

There is also the possibility of complex links between layers which are not in a direct constituency relationship, for instance between morphemes and clauses.

There is psycholinguistic evidence that syntactic complexity can contribute to comprehension difficulty. While coordinate or paratactic structures are somewhat more difficult than simple sentences, it is the subordinate or hypotactic structures that are most difficult. As we saw in chapter 2 operative documents can be extremely syntactically complex. Even for a legal audience, such texts can require work before they are understood in full. Felker et al. (1981: 43) provide a range of research support for the difficulty caused by complex grammar. We also saw in chapter 2 that there is a strong tendency to construct complex sentences based on the listing of conditions. The argument in favour of this is that sometimes reference is clarified, for instance a long single sentence beginning 'Whoever knowingly . . . ' applies this condition to all that follows. However there is little question that long and complex sentence structures also make the language more difficult to understand. Felker et al. (1981: B-7) show that text can be made much clearer if conditions are presented one at a time on separate lines, rather than being embedded in complex syntactic structures, and once more provide considerable research support for this. The rather over simple plain language recommendation is that sentences should be less than twenty-six words in length.

It is also noticeable that in the example from Cunningham et al. (1994) discussed in chapter 2 it is explicitly stated that sometimes the grammar of operative documents follows different rules from everyday English, which creates a likelihood of miscommunication with non-lawyers.

A related problem mentioned in Felker et al. (1981) is that of relative constructions with 'whiz deletion', for instance 'I saw the man standing over there at the scene of the crime' is said to be more difficult to understand than 'I saw the man **who is** standing over there at the scene of the crime'. Redish and Rosen (1991) make the point that the use of whiz deletion may mask syntactic complexity, and writers may become aware of this complexity only when the full form is used. While the second form is more explicit, removing all whiz deletions is not a good idea – see the debate between Huckin, Curtin and Graham (1991) and Redish and Rosen (1991).

Planning, particularly in legal drafting, also provides the motivation to avoid possible ambiguity by the placing of information in places where it would not occur in natural speech, often for example separating subject from verb. Felker et al. (1981: 47–8) note that there is an 'extensive and varied body of research' which shows that this interferes with comprehension.

With the exception of police over-elaboration, the interpersonal power asymmetry discussed in chapter 3 mostly affects comprehension indirectly, because it makes it more difficult for the public (who are usually in a less powerful role) to negotiate their comprehension problems with lawyers, particularly within the highly constrained context of a courtroom. The same could be said when the public need to convey their meanings to lawyers. In that chapter we noticed a tendency in legal language to use double or multiple negatives, including 'hidden' negatives such as 'unless' 'forbid' and 'deny'. Felker et al. (1981: 69–70) present research findings that show that the more negatives there are in a sentence, the more difficult it becomes to understand. The plain language recommendation is 'avoid multiple negatives'.

The genres discussed in chapter 4 can play a critical role in comprehension. In that chapter the research done on the role of schemas in reading was mentioned. A number of reading scholars (including Bower, Black and Turner 1979; Perkins 1987; Schank and Abelson 1977; Wallace 1990; and Weaver 1988) have provided convincing evidence that knowledge of both textual schemas or genres, and knowledge schemas (see below) play a critical role in comprehension. We also noted in chapter 4 that a group of lawyers found a legal agreement comprehensible, because their knowledge of the generic structure of that type of text allowed them to predict the content of a section, so that they were able to overcome problems caused by inadequate wording. Leading linguists, who lacked the same knowledge of legal genres, were unable to understand the text despite high levels of both linguistic knowledge and general education. A lack of knowledge of legal genres can therefore be a comprehension problem for non-lawyers if the lawyers drafting a legal text are not sensitive to this issue, or if for some other reason they fail to address it in their drafting.

Finally one should mention the possibilities provided by non-verbal forms of communication. Legal documents rarely make use of the communicative effectiveness of illustrations, charts and graphs, although maps and diagrams have a tradition of use in property documents dating at least from the Domesday Book.

Stygall (1994: 208) offers some words of caution. She notes that 'The metalinguistic consciousness in the legal community only admits words and phrases as problematic', making the case that the conceptual frame is a major source of communication difficulties between lawyers and others, but that this is less discussed because it causes some discomfort in acknowledging the lack of 'mutual intelligibility and access'. This brings us to the issue of knowledge schemas.

Knowledge schemas

The role of knowledge in comprehension is well attested (Anderson 1984; Anderson and Pearson 1988; Kintsch 1988). If two people share a knowledge base in a particular area, their communication is greatly facilitated. Sometimes a great deal can be communicated by few words, since so much can be assumed. If the knowledge is particularly specialized, full communication about it with a person who does not share that knowledge may difficult, or even impossible. A familiar example is the impossibility (for people like myself who know little of the subject) of understanding discussion among quantum physicists, or of discussing the topic with them in depth. It is equally the case that when lawyers engage in discussion of points of law in the courtroom, a lack of knowledge can make the discussion simply unintelligible for non-lawyers, and much lawyer–client interaction is spent negotiating ways round this lack of shared knowledge. In recent years this has emerged as a major source of the difficulties of communication between lawyers and other people. In chapter 2 it was also argued that even if the public understand every individual word that the lawyer says, the lack of a shared 'frame' or conceptualization of the world may lead to communication breakdown.

Having looked at some possible sources of communication difficulty, a brief introduction to the plain language movement will be given, and examples of complexity and its consequences will be drawn from four important legal genres.

The Plain Language Movement

The Plain Language Movement usually traces its origins to Sir Ernest Gowers' (1948) *Plain Words*, and his later influential *Complete Plain Words*, published originally in 1954, and in many revisions and editions since. There has been a continuing movement for plain language in Britain, spearheaded since 1979 by the Plain English Campaign, which since 1984 has been working with the National Consumer Council to advocate plain English law. The movement also became influential in the USA, reaching its height with the personal endorsement of President Jimmy Carter. The influential Document Design Center in Washington DC has produced thorough surveys of the evidence concerning the difficulty of individual linguistics features of legal English, as well as detailed guidelines on how to reduce its complexity (see particularly Felker et al, 1981). The implementation of these plain language principles is demonstrated in the examples later in this chapter. Eagleson (1991) describes developments in Australia, beginning with the reform of NRMA insurance policies, later followed by the important work on simplifying legislation described in the Law Reform Commission of Victoria (1987) report.

More recently in Britain the plain language movement has had a major success in persuading the government and mainstream English law authorities to implement change towards plain language. They have assisted the Master of the Rolls, Lord Woolf, in producing the 1998 *Civil Procedure Rules* (SI 1998 3132) which substitute many forms, documents and procedural wordings with clearer equivalents. Many of the idiosyncracies of legal language discussed in Chapters 1 and 2 have been addressed. A number of arcane legal terms have been replaced: for instance a *plaintiff* is now a *claimant*, a *pleading* is now a *statement of case*. Law Latin has been replaced with English – *ex parte*, *inter partes*, *in camera* and *sub poena* have become *with notice*, *without notice*, *in private* and a *summons*. Proper names such as an *Anton Piller order* have been replaced with more transparent titles such as a *search order*. These changes have yet to be adopted elsewhere.

Plain language movements are not limited to the English speaking world, however. For example, in both France and Germany there have been substantial movements for plain language.

Jury Instructions

Judges' instructions to juries are a common feature of Common Law jury trials. Some of these instructions come at the beginning of the trial and largely inform the jury of their obligations. Some, particularly those instructing jurors to take no account of pieces of inadmissible evidence, come during the trial. Most come at the end of a trial, when the judge provides the jury with information and directions they will need in handling the evidence, particularly testimony, and in reaching a decision within the framework of the law. Since jurors are rarely legally trained, this means that the judge needs to present the issues in a form that jurors can understand. Jurors have the responsibility of deciding innocence or guilt on the charge or charges, and therefore have considerable power, so their decision needs to be founded upon adequate understanding, to avoid the fairness of the trial being endangered.

The problem, which is common to the other legal genres used as examples, is that there are in effect two very different audiences for jury instructions. First there is the obvious and direct audience, the lay jurors. However, jury instructions can also serve as the basis for later appeals, and they may be used, in effect, to evaluate the accuracy of the judge in communicating the law. The second audience in this case consists of the judge's legal peers: fellow judges and lawyers. The jury instructions must pass muster for this audience too: in essence they must be legally watertight, bringing into play the issues examined in chapters 1–4 on the desire for precision authority and literacy in language, with their associated language features. There is, therefore, an underlying tension between the language appropriate to the lay jury audience, and the language appropriate to the specialist legal audience. This problem is referred to in this book as the **two audience dilemma**. While these tensions are in many cases reconcilable (it is often possible to produce language that addresses the needs of both audiences), they explain much of the seeming irrationality of using legal language to (mis)communicate with a lay audience that cannot fully understand it. As English and Sales (1997) note:

The legal system has also foisted upon jurors instructions that have been criticized as abstract and generic (Severance, Greene and Loftus 1984). Jurists persist in administering these instructions to jurors because they have survived on appeal to a higher court (Severance and Loftus 1982). The view that jurors remember and understand any instruction given them, and that therefore it is more important to focus on an instruction's survivability on legal appeal than on its comprehensibility, is ill-informed.

(English and Sales 1997)

In chapter 1 Stygall's discussion of jury instruction was mentioned, which showed that essentially written language was presented in oral form, leading to communication breakdown. She also shows that a lack of a shared conceptual frame can lead to poor communication between lawyer and juror.

In the United States there has been a long-term involvement of psycholinguists in the study of the comprehension and incomprehension of jury instructions. There are model instructions known as **pattern instructions** for a variety of types of legal cases, which judges often use to save time, and to avoid problems with appeals or any appearance of judge bias. An influential early study of pattern jury instructions by Charrow and Charrow (1979) exposed the role played by many of the linguistic features mentioned in previous chapters. They express their view as follows: '(1) that standard jury instructions – when viewed as discourse – are not well understood by the average juror; (2) that certain linguistic constructions are largely responsible for this hypothesized incomprehensibility; and (3) that if the problematic linguistic constructions are appropriately altered, comprehension should dramatically improve, notwithstanding the 'legal complexity' of any given instruction' (i.e. despite a lack of shared knowledge) (Charrow and Charrow 1979: 1300).

Charrow and Charrow tested the comprehension of fourteen standard civil jury instructions. The subjects for their (1979) study were people called for jury service in Maryland. They tested the pattern instructions by having the subjects paraphrase them. 'The analysis revealed the existence of numerous grammatical constructions, phrases and words that appear both to typify legal language and to affect jurors' comprehension adversely' (Charrow and Charrow 1979: 1311). Even the most generous form of measurement showed that only an average of 54 per cent of instructions were understood. Subsequent studies have showed that 'it is common to find over half the instructions misunderstood' (Lieberman and Sales 1997).

Charrow and Charrow specifically mention as sources of difficulty the following language features, all of which were shown to be typical of legal language in chapters 1–4, and were documented earlier as causes of comprehension problems. Charrow and Charrow (1979: 1360) note that 'all the grammatical constructions, discourse conventions, and vocabulary items that we isolated in the jury instructions commonly appear in other branches of legal language'.

- nominalizations;
- technical vocabulary;
- 'as to' propositional phrases (e.g. 'The order in which the instructions are given has no significance **as to** their relative importance.');
- unusual positioning of phrases;
- whiz and complement deletion;
- negatives, particularly multiple negatives;
- passives in subordinate clauses;
- doublets, triplets and longer 'lists of words';
- poor genre structure;
- formatting – particularly numbering;
- subordination, particularly multi-layered subordination, and use of a clause to replace a noun phrase (rank shifting).

They also found that the use of the modal verbs *must*, *should* and *may* enhances comprehension, and that passives in main clauses are not a comprehension problem.

Charrow and Charrow (1979) discount sentence length as a factor, showing that it accounts for little of the comprehension difficulty of the jury instructions. The Flesch readability formula based on sentence length showed no relationship to reading problems. They concentrated instead on the complexity of relationships. They were also able to discount personal variables such as age and sex – predictably only educational level had an effect.

Charrow and Charrow (1979) also looked at the difficulty of the legal concepts involved in the jury instructions, and found that this explained around 12 per cent of the total variation in performance on the task, but for subjects with a lower level of education this rose to 39 per cent. This gives an important indication of the role played by the **knowledge** factor in the comprehension of legal language. It is important, but by no means overwhelmingly significant. Note also the findings concerning the educational level of jurors discussed by Lieberman and Sales (1997).

In an attempt to find solutions to these problems, a follow-up study was conducted where jury instructions were modified to eliminate most of the linguistic features listed above, but 'we did not mechanically eliminate all passives or replace all complements or 'whiz's'. In certain cases, the passive construction was essential for proper focus, and where we used a truncated passive in a modified instruction, the agent was obvious from the context' (Charrow and Charrow 1979: 1335). The comprehension of subjects was 'significantly and substantially better on the modified instructions' (1979: 1331). This was the case even for more conceptually complex legal notions. Charrow and Charrow (1979) also provide detailed evidence that each individual language feature (with the possible exception of some types of whiz deletion) played a role in comprehension difficulty.

An issue that has arisen in subsequent studies has been the role of 'deliberation', where jurors or mock jurors are given the opportunity to discuss the instructions and their verdict (English and Sales 1997; Lieberman and Sales 1997). The process of negotiation of meaning among the jurors appears to enhance comprehension of jury instructions, providing another means of addressing poor comprehension.

Work on the comprehensibility of jury instructions has continued up to the present day, with many papers and books published in the area – for many references see English and Sales (1997) and Lieberman and Sales (1997). Lieberman and Sales (1997) note that Charrow and Charrow's findings have been supported by many other researchers, who have found 'Jurors do not understand a large portion of the judicial instructions delivered to them even when they are pattern instructions' and they note 'this is not surprising, because the emphasis in both non-pattern and pattern instructions has been on legal accuracy, with minimal attention paid to comprehensibility to anyone outside the legal community' (the two audience dilemma). Among the fundamental Common Law notions in jury instructions that jurors and mock jurors are likely to misunderstand are:

- reasonable doubt (in a Common Law criminal trial, guilt must be proven 'beyond reasonable doubt');
- presumption of innocence (a person is innocent until proven guilty);
- burden of proof (the defendant need not prove innocence, it is up to the prosecution to prove guilt).

For instance Dumas (2000) gives the following example of the 1995 Tennessee instruction for 'reasonable doubt'.

Reasonable doubt is that doubt engendered by an investigation of all the proof in the case and an inability after such investigation to let the mind rest easily as to the certainty of guilt. Reasonable does not mean a captious,

possible or imaginary doubt. Absolute certainty of guilt is not demanded by
the law to convict of any criminal charge, but moral certainty is required,
and this certainty is required as to every proposition of proof requisite to
constitute the offense.

(*Tennessee Pattern Jury Instruction – Criminal* 1995: 7:14)

This contains most of the features outlined by Charrow and Charrow
(1979), including unusual and low frequency vocabulary such as *engendered*, *captious* and *requisite*. The final sentence is syntactically complex
(there are around eleven clauses in the three sentences). There is a whiz
deletion before *requisite*. There are many passive structures, and also the
odd metaphors in 'Absolute certainty of guilt is not demanded by the law'
and 'let the mind rest easily as to the certainty of guilt'. There are also two
'as to' structures. To anyone who is not accustomed to reading complex
written language, this passage could produce major comprehension difficulties. Dumas (2000) offers a far more intelligible if somewhat longer
revised version.

A particularly disturbing area where lack of comprehension can occur is
in jury instructions concerning the death penalty. (As the USA is almost
alone among western democracies in using the death penalty, this discussion is limited to that country.) The issue is literally one of life or death,
and if a death sentence is applied in error, the error is not reversible. For
example, Diamond and Levi (1996: 231) note 'All these results support the
district court's original conclusion that James Free was sentenced to death
by a jury that received unnecessarily confusing instructions, but they came
too late for Mr. Free. He was executed on March 22, 1995.' Death sentences are arrived at in the USA by a two stage process. First the defendant must be found guilty of the offence. Secondly, factors which weigh
against a death penalty (mitigating factors) and factors which weigh in
favour of a death penalty (aggravating factors) must be balanced to see
whether the death penalty or imprisonment should apply. Levi (1993)
showed that the Illinois jury instruction concerning the second stage were
linguistically complex, and that jurors had problems with the following
linguistic features: technical and literate words such as *aggravating* and
preclude, as well as the vagueness of the word *sufficient* – it was previously
noted that words like *aggravating* that have an everyday meaning, but are
used in a technical sense are particularly prone to misunderstanding; the
discourse organization of the instructions; the use of passive verbs without
expressed agents, obscuring agency; the use of complex noun phrases involving nominalizations which similarly render both agent and action un-

clear (i.e. grammatical metaphor); and complex subordinating syntactic structures. In addition much of the information that needed to be included was in fact omitted.

Diamond and Levi (1996) rewrote these instructions to cope with these problems, then tried out both the original and the revised versions on groups of potential jurors, some of whom were allowed to discuss and deliberate on the instructions, while others were not. Their results indicate that Diamond and Levi (1996: 230) 'revising the instructions had the effect of increasing the performance of deliberating jurors on average from 52 percent to 67 percent correct (and decreasing the incorrect rate from 42 percent to 27 percent)'. For only half of the material to be understood is disturbing in a death penalty case, and it is worth noting that even on the rewritten material this rose to only two-thirds. Haney and Lynch (1994) similarly document comprehension problems with the words *aggravation* and *mitigation*. There is evidence that jurors with lower levels of comprehension are more likely to impose the death penalty. Furthermore, Levi (1993) shows that death is consistently the default option in the wording of the Illinois instructions. Tiersma (1995) also discusses similar problems in understanding *mitigation*.

There is a very large number of studies (see Lieberman and Sales 1997) which show that rewriting jury instructions on plain language principles enhances understanding of them, and therefore can go some way towards addressing this problem. There have been considerable efforts to reform pattern jury instructions along these lines in Arizona, California, the District of Columbia and Tennessee – see Dumas (2000).

Up to this point jury instructions have been discussed only as a linguistic issue. There is ample research to show that linguistic issues are a part, but not all of the problem. There may also be psychological issues in juries' understanding and acceptance of instruction. Jurors are likely to misunderstand or not respond in the way anticipated to instructions concerning evidence, particularly instructions as to evidence they are not allowed to consider. People tend to react negatively to being told not to do things (in the case of jury instructions, not to use information that they have), regarding this as a threat to their freedom. Indeed there may be a 'backfire effect' where instructions to ignore evidence lead to greater attention being paid to it (Cox and Tanford, 1989). Psychologists who study this phenomenon (called 'reactance') find that people may react by doing more of the forbidden behaviour. Instructions to ignore pre-trial publicity are similarly ineffective (Kramer, Kerr and Carroll 1990). Lieberman and Sales (1997) discuss other psychological explanations for such resistance.

A related area of the comprehension process, as noted earlier, is the system of attitudes, belief and knowledge of jurors – their schemas. There are two issues here, first whether the jurors' existing state of knowledge of the law will make instructions difficult or impossible to carry out. English and Sales (1997) note 'Most jurors have gleaned at least some naive representations of the law from friends, personal experiences, or the media. For example, in a study where subjects were required to write narratives describing certain crimes and the events surrounding them, Finkel and Groscup (1997) found that the stories were prone to be extraordinary and reflect the types of stories more commonly associated with the news media, TV, and Hollywood. This prior knowledge has been shown to persist not only in the face of a judge's instructions, but to subsequently influence juror decision making'. Smith (1993) in particular presents evidence that rewriting instructions according to plain language principles, while it makes clearer to jurors what the legal conception of a crime is, does not ensure that they will replace their existing schema with the legal one, but rather that they will often persist with applying their pre-existing non-legal schemas in reaching a verdict. (English and Sales (1997) raise some methodological issues in regard to Smith's findings).

Secondly, and this is not a comprehension problem, when jurors do understand instructions, their belief system may lead them to a verdict different from the one they know is intended by the law. When this occurs jurors are often opting for what they view as just, rather than what they see as lawful. Finkel (1995) speaks of 'vengeful nullification of the law in favour of the prosecution'.

In chapter 4 we saw another type of instruction, the guilty plea warning described by Philips (1998). In Philips' (1998: ch. 4) discussion we find another manifestation of the two audience dilemma, in that Philips shows that liberal judges tend, in their realization of the elements of the 'Substance of Procedure' stage, to target their language towards the accused person who is entering the guilty plea, while more conservative judges orient their language to fellow judges of the appeal court, in other words they wish to ensure that their cautions and 'reading of rights' pass muster in the appeal court, and are much less preoccupied with the accused person actually understanding these. Furthermore Philips (1998: ch. 4) shows that conservative judges vary the genre slightly, consistently omitting certain elements.

Legislation

The Law Reform Commission of Victoria (1987) report is a good example of material that has emerged from the Plain Language Movement. In line with the examples we have already seen, it presents (in Appendix 1) language features that are likely to need consideration in drafting legislation.

Chapter 2 looked at the linguistic characteristics of the text in table 2.1. In table 5.1 the right-hand column contains the plain language revision of that text produced as part of the Law Reform Commission of Victoria (1987) report.

Table 5.1   Original and plain language versions of part of The Companies (Acquisition of Share) (Victoria) Code, section 40 (1985)

Original version	*Plain language version*
Subject to sub-section (3) during the period commencing when a take-over announcement is made in relation to shares in a company and ending at the expiration of the period during which the offers constituted by the announcement remain open the on-market offerer, or a person associated with the on-market offerer, shall not give, offer to give or agree to give to a person whose shares may be acquired pursuant to the take-over announcement, or to a person associated with such a person any benefit (whether by payment of cash or otherwise) not provided for under the terms of the take-over announcement or, if those terms have been varied under section 17, under the terms so varied.	An offerer or an associate must not give, or offer or agree to give, to an offeree or an associate of an offeree a benefit not provided for under the offers – a) within 28 days after the Part A statement is served; or b) if offers are made within that time – within the offer period; or c) after the takeover announcement is made until the end of the offer period.

The modifications are along the lines described previously. At the grammatical level the sentence is much shorter and simpler in structure. The extreme syntactic dislocations discussed in chapter 2 (such 'Subject to sub-section (3)' being far distant from the verb 'give' which it modifies) have also been remedied. At the phrasal level the whiz deletion 'a person associated with' has been replaced with 'an associate of'. At the lexical level, 'expiration' has been replaced with 'end' and other rare and unusual expressions such as 'persuant to' have been deleted.

We noted previously the far-reaching revisions to the language of the legal system in Britain introduced by Lord Woolf.

Contracts

As noted previously contracts are a broad category of documents, including credit card agreements, insurance policies and public transport tickets. Two careful studies of the lack of intelligibility of such documents are described in Labov and Harris (1994). One study, the US Steel Case, looked at a letter sent to African American steel workers, most of whom had a limited education (they were the audience for the letter). They had been limited to junior and lower paid positions, and the court had ruled that they should be compensated for this discrimination. They received a letter with a cheque for compensation, provided that they renounced their right to further action against the company. The last page of the letter consisted of a legal waiver in one very long sentence. The letter, including this waiver, was analysed using both readability measures and measures of syntactic complexity. The waiver, and related matter in the body of the letter, were far more complex and difficult to read than the balance of the letter. In the sections which were less complex, Labov and his associates were able to establish linguistically that these were clearly biased in favour of acceptance of the offer. Another case described in Labov and Harris (1994) was the Thornfare case. This case was not a contract as such, but a letter concerning the right to welfare benefits. Once more, a carefully constructed questionnaire to the targets of the letter, welfare recipients, showed that they had only a limited understanding of a letter written in complex bureaucratese. These methods – the analysis of linguistic complexity, objective readability measures, and questionnaires to the target audience – are the principal means by which the intelligibility of legal language can be examined.

There has been a considerable effort by Plain Language Practitioners to improve contracts that are intended to be read by a lay audience. Redish (1986: 126) provides the example shown in table 5.2 which is taken from the 'covenants and conditions' section of a hire purchase agreement for a car.

Table 5.2 Original and plain language versions of part of a hire-purchase
agreement

Original version	Plain language version
The buyer further promises to pay the holder hereof a delinquency and collection charge for default in the payment of any instalments above recited, where such default has continued for a period of ten days, such charge not to exceed five per cent of the instalments in default or the sum of five dollars, whichever is the lesser.	You also promise to pay a late fee if your payment is more than 10 days overdue. The late fee will be five percent of the amount overdue or five dollars whichever is less.

Notice the combination of linguistic modification, redundant information reduction, and formatting to clarify the text. The linguist, Robert
Eagleson, in Australia has similarly been extensively involved in rewriting
insurance contracts for the large New South Wales insurer NRMA Insurance.

Davies (forthcoming) provides an analysis of the differences between an
older form of contract used by furniture removal men, and a form revised
on plain language principles, given in table 5.3. The issues here are of
some everyday importance. The contracts used by removal men are typically presented when they arrive to move household contents. The client is
usually worried and stressed, and may be under time and/or financial
pressure to get the removal quickly underway, and therefore it will be
difficult to scrutinize the contract. Under such circumstances a form written in legalese is unlikely to be well understood even by a well educated
client. The client is then the first audience. The second audience is however the legal profession – if there is a problem the contract may be
brought to court. The contract needs to contain all the relevant legal
matter, and to be legally watertight. As noted above this can entail the
language features associated with literacy, specialization and authority. Once
more then the problem is one of writing for two audiences – the **two
audience dilemma**.

Davies (forthcoming) notes that the two forms of the contract give
priority to different audiences. The older form of the contract, written in

legalese, clearly prioritizes the legal audience. The newer form, written in formal, but much plainer language, prioritizes the client audience. Both forms should in principle serve both audiences, because legal documents need to be legally watertight (the legal audience), but on the other hand, there is a clear risk of injustice to the client (the non-legal audience) if s/ he signs a contract, thereby perhaps sacrificing various rights and entering into commitments, without understanding what is going on. Davies' linguistic analysis revealed the older version contained legal vocabulary such as *parties*, *award*, *deemed* and *precedent*. It also used archaic deictics (see chapter 2) such as *aforesaid*, *hereby* and *thereof*. The plain language version used some sub-technical jargon of a type likely to understood by an educated lay audience, such as *arbitration*, *barrister* and *dispute*. The older version also consistently used the archaic *shall* for obligation. Looking at grammatical elements, the older version had an average sentence length of 74.3 words, and various complex subordinating syntactic structures. The plain language version had an average sentence length of 9.5. With regard to the issues related to the degree of 'writtenness' of the two versions, Davies (forthcoming) notes that the plain language text 'is in some ways nearer the spoken mode than T1 [the older text], if only because it is quite easy to read it aloud, whereas this is much more difficult to do (if not almost impossible) in the case of T1.' Another aspect of this mode difference is that the old text uses much more complex noun phrases: on one of Halliday's measures of 'lexical density' which examines this issue, the old text is twice as dense as the plain language text. The score for the plain language contract is within the range that Halliday suggests for written language, but it is far nearer spoken language than the old text. On both the measures of readability used by Davies, the plain language text is much easier to read and understand, while still being formal and sub-technical.

However, one worrying aspect of the plain language version of the contract was that certain elements present in the old contract concerning the stages of the legal process were missing from the new one. This is shown in table 5.3. The underlined sections are elements of information in the original which are not retained in the plain language version. The plain language version therefore removes: the limitation of the initiation of this procedure to the customer; the specification of a barrister with at least ten years experience; the need to go through arbitration before taking the matter to court; and the flexibility to have the arbitration in a town other than where the contract was made with the agreement of the parties. There is an obvious risk involved in these omissions.

Table 5.3 Original and plain language versions of part of the British Association of Removers Contract (1982)

Extract from British Association of Removers contract	*Plain language version*
ARBITRATION – If any dispute, difference or question shall at any time hereafter arise between the parties hereto or their respective representatives in respect of any claim or counterclaim <u>put forward on the part of the customer against the contractor</u> in connection with or arising out of this contract or <u>any extension thereof</u>	**Disputes** If there is a dispute arising from this agreement,
the claim shall be referred to the arbitration of a single arbitrator to be agreed by the parties or failing agreement to an arbitrator, being barrister <u>of not less than ten years calling</u> to be appointed at the request at the time being of the British Association of Removers Limited	the two sides will refer it to an agreed arbitrator. If they cannot agree on one, the President of the British Association of Removers at the time of the dispute will appoint a barrister to arbitrate.
according to the laws for the time being governing the resolution of disputes by arbitration in the State or Country within which the Contractor's office concerned with the making of this contract shall be deemed to have been made.	The arbitration will take place in accordance with the law of the country where the contract is made (see clause 22).
The cost of any such arbitration shall be in the discretion of the arbitrator	Costs of arbitration. The arbitrator will decide who pays the costs.
and the award of such arbitrator <u>shall be a condition precedent to any legal proceedings in a court of law</u> in respect of any matters hereby agreed to be the subject of arbitration.	
The arbitration <u>shall unless otherwise agreed</u> be held in the town in which the Contractor's office from which the contract was deemed to have been made aforesaid is situated.	Place of arbitration. The place will be in the town where the contract is made (see clause 22).

In this case the pursuit of clarity led to the omission of information. This is not part of the agenda of the plain language movement, but the legitimate aim of removing superfluous and repetitive detail can carry this danger.

What emerges clearly from Davies' analysis is that the underlying notion in plain language modifications is one of register shift, from more written to more spoken, from more technical to more everyday, from more formal to less formal.

Police Cautions

Legal language is not used only by lawyers. It is also used by the police in certain circumstances. However, if poor communication is the result of the use of legal language, there is a risk of injustice, since a reality of the legal system is that much of the power to prosecute suspects lies in the hands of the police. In Common Law local or magistrates courts where minor offences are tried, if the police present evidence that a person is guilty, this is often accepted without extensive further investigation or argument. The same is true perhaps to an even greater extent in Roman Law systems – for instance in cases brought by the police in China the main concern of many local courts is sentencing rather than decisions concerning guilt or innocence. Police procedures are therefore a central factor in the avoidance of injustice.

Where the police have to meet statutory requirements concerning their language procedures, the wordings they use must be legally watertight, and able to resist a legal challenge that suspects have not 'been given their rights'. The need to retain admissibility in court explains, in part, inertia and even resistance when it comes to using plain language. The first target audience then is the courts – lawyers and judges. The other target audience is the people who are interviewed. Once again, the genuine difficulty of drafting material for disparate audiences (the two audience dilemma) may explain any inadequacies in the intelligibility of police language. There may be a clash between the need to meet legal requirements and the need to communicate with the public, particularly concerning rights during a police investigation.

In Common Law countries police interviews contain a number of 'scripted' elements intended to inform interviewees of their legal rights and obligations during the interview. In the USA these are generally referred to as 'warnings' and the most widely used warnings are the 'Miranda Warnings'. In most other Common Law countries, including England, Australia and Malaysia, they are known as 'cautions', and derive from an original English source which over time has evolved differently in these varied contexts. They are usually written by lawyers, and traditionally use legal language, with all the problems of intelligibility associated with it. However if the cautions are not intelligible to those cautioned, they have failed in their primary purpose of cautioning. There is a literature on inadequacies in cautions, particularly their lack of intelligibility for interviewees, not only in New South Wales (Gibbons 1990), but also in the USA (Brière 1978; Shuy 1998a; American Civil Liberties Union 1997) and Britain (Kurzon 1996). The issue of the comprehensibility of cautions can be clouded by the fact that they are familiar to many people. Viewers of television police dramas are usually familiar with cautions, so they are part of their background knowledge. However, in fact, many of them do not really have a full understanding of the significance and meaning of the cautions, as can be seen from the examples that follow.

The illustration used here concerns the cautions used by the New South Wales Police Service. This is given as a detailed study of the issues and processes involved in arriving at plain language in legal contexts. I was given an opportunity by the NSW police to work with them in 1996–7 to revise language aspects of their procedures and cautions. (It is to their credit that they involved a public critic of their procedures in the revision process.) The account provided here describes the original versions, and their linguistic complexity. Given their familiarity to most English speakers, ethnographic evidence is provided from transcripts of real police interviews that these cautions are not always well understood by either first or second language speakers (the examples of second language speakers are taken from transcripts of interviews in Gibbons (1996) and those of native speakers are from transcripts kindly provided by Philip Hall). The revisions to the cautions and their linguistic basis are discussed. Finally an account is given of their testing on limited proficiency English speakers. This was important because approximately a third of the population of New South Wales, and around half of the population of Sydney are not from English speaking backgrounds.

The revisions of language procedures were part of a major New South Wales Police Service review. This was in turn a consequence of: a move towards 'community policing'; the Woods Royal Commission which found large scale corruption of NSW police procedures; and the introduction of a new Evidence Act, based on one brought in previously by the federal government. The new Evidence Act and the reforms of police procedure were also influenced by the Police and Criminal Evidence (PACE) Act of 1984 in the UK, and the police reforms it entailed.

The review of police procedures in New South Wales led to a new *Code of Practice for Custody, Rights, Investigation, Management and Evidence* (*CRIME*), hereafter referred to as the *Code of Practice*. This is a set of guidelines concerning police procedures. It was developed to replace various guidelines and instructions concerning police procedures. The process of development had several stages:

1. the police sent out the old versions and I and others suggested revisions in writing;
2. the police produced a draft revised *Code of Practice* which was sent out again for comment;
3. the police made some changes on the basis of the comments;
4. the revised draft was discussed at a large meeting involving many interested parties at Police Headquarters;
5. the police produced the final version of the *Code of Practice* without further consultation.

While this process was clearly consultative, I was uncomfortable about the fact that there was never an opportunity to sit with the drafters and work on the changes, nor was there an opportunity to discuss the legal status of the changes with police lawyers. What emerged contained improvements, and inevitably compromises and errors. In what follows, where appropriate the quotations will be labelled as: the original or 'old' version; suggestions for revision; and the final *Code of Practice* version.

A person interviewed by the NSW Police has certain rights: the right to silence, for instance, and the right to take away a recording of the interview. The police also need to cover themselves against false charges of malpractice. For example, that someone was sitting out of view of the video camera making threatening gestures or holding cards with responses written on them. Police also need to cover themselves against claims that interviewees were intimidated or bribed. To cover these rights and to avoid accusations, the police are advised to use certain prepared cautions, or scripted questions.

In the original police guidelines there were forty-one scripted cautions, but since many of them were slight variants of a few common patterns, the number was eventually reduced to five in the revised *Code of Practice*. The process of simplification will now be illustrated. Caution 1 is used at the beginning of the interview process; Caution 2 is used when an interview is resumed after a break; Caution 3 is also a 'resumption' caution, but used specifically when video taping: Caution 4 is used at the end of the interview. A fifth caution, also used at the end of interviews, was included in the *Code of Practice*, but was not subjected to the revision process.

Caution 1

Caution 1, used at the beginning of the interview process, may be familiar because it appears in various forms in television police dramas.

> *Original version*
> I am going to ask you certain questions which will be recorded on a video-tape recorder. You are not obliged to answer or do anything unless you wish to do so, but whatever you say or do will be recorded and may later be used in evidence. Do you understand that?

This caution was used at the beginning of interviews in police stations. At the time of arrest the first sentence is left out.

The linguistic complexity of this caution include the following. First, the second sentence has a complex syntactic structure, with several layers of subordination and coordination: 'you're not obliged to answer' is conjoined with 'or do anything'. Furthermore, 'whatever you say or do' is a full clause, but it is rank-shifted to be the subject of both 'record' and 'use' (see figure 5.1).

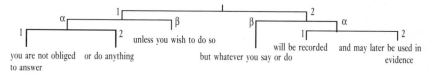

Figure 5.1 Syntactic structure of Caution 1

Another problem is passives without expressed agents. One presumes that it is the police who are 'not obliging', who are 'recording' and are 'using', but there is no expressed agent. (We noted previously that there is pyscholinguistic evidence that passives without expressed agents can be harder to process.) There are also some lexical difficulties – 'in evidence' is legal jargon, and the word 'unless' can cause problems for second

language speakers (it conflates 'if . . . not'). 'Obliged' is also a low frequency word.

Another problem with some cautions is that they combine different
concepts rather than just going through them one at a time (i.e. saying,
'Concept A, do you understand?; Concept B, do you understand?; Concept
C, do you understand?'). In this caution, two concepts – the right to
silence and the recording process – are combined.

It is not single complexities that cause the problems, it is their accumu-
lation. In the written form, this caution might cause less processing problems, because there is time for a reader to go through it element by element.
However, when read aloud only once, often in a time of trauma for the
interviewee, it can cause the problems documented in Gibbons (1996).

Phillip Hall provides the following interview segment between police
and a native speaker suspect, showing that neither side appears to have
fully internalized the nature of the caution – notice that the police officer
proceeded with questioning despite the suspect clearly indicating he was
taking his right to silence (the questioning in fact continues).

Police officer: You are not obliged to say or do anything unless you wish
                   to do so, but whatever you say or do will be electronically
                   recorded and may be used in evidence. Do you under-
                   stand that?
Suspect: Yeah.
Police officer: Do you agree that prior to the commencement of this
                   interview I told you that I intended asking you further
                   questions about this matter?
Suspect: Yeah but =x=
Police officer: =x= Well, do you agree that =y=
Suspect: =y= I don't want to say nothing.
Police officer: OK.
Suspect: Cause I can't remember.
Police officer: That's all right, but do you agree that prior, before I com-
                   menced this interview, in the presence of Mr Kennett, I
                   told you that I was going to ask you some questions about
                   =x=
Suspect: =x= Yeah. Yeah. Yeah.

The initial revision, which gave the police some options, was:

Suggested revision
> I am going to ask you some questions. You do not have to answer if you
> do not want to. Do you understand that?

> We will record what you say. We can use this recording [in court/against
> you/against you in court]. Do you understand that?

This breaks the caution into its two constituent concepts. The possibly
ambiguous 'certain questions' is replaced by 'some questions'. Addressing
the vocabulary issue, 'are . . . obliged' is replaced by 'have . . . to', and
'unless' by 'if not'. And finally, it is followed by 'do you understand that?'
This rewording is almost identical in meaning, and in the options makes
explicit elements that were buried in the original.

During meetings with the police it emerged that they also wished to add
the notion that the interviewee did not have to do things (e.g. provide
samples of blood) unless s/he wished to do. Therefore the final version,
adopted into the *Code of Practice* (p. 24) was:

Final Code of Practice version
> I am going to ask you some questions. You do not have to say or do
> anything if you do not want to. Do you understand that?

> We will record what you say or do. We can use this recording in court.
> Do you understand that?

This was probably the most successful of the revisions.

Caution 2

This caution is a 'resumption' question, used when an interview has been
interrupted and is about to recommence.

Original version
> Do you agree that prior to the commencement of this interview I told you
> that I intended asking further questions about this matter?

The major grammatical feature of this caution is the layers of projection
(akin to reported speech): 'Do you agree that', 'I told you that', 'I intended' and 'asking you'. The point of the utterance, that more questions
will be asked, appears at the end after several layers of projection. For a

second-language speaker, processing could simply break down before this point is reached. Furthermore 'prior to commencement' is left-dislocated (see figure 5.2).

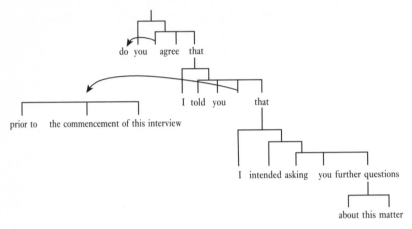

Figure 5.2   Syntactic structure of Caution 2

There also are some unusual vocabulary choices. Why say 'prior to' instead of 'before'? 'Further' has a different everyday use (e.g. 'Is it much further, daddy?' in the car). Here, it means 'extra'. 'Matter' in everyday language is usually a verb (e.g 'it doesn't matter'). For a second-language speaker, the less common uses or these words are less likely to be known, and might be a source of confusion. There are also some nominalisations, particularly 'commencement'.

The following example of a second language speaker's (SLS)'s response to this caution reveals comprehension difficulty.

P: ... Do you agree that prior to the commencement of this inter-
        view, I told you that I intended asking you further questions about
        this matter?
SLS: I say yes? – yes.

Phillip Hall provides the following interesting transcript, where a native speaker suspect is having difficulty relating his agendas to the cautions, and the Police Officer feels it is necessary to recast the caution.

P: Right. Do you agree that prior to the commencement of this record of interview, I told, told you I intended to ask you further questions about this matter?

W: Yeah. Should I um, I don't know –

. . .

P: And do you agree I, I'm going to ask you further questions about this matter? I want you to understand that you're not obliged to say anything about it, unless you wish, as anything you say may later be used in evidence. Do you understand that?

W: Ah, yeah, what should I do though?

P: Well, mate, it's a matter for yourself. But you remember prior to starting, you said that you had no objection to us talking on the, on the tape?

W: Yeah. I don' t know [long pause] I don't know.

My original suggestion was that this 'adoption question' lose parts of its content which were not directly relevant to the point of the question, discarding 'prior to the commencement of this interview' and 'about this matter'. Additionally 'further' would be replaced by 'more', and 'intend' by 'going to'.

> *Suggested revision*
> I am going to ask you some more questions. Do you understand that?

During discussion, as a consequence of the removal of the back reference, the police felt it necessary to insert part of the original caution. They incorporated some simple wordings that were in my draft suggestions. The *Code of Practice* version (p. 24) is:

> *Final Code of Practice version*
> I am going to ask you some more questions. You do not have to say or do anything if you do not want to. Do you understand that?
>
> We will video-tape/tape record/type up our questions, your answers and what you do. We can use this recording in court. Do you understand that?

My feeling about this revision was that it was two steps forward and one step back, but perhaps its greater explicitness was a virtue.

Caution 3

Another adoption question for video-taped interviews is also sometimes used.

Original version
> What I propose to do is ask you further questions in relation to this matter. My questions and any answers given by you will be electronically recorded on tape as the interview takes place. Do you understand that?

This caution is possibly even more complex than the previous one. Looking first at the grammar, the subject of the verb 'is' in the first sentence is a clause 'What I propose to do', which in turn contains a left dislocated object of the verb 'do' – namely 'What', and 'do' is itself subordinated by 'I propose'. In similar fashion the subject of the verb 'record' in the second sentence is 'My questions and any answers given by you' – there is a danger that people would have lost the thread of the syntactic structure before the verb appears. Furthermore 'given' is a passive that has been subjected to whiz deletion – a well established source of comprehension difficulty. The verb 'record' is once more in the passive voice without an expressed agent.

Concerning vocabulary, 'propose' in not a common word, and it is factually inaccurate – if the police have already begun the interview, they are in reality about to ask more questions, so this is not a proposal. Why would one ask questions 'in relation to' a matter, rather than 'about' a matter? This is an extreme case of the unnecessary use of elevated style, which was a characteristic of police language discussed in chapter 3. 'Matter' and 'further' are discussed above. 'Electronically' is not only a jargon term inserted in the middle of a verb complex, it is also redundant, since it is the only obvious means of recording on tape.

I suggested that Caution 2 be used for this purpose, and this was adopted.

Caution 4

The fourth basic caution, for use at the end of an interview, is:

Original version
> Has any threat, promise, or offer of advantage been held out to you to give the answers recorded in this interview?

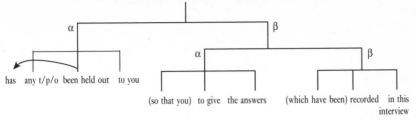

Figure 5.3   Syntactic structure of Caution 4

Once more this caution has some syntactic complexities. There are three clauses in my parsing of this sentence, but two of them 'give' and 'recorded' have been reduced so that their agents are deleted – my reconstructed form has 'so that you give' and 'which were recorded'. The latter has both a whiz deletion and a passive with no expressed agent, of the type discussed earlier in this chapter.

At the lexical level, holding out a threat is an odd literary metaphor. The previous version of this caution was 'threat, promise or inducement', but 'inducement' was changed to 'offer of advantage' – a questionable improvement. There are many examples of grammatical metaphor: 'threat', 'promise', 'offer' and 'answer' are all verbal processes, so congruently, they would be verbs. Furthermore, they are separate possibilities conflated in a single caution.

The following is an example of a second language speaker (SLS)'s response.

P: Has any threat, promise or inducement been held out to you to give the answers as recorded in this interview?
SLS: Yes.

When the interviewee says simply 'yes' (presumably not the answer that the police were expecting!) he reveals his incomprehension. The police officer then rephrased the question into simpler English, revealing that he was aware of the complexity of this question. Phillip Hall also provides the following transcript of a native speaker interviewed by police.

P: Has any threat, promise or offer of advantage been held out to you to take part in this interview?
W: No.

P: Do you understand what all of those three terms mean?
W: What?
P: Do you understand what 'offer of advantage' is?
W: No.
P: OK. Have I promised you anything to take part in this interview?
W: No.

This last caution proved difficult to revise. Three separate versions were suggested (the last by a student):

Suggested revision
   A: To make you do this interview, did anyone threaten you, or promise you something, or offer you something?

   B: Did any police officer threaten you? Did any police officer promise you anything? Did any police officer offer you something?

   C: Did you do this interview because: we threatened you? We promised you something? We offered you something?

In all three variants passive has been made active, whiz deletions are removed, and nominalizations have been replaced with verbs. I preferred B since it deletes 'do the answers recorded in this interview', and turns three concepts into three questions. Version B is broader in meaning than the original, but it makes the reasonable assumption that in any case police officers should not threaten people, promise them anything or offer them anything.

   Possibly because of the difficulty involved in revising this caution, in the draft version of the *Code of Practice* it was left unchanged. Perhaps Version B with its explicit mention of police officers threatening, promising and offering, was too direct. After some display of disquiet on my part about the lack of changes, the following emerged as the final *Code of Practice* version:

Final Code of Practice version
   Has any promise been made to you to make this statement?
   Has any threat been made to you to make this statement?
   Have you been induced to make this statement?
   Has anything been offered to you to make this statement?

The gain in this version is that the issues are presented one at a time, and nothing is being 'held out'. The losses are that there are still passives, the syntax is not simple, and the word 'induce' is used (in my idiolect this word is limited to unborn babies). Once again, some gain has been made, but there is still work to be done.

Caution 5

In the final version of the *Code of Practice*, another scripted caution was inserted without consultation. It took the following form:

> Were you told before you made this statement you did not have to unless you wanted to?

It shares with the old cautions a range of grammatical complexities. It has four clauses in complex syntactic relationships: 'told' subordinates 'you did not have to . . .' from which it is separated. There is a double negative, and once more the use of 'unless' – see Caution 1. After the efforts discussed above, I was unimpressed with the inclusion of this unheralded new caution.

Reactions

These revisions have been instituted in the police *Codes of Practice* for New South Wales. They have had a mixed reception from police officers. Some were pleased, because they thought the old cautions were absurd. Other officers dislike the changes. Two possible reasons for this dislike emerged in discussion. First, the revisions may make it clearer to people what their rights are, so, for example, more people might take the right to silence. Second, as noted previously, the complex and technical language of the original versions carries a social message concerning the power and authority of the police. Most work in this area has assumed that only propositional information is communicated by police cautions. It is clear however that complex and technical language also carries a social message enhancing the power and authority of the person using it. Resistance to a lessening of this power and authority would not be not surprising. (We noted in chapter 3 that the police use over-elaborate language when it is unnecessary.) The revised versions lessen this power and authority, and reduce the power asymmetry between the police and the interviewee – something that some police officers find undesirable.

Testing the new versions of the cautions

There is a common sense feeling that the revised versions of these cautions are simpler and clearer. What is more, they remove many linguistic features that were shown earlier to be well attested sources of comprehension difficulty. Nevertheless it is important to test out such revisions. Sixty-two intermediate speakers of English as a second language completed questionnaires on the cautions. For each of the first four cautions they were asked to rate the caution for its comprehensibility and they were asked a 'scenario' comprehension question to see whether they understood the caution. Half of the subjects received the old versions of cautions 1 and 2, and the revised versions of cautions 3 and 4, while the other half received the revised versions of cautions 1 and 2, and the old versions of 3 and 4. On all cautions the revised versions were rated more comprehensible, and on all cautions more correct answers were given on the comprehension questions for the revised cautions. It seems that both subjectively and objectively the revised cautions were more intelligible.

There are other types of warnings and cautions directed to the general public that also need to be intelligible if they are to serve their primary purpose of warning – see for instance Dumas' (1990) discussion of the warnings on American cigarette packets.

Conclusions

In this chapter we have seen evidence from psycholinguistic testing, from linguistic analysis and from ethnographic data that the language of the law is difficult for non-lawyers. Much of the time it fails a primary purpose – that of simply communicating. The underlying cause seems to be that the language is written for two audiences: the **two audience dilemma**. Language in legal contexts often needs to be able to resist challenge in court – the legal audience. On the other hand it also often needs to be intelligible to non-lawyers. We have seen here plain language that fails the first requirement (although this is not necessary), but far more often, language that fails the second audience.

The linguistic complexity of legalese derives from the factors described in preceding chapters – the properties of written language, specialization and technicalization, the need to establish authority, and genre structures needed to achieve legal purposes. At the lexico-grammatical level, difficulty is produced by the features listed in the introduction, and exemplified in the sections following the introduction. The difficulty engendered by unknown generic structures is evidenced. Surface presentation features, such as lay-out and other non-verbal signalling of content structure are of considerable importance. Linguistic complexities may serve purposes other than the communication of ideas, such as the elevation of the status of those involved in the legal system and the assertion of their authority since it is difficult to challenge what one cannot understand. As van Dijk (1993: 256) suggests 'one of the social resources on which power and dominance are based is the privileged access to discourse and communication'.

There are other sources of difficulty that are beyond the ambit of the linguist. Most important of these is the knowledge base of the non-legal audience. The mastery of some legal concepts may demand concentrated study and intellectual ability. Some legal documents contain such legal concepts, as well as complex information in complex relationships with other information. Linguistic approaches cannot affect these informational complexities, nor should they attempt to do so if such complexity is necessary. Nevertheless, in the body of this chapter it has been demonstrated repeatedly that legal texts can be made easier to understand when linguistic principles are carefully applied. Legal texts and processes can often be made more accessible to both audiences, lawyers and the general public, without sacrificing legal exactness. It is clearly socially desirable that such changes be made, remembering the dilemma with which this chapter began, that ignorance of the law is no excuse. When what could be done is not done, this omission may be serving agendas of status, financial advantage and power. Without public understanding of it, the law is in constant danger of becoming a mechanism for oppression rather than order, for injustice rather than justice.

6
Language and Disadvantage
before the Law

We have not the slightest faith in the legal or judicial process. We
know the law is for big people.

Ram Khiladi (an Indian Dalit), *The Hindu*, 11 July 1999

Counsel: You went to, went and got into the car outside your
home, I withdraw that, whereabouts in relation to your
home did you get into the car on this morning.
Child: Well on the, when?

Brennan (1994)

Why should they make deaf people suffer more? Why?

Deaf prisoner (Brennan and Brown 1997)

Introduction

Chapter 5 discussed the problems that may arise when there is a communication gap between speakers in legal contexts. We noted that these problems can have two sources. It may be non-lawyers' limited command of the
language of the law, or lawyers' limited command of language other than
the standard language of the legal system.

Looking first at **comprehension** problems caused by the language of
the law, we saw in chapter 5 that these are in part a consequence of
differences in the use of register between lawyers and non-lawyers, and
between legal institutions and the general public. This places the public at
a considerable disadvantage when trying to understand lawyers and the
legal system, because the decontextualized, formal, specialist and power
laden language of the legal system is distant on all four of those parameters
from everyday conversational language, which tends to be contextualized,
informal, non-specialist and low in power differences. Concerning the demands for language **production** made by the legal system, the courtroom

(and to a lesser degree the police station) is a linguistic context which demands testimony that is decontextualized (since it operates in the secondary reality) and formal (among the most formal situations that many witnesses will ever encounter), requiring formal language. We saw in chapter 3 that many speakers have problems with this, and some may overreact, using excessively elaborate language.

Both comprehension and production are issues of language proficiency. We noted earlier that education is a primary context for the acquisition of high register, so people with a lower level of education will tend to have a lower level of control over it. Other people who may have a limited command of high register are children and those who speak a non-standard variety of language due to social class and geographical factors (sociolect and dialect), and speakers of more radically different forms of a language such as pidgins and creoles. Even more disadvantaged are the functionally illiterate, who constitute around 7 per cent of the population in many countries, and may be over-represented among those who are accused of criminal offences (see Hayes 1993). Second language speakers, including the deaf, may not even have a full command of conversational language. In Roman Law systems, where much testimony is provided in written form, people who have a low level of literacy, often in combination with a poor command of formal language, may have particular difficulty in communicating with the court, particularly if they cannot obtain the help of a lawyer in presenting their evidence.

Since the processes of the Common Law system are mostly oral, literacy may seem to be less crucial, but laws, regulations and contracts are encoded in writing, and this manifests itself continually in the spoken language of the law. Disadvantage caused by poor command of High Register may be compounded by the adversarial nature of examination in court. Cross-examination in particular is intended to subject both evidence and witness to testing. Even for the most educated, articulate and confident witness, the process is difficult, and frequently humiliating, as we saw in chapter 3. For witnesses who, for whatever reason, are less educated, confident and articulate, this is magnified. Examination is a linguistic process, and both confidence and language competence are needed to cope well with examination, and to express one's version of events. The courtroom is, as we have seen, a place where power is unequally distributed, being overwhelmingly in the hands of the legal professionals. The discourse rules of the legal process may also be radically different from those of non-cognate cultures.

Finally there is an attitudinal element. Language difference can be perceived as an indicator of cultural and ethnic difference, and differences are a basic component of social attitudes, including prejudice see (Giles and Powesland 1975). People involved in the law will have the normal range of social attitudes, and this may affect the way they treat each other: for instance the prejudice against lawyers as a powerful self-interested group manifests itself in lawyer jokes. Likewise judges' prejudices are the object of frequent media reports, and may affect their language behaviour (Philips 1998). Unfortunately there is only limited information on when and how people's 'construction' of social categories is triggered by language in legal contexts.

There are those who say that people are generally treated the same by the legal system, and therefore disadvantage before the law is not a major issue. This position ignores some important issues. First, the law has the potential to be a mechanism for oppression and persecution, rather than a means of achieving justice, if vigilance is not exercised – there are many examples of this, including the persecution of dissidents through the legal system by Stalinist regimes. Second, providing the **same** treatment does not equate with providing **just** treatment. A second language speaker who does not speak the language of the court, and who is not provided with interpreting services may receive the same treatment as native speakers, but such a process is clearly unjust, in that s/he can neither understand the proceedings, nor make a case. The same is true to a lesser degree of all the minorities that will be discussed in this chapter and the next.

This chapter will look at studies of the contacts between the groups mentioned above and the law. Where information is available, the nature of communication problems will be examined, then possible solutions will be described. The types of differences that may lead to problems can be broadly grouped into those within a single language, and communication challenges between different languages and cultures. Differences between whole languages often come down to issues of legal interpreting and translation which are discussed in the next chapter.

Children

There is research to show that the reliability of children's testimony is similar to that of adults, if they are questioned in a way that helps them to produce their version of events (Zaragoza et al. 1995). In the words of Walker and Warren (1995) the linguistic issue is 'asking the questions, understanding the answers', and the role played by language in disadvantaging children in contact with the legal system.

There is a disturbing study by Brennan (1994) of questions put to children in sexual abuse cases. Brennan attempted to examine children's understanding of lawyers' questions. He asked children aged 6–15 to repeat questions from counsellors, teachers, questions selected randomly from lawyers, and questions from lawyers that Brennan judged to contain particularly difficult (in Brennan's term **strange**) language. Counsellors' questions were almost always reproduced with their sense intact. Teachers' questions were reproduced with the sense intact 80 per cent of the time. In random questions from lawyers, the main sense is missed 43 per cent of the time. In the difficult lawyers' questions, the main sense was reproduced only around 15 per cent of the time, indicating almost complete communication breakdown. The figure of 43 per cent of questions not being understood is perhaps the most important one. The comparison data from counsellors' questions shows clearly that the problems lie in the way the questions are put, rather than some inherent problem in other aspects of adult–child communication. In other words the comprehension issue is largely linguistic.

Children may be more suggestible. For instance Mary Brennan and Richard Brown (1997) discussing the confusing answers signed by a deaf child write 'he [the interpreter] realised that the child may have been influenced in his way of answering by what typically happened in the classroom. The teacher described how he would ask the child a question. If the child gave a wrong answer the teacher would ask the question again. This would continue until the child got the answer "right". It could well be, then, that the child sensed his answers did not "fit" what was expected and therefore tried to please the adults by giving different answers until the right one was arrived at.' The legal consequences of this could be serious.

In addition to this, however, we have the problem of interpersonal power and coercion. A reality of life is that children generally have much less power than adults, and much less skill in using language to maintain an equal power relation. Mark Brennan (1994) notes several such problems with the questioning of children in sexual abuse cases. The first is that the children may have been frightened into silence. Linguistic problems include coerciveness and complexity. Looking first at coerciveness, in chapter 3 we noted the suggestibility of people subjected to formal questioning: in the case of children this is a particular problem (Saywitz and Moan-Hardie 1994). When framed as yes–no questions, interrogation is likely to provide the response sought by the questioner rather than the facts – proof rather than truth. We also noted in chapter 3 the ways that questions can be made more coercive of the interlocutor, or more controlling of the information. Brennan (1994: 212) gives the following example of a yes–no question to a child that contains nearly all the relevant information, and also uses two coercive tags:

C: Now you had a bruise, did you not, near one of your breasts, do
            you remember that?
Child
(12 yrs):   No

The child's reply is damaging to her case, since it indicates either that she was not bruised, or that she cannot remember details of the incident.

The other problem is linguistic complexity. This may derive from the various sources of difficulty discussed in chapter 5, including complex grammatical structures with a number of clauses, particularly reported speech constructions. Brennan (1994: 213–15) gives the following examples of questions of extreme syntactic complexity addressed to 10-year-old children.

C: And did your mother ever say to you that if somebody asks you the
     questions I am asking you, you should say that we didn't say what
     was going to be said?

C: Well I know, I understand what you say you have been talking to her
     today but you see what I am asking you is this, that statement sug-
     gests that you said those things that you now say are wrong to the
     police. Now did you say it to the police or did you not?

C: Remember that you told us before the lunch break that you had never
     been out with Martin before this particular day, 8th of November, do
     you remember saying that, before lunch, do you remember or do you
     not?

Notice also the extreme coerciveness of the last question, with three repetitions of 'remember', and a long forceful question tag.

Another source of difficulty can be the use of technical language, and other unnecessary lexical complexities of 'lawyerspeak', for instance 'withdraw' and 'whereabouts in relation to' in the following.

C: You went to, went and got into the car outside your home, I **withdraw** that, **whereabouts in relation to** your home did you get into the car on this morning.

Child: Well on the, when?

The child's reply clearly indicates a lack of understanding.

Finally (and as we shall see this can also be a crosscultural problem) Brennan notes that questions often ask for specific information concerning time and location that children are unlikely to be able to provide.

C: I am sorry, you might not understand me, the first time and then it's finished, **how long until the next time** that your father put his penis in your vagina?

        (*To child aged 7 years.*)

Brennan (1994: 216) shows that 'the credibility of the child witness is systematically destroyed by a combination of language devices and questioning styles'. Truth is unlikely to emerge from such processes, and as Brennan notes, the child is 'abused again' by coercive and insensitive questioning.

Indigenous Minorities

There is a substantial literature on this topic, so the discussion here will highlight communalities between such communities, and will illustrate the issues from some important studies.

Information concerning the disadvantage suffered by Australian Aborigines and Torres Strait Islanders in contact with the law is particularly rich. To avoid any suggestion that this is a liberal self-indulgence, it is interesting to note that in June 2000 the Magistrates Courts of Victoria made an official apology for injustice suffered by Aborigines in their courts. Eades has carefully documented over the last 15 years communication problems between Australian Aborigines and the law (see for instance Eades 1992, 1993, 1994a, 1995a, 2000). She describes the problems that speakers of Aboriginal English have with the legal process. A fundamental underlying issue is what is known as the 'knowledge economy' in Aboriginal society.

In traditional Aboriginal societies material goods were mostly held in common, and status, rather than deriving from wealth came from the possession of secret knowledge (this situation is also found in other indigenous communities). The result is that attitudes to knowledge are quite different from those found in western societies. Much knowledge is not to be shared freely. Some of it is available only to those who have been ceremonially initiated into it. It may be the property of only women or men (women's/men's 'business'). Even if such knowledge becomes known to those who should not know it, to display the knowledge is unacceptable. The consequence is that questioning in Aboriginal societies is generally done with great caution, often indirectly by raising a topic, and leaving it open to the interlocutor to contribute what knowledge s/he is willing to share. Direct questioning is regarded as rude and intrusive. Answering is not obligatory, since a direct answer may involve secret material or may grant the questioner unearned status. Silence is often an appropriate response. The clash with police questioning and courtroom examination is evident, because police investigation and trials are largely dependent on the right to question and the obligation to answer. Eades mentions the problems caused by Aborigines who frequently say 'I don't know' or 'I don't remember' which Eades (1994a: 242) says 'would translate into Standard English as something like 'This is not an appropriate way for me to provide information of this nature'.

Concerning silence, the Criminal Justice Commission of Queensland report (1996: 24) provides this example, and the comment that follows.

C: ... I suggest the reason to you, because you don't want everyone to know the little criminal that you are, do you? That's the reason, isn't it? Isn't it? Isn't it? Your silence probably answers it, but I'll have an answer from you. That's the reason, isn't it?

W: (silence)

J: D ... [witness's name], I am asking you to answer the question. Ask the question again, please, Mr X.

C: I'm suggesting to you that you don't want the court to know the little criminal that you are. Isn't that right?

W: Yes.

The reliability of the witness's answer (as evidence of the truth of the proposition in the question) is arguably suspect. ... The use of silence may indicate several things, including dissent. The final 'yes' answer may be an example of gratuitous concurrence. The fact that the answer was only made in response to sustained questioning [and after the judge's intervention] may also cast some doubt on its reliability. Both the silence and the eventual concurrence are consistent with the witness's discomfort and alienation.

I would add that the use of the highly coercive question form and the humiliating person oriented status reduction might be additional sources of the witness's unwillingness to reply. In Common Law, silence is not an available option in this situation.

Eades also discusses the fact that Aboriginal culture does not use measurement expressions, particularly to discuss time. So, for instance, a date is referred to by a significant event that took place around that time, not by a calendar date. By contrast courtroom and police questioning often focuses strongly and specifically on the timing of events. The Criminal Justice Commission of Queensland Commission report (1996: 26) provides the following example of an Aboriginal man providing an answer which says that he arrived at a pub at 10 p.m., left at 10 p.m. and spent two hours there.

C: What time did you go to the hotel?
W: About 10 o'clock at night.
C: What time did you leave the hotel?
W: About 10 o'clock that night.
C: How long had you been there?
W: I was there for a couple of hours.

Walsh (1994) raise issues concerning Aboriginal interactional style. He shows that Aborigines tend to operate in a less dyadic and more 'open broadcast' style, where people speak at the same time or not at all – long periods of silence are acceptable, rather than uncomfortable as in anglo conversation (Sacks, Schegloff and Jefferson 1978). Listeners are free to tune in or tune out, and to contribute to or ignore the group polylogue. Eye contact is infrequent and unnecessary. Once more the contrast with legal interaction could not be more extreme, where for example silence is only permitted in rare and limited circumstances, otherwise failure to provide an answer can be incriminating or punishable. Both police questioning and courtroom examination are intensely dyadic, even when there is a larger audience. Witnesses are expected to attend and respond immediately (see 'silence' in chapter 3). Eades notes the problems caused in police and courtroom questioning by Aborigines who refuse to make eye contact with interlocutors, thereby giving an impression of 'shiftiness' or even guilt which may be compounded by long periods of silence. Walsh (1994) in his discussion of Aboriginal land claim hearings notes a judge being dismayed when several Aboriginal people answer a question at once, shouting from any part of the location. He also notes that (Walsh 1994: 229) 'one Aboriginal witness was extremely reluctant to reveal information restricted in Aboriginal law'. These problems result from the different interactional styles and the knowledge economy discussed previously.

An issue that may exacerbate these problems is that in traditional Aboriginal communities, as a consequence of disadvantage and poor health care, around 40 per cent of the population suffer hearing loss, and up to 98 per cent of young people suffer hearing diseases (House of Representatives Standing Committee on Aboriginal and Torres Strait Islander Affairs enquiry). This means that witnesses may have problems hearing questions.

Another area of difference lies in the nature of narrative in Aboriginal culture. Christie and Harris (1985) show that Aboriginal narratives do not have the same genre structure as western narratives. The elements of the narrative, their sequencing, and the assumptions behind the narrative are different. The central role of western-style narrative in legal processes was described in chapter 4. Since expectations of genre structure usually operate below the level of consciousness, there is a clear possibility of this cultural linguistic difference producing miscommunication between Aborigines and non-Aborigines in legal contexts. Eades documents the confusion caused in courtrooms by Aborigines who do not organize their information in conformity with western 'logic', and therefore are viewed as incoherent and have their testimony discounted.

There are also some important linguistic differences between standard English and some forms of Aboriginal English which fall between creole and standard English in the post-pidgin continuum found in Northern Australia. Liberman (1981) notes that Aborigines in contact with the law are prone to 'gratuitous concurrence', of saying *yes* to everything, in order to avoid further pressure or questioning by white officials. Eades (1994a: 245) says 'Thus a very common strategy for Aborigines being asked a number of questions by non-Aborigines is to agree, regardless of either their understanding of the question, or their belief about the truth or falsity of the proposition being questioned.' This phenomenon is common across the Asia-Pacific region. Naturally the consequences can be disastrous for the individual who is being accused of a crime by a lawyer or police officer. Prince (1990: 284) mentions that even for native English speakers 'items like "yeah", "uh huh", "mm", "I see", "right" . . . communicate something like "I have processed, or purport to have processed the preceding clause; you may now go on".' Eades recounts the story of an Aboriginal man who was called as a witness to a traffic accident appearing in court and saying 'I plead guilty, eh'. Coldrey (1987: 84–5) gives the following example from a police record of interview with an Aboriginal man.

P: Right. Now Cedric. I want to ask you some questions about what happened at Jay Creek the other day. Do you understand that?
W: Yes.
P: Now it's in relation to the death of X. Do you understand that?
W: Yes.
P: Right. Now I want to ask you some questions about the trouble out there but I want you to understand that you don't have to answer any questions at all. Do you understand that?
W: Yes.
P: Do you have to tell me that story?
W: Yes.
P: Do you have to though?
W: Yes.
P: Do you, am I making you tell me the story?
W: Yes.
P: Or are you telling me because you want to?
W: Yes
P: Now I want you to understand that you don't have to tell me, right?
W: Yes.
P: Now do you have to tell me?
W: Yes.

It was only because the police officer checked the understanding of the witness that this problem emerged – often such gratuitous concurrence could go undetected.

A related phenomenon, particularly important for examination and police interviews is that in order to agree with a negative question, some speakers reply *yes* (or in the affirmative) (in linguistic terms an agreement with the speech act force rather than the propositional content). This is common throughout the Asia-Pacific region (see Lane 1993). Cooke (1995b: 108–9) give the following example of a negative question to an Aboriginal man from a coronial inquiry in the Northern Territory.

C: But the old man didn't go in the boat, did he?

W:	Yes.
C:	I beg your pardon.
W:	Yes.
Interpreter:	Yes, he's affirming he didn't go in the boat.
Coroner:	The old man didn't go in the boat.
Other Counsel:	He's answering you exactly on point.
Coroner:	You ask these questions that way and that's what you get.

It is perhaps worth noting that the problem arises here from both the Aboriginal source – the type of answer – and from the legal source – the type of question, as the Coroner's comment indicates. (See also chapter 3.)

Another example that can be sourced primarily to the lawyer is the following question from a solicitor to an Aboriginal witness (Criminal Justice Commission of Queensland 1996: 23)

S: All right then. So he was – he was pretty cranky about the door being opened and I'm just saying to you – suggesting that what happened; he was cranky, you'd made him coffee, you had this disagreement about the door being opened, he got up, grabbed his cup, lifted it off the table and as he was walking out just lost the grip on it and it came out of his hand and was flung across to you and cut you and actually hit your cup and smashes and caused your leg to be cut?

PC: Well perhaps that might be broken up a little bit Your Worship.

J: Yes.

PC: There's about twenty different things she could answer yes or no to in [that].

Notice a number of the features of complex questions discussed in chapters 2 and 3, particularly direct and indirect projection, and many clauses. It is also a clear case of a lawyer putting a 'story' for confirmation (chapter 4).

There is an obvious danger that what is discussed above may lead to miscommunication and miscarriage of justice. Some possible means of alleviating (but not entirely solving) this problem are discussed in the next chapter.

Second Language Speakers

It is obvious that people who do not have a native command of the language of the legal system may have communication difficulties in their contacts with the law, and hence be disadvantaged. This section therefore will be concerned with demonstrating and describing this miscommunication. A major remedy for these problems is the provision of interpreting and translation services, which are discussed in the next chapter.

In demonstrating that there are communication problems, we need first to consider what indicators there might be of these problems, and second their possible source. The linguistic sources of complexity and possible miscommunication were presented in chapter 3. Indicators of possible communication problems in interaction include the following:

- overt statements of incomprehension: in Conversational Analysis terms these are a form of 'other initiated repair moves' (Schegloff, Jefferson and Sacks 1977);
- asking what to say;
- responding with apologies: 'sorry?' 'I beg your pardon';
- clarification requests;
- absent or inappropriate responses.

These are exemplified in the following case of a young Tongan-Australian man who was being charged with murder (first presented in Gibbons 1996).

The young man spoke English as a second language, and his defence had concerns about possible miscommunication when he was interviewed by the police in English. To assess his spoken English, I interviewed him using the oral scales of the *Australian Second Language Proficiency Rating Scales*, which are designed by the Adult Migrant Education Service specifically to give a proficiency rating from an interview. They consist of a set of descriptors of stages in the development of English as a Second Language. He was at level 1+ to 2 on the five point ASLPR scale, that is between survival proficiency and minimum social proficiency. Both his comprehension and his production of English were severely limited, despite some superficial fluency. With regard to grammar for example, he commanded only parts of the English tense system and had some difficulties with articles 'the', 'a', etc.; he had problems with complex sentence structure, a noticeable accent and his vocabulary was limited mostly to the everyday. In other words his proficiency and register range were adequate only for everyday communication. During the recorded interview with the police he pointed out his limited English on two occasions.

not speaking good
'cause I never speaking good English

The interviewee was born and lived in Tonga until age 10–11. He learned only a little English in school. He then moved to New Zealand, where he received some schooling, but dropped out of school at age 13. Most of his English was learned through social contact with English speakers in New Zealand and subsequently in Australia. He had received little formal instruction in English. According to his Tongan interpreter, his Tongan was also underdeveloped, not surprising given his life history and limited opportunities to master complex adult language. It was, however, considerably better than his English.

The psychologist in the case rated his IQ at 40, giving him a mental age of less than 6 years, and placing him in the bottom 0.1 per cent of the population. This result may be explained in part by his limited language for testing purposes, but it is also well established in the bilingualism literature that people who do not attain a full native ability in any language are in danger of suffering cognitive deficits. In this case we do not know whether limited intellectual ability hindered language acquisition, or whether limited language hindered intellectual development, but it seems likely that the two factors were mutually reinforcing.

The man's limited proficiency in English, and his limited formal instruction in the language, were likely to seriously affect a police interview conducted in English. Compounded with his poor intellectual development, one would predict numerous communication difficulties and breakdowns, including incorrect understanding, absence of understanding, or insufficient understanding on the part of the man, and some misunderstanding of the man by the police. In other words, communication was likely to be both limited and inaccurate.

In the case in question a homicide had taken place, but the fatal blows had not been struck by this man, so the real question was whether he had collaborated in the murder. In order to obtain a conviction, the police needed to establish that he was actively complicit in the murder. Since he did not commit the murder, there was no material evidence. Only testimony (i.e. language) could provide grounds for a conviction, so the police interview was a major element in the outcome of the case, and good communication in that interview was essential.

The police interviewed the man without the intervention of an interpreter or other support person. They recorded the interview using the official ERISP video taping system.

Evidence of power asymmetry and imposition of a 'story'

The possibility of a 'confirmation story' being fed to this man, would be manifested in confirmation questions eliciting a yes or no answer. Since this was verbal interaction, it was possible to look at the responses as well as the questions. When this was done it became apparent that many of the questions were polar in function if not in form, certainly this was the reading placed upon them by the interviewee (i.e. this was their perlocutionary force). In fact 145 questions out of 449, or 31 per cent, were answered by a simple 'yeah' or 'yes'.

Asking what to say
On several occasions the man also asked the police whether he should agree, as shown in these examples.

P: All right. You may have to speak clearly when you answer please. Do you agree that prior to the commencement of this interview, I told you that I intended asking you further questions about this matter?
W: I say yes? – yes.

P: Do you agree that earlier tonight you told us that it was your idea to rob these men?
W: What do you want to say?

P: But isn't it the case, that you decided prior to approaching those men, to steal from them?
W: I . . . say yes . . . or what? ['or what' not transcribed by police]

These responses by the man reveal problems of complexity (discussed later), and the fact that the man asked the police what he should answer reveals power asymmetry.

Evidence of communication problems

Turning now from the issue of the story and the affirmative responses, other evidence from the interaction will be presented to show that communication was poor.

Responding with an apology

Responses can take the form of **apologies**, as in the next ten examples. A tentative interpretation based on the framework established in chapter 2 of the sources of the communication problem are given below the extracts in italics.

P: Did you approach these men?
W: Your pardon?
Specialist lexicon – *'approach'* (why not 'go near' or 'go to'?)

P: Did you sustain any injuries as a result of that initial fight?
W: Pardon? I don't . . .
Phrasal complexity *'as a result of that initial fight'*. **Grammatical metaphor** *'as a result of'* = *'because of'*. **High Register**: *'sustain'*, *'initial'*.

P: Did you see what injuries the little man had?
W: Pardon?
Syntactic complexity.

P: What were they doing to the man that made you fear that they may kill him?
W: What did you say, pardon?
Syntactic complexity (see figure 6.1).

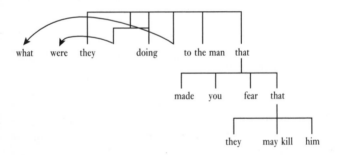

Figure 6.1   Syntactic complexity in police question 1.

Responding with a clarification request

Another signal of incomprehension is when **the police question is answered with another question** requesting clarification.

P: What happened when the men arrived in the car?
W: What happened?
Complex question.

P: Can you describe that weapon?
W: Who? – me or them?
Understands 'describe' as limited to people?

P: Where did you hit him with the piece of wood?
W: When I hit him?
Confuses question words when and where.

P: What part of the house did you hit?
W: What do you mean?
Complex embedded question.

P: Can you tell me why, when these men were on the ground and
     apparently defenceless, you continued to hit them with a piece of
     wood?
W: You say, why are you hitting him for?
Technicality: *'apparently defenceless'.*
Syntactic complexity (see figure 6.2).

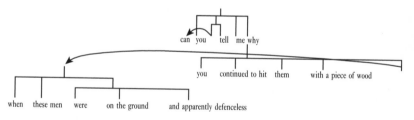

Figure 6.2   Syntactic complexity in police question 2.

P: You have any complaints?
W: Complaints?
Lexicon: *'complaints'*

Absence of response
Another possible signal of comprehension difficulties (often clearly
handled as such by the police) is the **absence of a response,** of which

there are thirteen examples on the tape. Rather than repair initiation, in CA terms this is a marked non-compliance with turn taking conventions of English (see Sacks, Schegloff and Jefferson 1978).

Inappropriate response
Another indication of problems with understanding is the **inappropriate response** which clearly violates Grice's maxims (Grice 1975). There are a number of occasions where the interviewee seems to confuse the interrogatives 'who', 'why', 'when', 'where' and 'how' (it is worth noting that some pidgins replace these words with 'what man', 'what for', 'what time', 'what place', 'what fashion', and Chinese does something similar, reflecting their semantic complexity). See the next two examples below, and some of the previous examples.

P: Ten schooners. And where did you consume that alcohol?
W: My cousins and me.
Semantic complexity: confuses question words *who* and *where*. Technicality: '*consume*'.

P: How did they come back?
W: Come back.
P: Were they in a vehicle?
W: Maybe they angry or –
Confuses question words *how* and *why*. Technicality: '*vehicle*'

P: When did he go home?
W: . . . by train or taxi, I don't know
Confuses question words *when* and *how*.

Another candidate for a vocabulary problem is 'full' in the next example.

P: . . . What is your full name?
W: William [first name changed]

The next example shows a likely misunderstanding of the meaning of tense and aspect – he seems to understand 'what were they doing' as 'what did they do'

P: When you told them to stop, what were they doing?
W: They – hop on in the car, then they start driving.

In the following example he apparently reads the request as a question, recognizing only the question form, and not its functionally metaphorical use as a request speech act.

P: Yes. Can you describe those two men?
W: Um – yeah. Yes.

The above examples provide clear evidence that there was miscommunication, and that an interpreter was desirable in order to improve communication. However, perhaps the most worrying aspect of the interviewee's comprehension is that there are many examples where he understood one or two words, sometimes repeating them, and used a strategy of giving a reply on the basis of those. As another second language client expressed it 'Sometime when you speak to me, sometime I don't understand. Sometime I understand two three words, and I think [i.e. attempt to work out] what you say'. Often these interviewee responses based on limited comprehension appear relevant and appropriate. Hence poor comprehension is masked, and even when relevant and appropriate replies are given, there is no guarantee that the interviewee has fully understood the question.

One question that arises is whether the police are always aware of communication difficulties. One obvious signal is repair sequences which take a number of turns, showing a recognition of poor communication. If these repair sequences take the form of linguistic modification involving substantial linguistic simplification, we also have evidence that the police are aware of the source of the communication problem, namely the interviewee's limited English proficiency. We have already noted some cases of police **rephrasing into simpler English**. In the following additional examples the rephrasings are marked by an arrow, and detailed underneath in underlined form.

P: Did you sustain any injuries as a result of that initial fight
W: Pardon? I don't –
P: Did you – were you hurt as a result of that initial fight?
W: Hurt?
Did you sustain any injuries → were you hurt

P: . . . I'd just like to suspend the interview while I go and get that piece of wood that I showed you earlier. Do you understand that?
   [*no audible response*]

P: I want to suspend this and go and get that piece of wood and show
       you again . . .

I'd just like → I want
the interview → this
while+subordinate clause → and + conjoined clause
that+subordinate clause → and + conjoined clause
earlier → again

P: . . . Do you agree once again, that we're the only three people in this
       room?
       [*no audible response*]
P: We're the only three people here?
W: Yes.

Deletion of 'Do you agree once again, that', i.e. removal of subordination
'in this room' → here

On the basis of this evidence the police were aware of communication
problems, and the fact that they solved them by simplifying their language
shows that they were aware that the interviewee's English was a source of
the problem. These are also remarkable examples of the ability of native
speakers with limited conscious linguistic knowledge to perform far reaching simplifications.

There is evidence from the discourse that the police were providing a
version of events for affirmation rather than eliciting the interviewee's own
version, and secondly that they were proceeding with an interview when
they were aware that the interviewee's English was causing substantial
communication difficulties. These are distortions of due process. Partly on
the basis of evidence of incomprehension by the interviewee, the police
interview was rejected as evidence, the man was found not guilty. In this
case, as in a number of others in which I have been involved, the distortions of the interview process were self-defeating, in that when these problems were exposed, evidence vital to the prosecution could not be used in
court. Furthermore, without the intervention of the psychologist and myself, the man could have been sentenced to life imprisonment on the basis
of evidence derived from a distorted process.

Such problems are also found in courtroom interaction. Lane (1985:
201) offers the following example of a Samoan man in a New Zealand
court. The man is a friendly witness, yet counsel is compelled to ask the
same question (to which the counsel clearly knows the answer) three times

before communication finally occurs. (Notice too that resolving the problem is made difficult by the prohibition on leading questions.)

C: Did you go anywhere else with him?
W: My brother and my sister-in-law came with me on that night.
C: Did you decide to go somewhere else when you were in the car?
W: No
C: When you were in the car did you decide to go somewhere else?
W: Yes when we arrive home, I ask him because that time I have this dance ticket. I asked him please can he drive me down to the dance.

Gumperz (1982) describes the perjury trial in the USA of a Filipino doctor attached to a US Navy Hospital. He was charged with perjury because his sworn testimony in a child abuse case was in conflict with his statement to an FBI agent. Although the doctor spoke very good English, there were misunderstandings. Gumperz (1982: 176) gives the following two examples of Dr A answering the speech act rather than the propositional meaning (italics are in the original).

Q: It's the testimony by Lieutenant Commander Gilbert that you did not attend the briefing.
A: *Yes*
Q: You did attend it?
A: No.

Like the agreement phenomena discussed earlier, the 'yes' agrees that this was Gilbert's testimony, not that he attended, as the follow up question demonstrates. The next example is similar.

A: When the child came, I initially examined the patient and I noted the moistness of the tongue, sunken eyes, the skin color, and everything was okay.
Q: Are you suggesting that there were no sunken eyes?
A: *No*
Q: I think we better slow down a little bit more and make sure the record ... did you observe sunken eyes?
A: No.

Gumperz (1982: 179) writes 'Note for example that the 'no' ... could be read as "no, that's not what I am suggesting" or "no, there were no symptoms of sunken eye'". Such inherent ambiguities are often resolved by culturally specific discourse conventions which in inter ethnic settings can lead to misunderstandings.' The 'everything was okay' demonstrates that the patient did not have 'sunken eyes' and therefore 'noted' is not the appropriate verb since it presupposes the conditions – it should have been expressed with a verb such as 'checked (for)'. Notice that both questions are in reported speech or projected form, which opens the question to ambiguity, as the coroner commented in the quote given earlier in the section on indigenous people.

Gumperz also argues that the many examples of unclear use of pronouns may be the result of transfer from Philippine languages, where a much richer pronoun set permits them to be used in contexts where the reference of English pronouns is unclear. There are also various problems with the misuse of tenses, like the examples discussed earlier. Gumperz shows the problems caused by the transfer of Philippine language intonation patterns to English, making the salience of information unclear to English speakers, and documents how social norms concerning interference in the affairs of other families made the doctor seem uncaring about the plight of the burn victim. On this basis, Gumperz argued in court that the seeming contradiction between Dr A's interview with the FBI, and his courtroom testimony was a result of misunderstanding during the FBI interview not perjury. His evidence was accepted and the case was dismissed.

Pauwels, D'Argaville and Eades (1992) describe communication difficulties in lawyer–client interviews similar to those described for police interviews and courtroom discourse.

In prisons, second language speakers may, like the deaf prisoners discussed later, face prison procedures and have little possibility of understanding them. In New South Wales, the Department of Corrective Services began in 1997 a process of review of the treatment of 'ethnic inmates' in prisons. A report by Maher et al. (1998) based on recordings of discussions in focus groups involving eighteen women. Unfortunately some of the women knew little or no English, and the prison failed to provide the requested interpreters. Those who were able to communicate reported that on reception to the prison:

> I didn't understand anything. They never rang an interpreter. I spoke no English. I didn't understand. They asked you to sign and rush through and you have to sign it [papers] and rush in reception.

All information in the prison is in English only, apart from emergency procedure signs in sixteen languages (perhaps an indicator of the linguistic diversity of NSW prisons). Many prisoners, while able to communicate orally to some degree, find it much harder to cope with official documents:

> They just say read this and sign it. You might understand if they speak it to you, but not written

Often other prisoners interpret, rather than an accredited interpreter:

> If someone can't speak English they call an inmate to interpret

The problems are not only found at reception. The report adds (Maher et al. 1998: 5) 'it was clear that difficulties in relation to language and access to interpreter services were not confined to the reception period. Indeed, women continued to have ongoing problems in everyday dealings with custodial staff, Corrections Health Service, Welfare, Psychological Services, Education, Industries, legal services and classification committees'. The resemblances to the problems of the deaf are a result of the fact that both groups are second language speakers.

The remedies for these language problems are similar to those for indigenous minorities. However there is a major additional resource – the interpreter and translator. Legal interpreting and translation are the topic of the next chapter.

The Deaf

'Deaf' is a term that can refer both to a physical condition – an inability to hear well – and to membership of the deaf community. For the purposes of this book, I am using the term in the first sense. Much of what is said here is based on the important work reported in Brennan and Brown (1997). Given adequate opportunities, most deaf people develop a sign language as their mother tongue. Sign languages are not signed variants of spoken languages, but are distinct languages in their own right, with a high level of regional variation. Their vocabulary syntax and morphology differ greatly from the spoken languages around them. The deaf also often view themselves as a separate community with a different culture from the hearing community.

The deaf are a special case of second language speaker, but they are different in that people born deaf rarely develop a full command of speech, which makes it unlikely that they will fully master the grammar, vocabulary and discourse of a spoken language. Brennan and Brown (1997: 12) summarize this by writing 'The Deaf community . . . can never have full and equal access to spoken languages.' Furthermore deaf cultures are at present effectively non-literate since writing systems for sign languages are only developing now, so literacy among the deaf is literacy in non-sign languages that they rarely fully command. Brennan and Brown (1997: 92) write 'many Deaf people simply cannot read and write well'. The communication barrier between the deaf and the dominant hearing community has been reinforced historically by the hearing community's lack of knowledge and understanding of the deaf, and consequent negative stereotyping. The result is a significant cultural and attitudinal barrier maintained by both sides.

Looking back once more at the characteristics of legal language discussed in previous chapters, we can see immediate problems, even when sign interpreters are used (which is by no means always the case). Concerning technicality, there may not be signs for certain technicalities, since there is no signed legal system. In such cases the deaf 'borrow' words from the spoken language, by finger spelling or using lip shapes ('mouthing' the word). Sometimes this goes so far as to be spoken language reproduced by signs ('signed' English/French/etc.) or a 'sign supported' version of the spoken language. Deaf people with limited command of the spoken language may not understand these well. With regard to literacy, low levels of literacy make it unlikely that deaf people will master the written register typical of operative documents, so signed interpreting will be of limited help. Interestingly also, according to Brennan and Brown (1997), British Sign Language lacks many of the honorifics and other markers of power relationships, making address forms such as *Your Honour* difficult to sign, and sometimes preventing the signed testimony of the deaf from sounding appropriately respectful. This means that the main characteristics of legal language discussed in chapters 1–3 (technicality, writtenness and power) will cause severe communication problems for the deaf in various legal contexts.

The disadvantage suffered by the deaf in contact with the legal system can have both the expected problems, similar to those of other second language speakers, and others that are radically different. For instance in contact with the **police**, a signer who is handcuffed is effectively gagged; a signer who is restrained may be misinterpreted as 'struggling' when attempting to sign, with easily imaginable results; unless the police have text telephones, a deaf person is effectively denied the statutory telephone call when taken into custody. In **prison**, in the absence of text telephones, deaf prisoners cannot make permitted telephone calls to their families, unlike other prisoners; if there are no other deaf prisoners then there is no one they can fully communicate with, a situation verging on solitary confinement; the education and training opportunities in prison are rarely appropriate to the deaf; isolation and boredom are increased both because they cannot listen to radios, and televisions usually lack text facilities; there may be no provision for flashing time indicators (the visual equivalent of a bell) or flashing fire alarms; they are also rarely given interpreters for contacts with the prison authorities at initial orientation, parole boards, psychiatric assessment or sentence reviews – consequently they may serve longer sentences. Judge Stephen Tumin, a British ex-Chief Inspector of Prisons stated in a television interview (quoted in Brennan and Brown 1997: 109) 'There are completely inadequate provisions for deaf people in prisons. There is no central arrangements or rules or provision organised centrally for disabled people at all.' In effect deaf prisoners suffer more than hearing prisoners, justifying the disquiet expressed by the deaf prisoner at the beginning of this chapter.

Apart from the legal register issues mentioned previously, the main problems in **courtrooms** have to do with interpreting, which is handled in the next chapter, but it is worth mentioning that in addition to linguistic problems, deaf people must look at the interpreter, thereby missing many non-verbal cues from the source speaker, and deaf people in the public gallery may be too distant, or at the wrong angle to see signed interpreting.

Social Class

Social class can be a problematic category. Here it is used to refer to broad employment categories – unskilled manual labour, skilled manual labour, white collar, and professional and managerial. The language consequences of these types of employment is the degree to which work demands and involves the use of High Register, particularly in literacy practices. There are strong (but not absolute) relationships between employment category, level of education and command of High Register. The section on jury instructions mentioned the greater communication problem that people with lower levels of education have with the language of these instructions. The same can be assumed for other aspects of the law – that people from the working class will, often as a consequence of their lower level of command of High Register, have greater difficulty in understanding legal processes and in putting their views and stories across, in participating in general.

Social stereotyping can also contribute to unequal treatment in the justice system. Cicourel (1976) shows how teachers, police officers and probation officers tend to attribute antisocial or illegal behaviour of working class youths to 'bad attitude' leading to a 'punishment frame', while similar behaviour by middle class youths is attributed to a 'depressed state', leading to a 'treatment frame'. In particular he contrasts the cases of two youths who have suffered similar experiences, but while the middle class youth is repeatedly offered a second chance, the working-class youth is not.

Wodak-Engel (1984: 98–100) gives two samples from Austrian traffic courts of the trials of a middle class man and a working class woman with the same judge (gender issues may also be involved). A major language difference between the two speakers not apparent in the (translated) transcripts is that the judge is forced to switch to dialect to communicate with the working class woman, and is displeased about doing so – perhaps seeing this as inappropriate to both the legal context and his status as a judge.

The differences in the transcripts are of interest in various ways. Looking first at the language of the two defendants, the middle class speaker uses High Register including grammatical metaphor, for instance: 'I had subjectively the impression . . .' (not *I thought*); 'the deformation of the wings' (not *bent*); 'I would be able to orient myself' (not *know where I was going*). This defendant gave a well constructed 'story' with an ideological slant towards his lack of blame. The working class woman's account is much more direct, and the judge's interruptions mean she is not given the opportunity to construct a coherent 'story'.

It seems that the judge's social prejudices are activated by these differences, since he engages in status support (see chapter 3) with the man in discussing his high status employment and good salary, and status reduction with the woman, particularly in the patronizing information 'Every vehicle has a steering wheel'. The woman provides a reasonable everyday definition of *swerve* after saying 'no' to a question on swerving, but her lack of elaboration allows the judge to believe that she cannot understand the word. The questioning style adopted with the two defendants is also noticeably different in politeness: compare the judge's 'You are a PhD?' on the man's education, to his 'form filling' question to the woman 'and now we need the education'; and when asking for their account of events 'Now, what happened?' addressed to the man, but 'and what else?' to the woman. Concerning the judge's question about the PhD, consider Philips (1998: 61) comment 'attributions involving education can be understood to function sometimes as "code" for attributions associated with class and race.'

The middle class defendant had to pay a nominal fine, although he was guilty of manslaughter. The working class defendant received a three-month jail sentence, although she was less responsible for the accident in which she was involved than the middle class defendant.

Women in Sexual Assault Cases

Liebes-Plesner (1984) and Matoesian (1993, 1997) show in some detail the way in which women in sexual assault cases are disadvantaged and sometimes traumatized by the style of questioning to which they can be subjected in court. Matoesian (1993: ch. 5) provides transcripts of the cross-examination of rape victims which contain many of the 'power' language features discussed in chapter 3, that are intended to pressure witnesses into an account of events with which they are not in full agreement. He describes the lawyers preventing witnesses from producing a coherent ('multi-unit') account, including interruption and taking the turn away from the witness; lawyers' use of silence to emphasize particular statements or create doubts about the credibility of witnesses; the use of coercive question forms; and topic and information control. In the examples given by Matoesian these are used to construct a version of the sexual encounter in which the woman is a willing participant, sometimes drug or alcohol affected. To give an example, the following extract (Matoesian 1993: 161) comes from a trial where the defence counsel (CD) had previously attempted to establish the word *partying* as meaning drug and alcohol use and possibly sexual activity (the symbol [[here indicates that the counsel and the witness speak at the same time).

CD: O.K. you went outside and you waited for at least ten minutes for one of these friends to emerge, is that correct?
    (1.2)
W: Mmhmm
CD: Who were you waiting for?

(3.9)

W: I dont remember who it was.

CD: Aren'tchu just trying tuh come up with an excuse for why you had
      to wait outside there?

      (0.6)

W: No

      [[

CD: Weren't you in fact waiting outside for somebody to go pardying
      with (.) <u>anybody</u>

CP: <u>Objection</u> yer honour

J: Overruled

W: No

Notice here the use of questions where the expected answer is *yes*, the use
of a turn taking violation to override the woman's 'no' response, and the
indirect construction of the witness as intending to be promiscuous.

A commonplace of lawyers defending men accused of sexual assault was
to ask women about their previous sexual experience. This tactic had
several purposes. First it was intended to suggest that the woman was a
willing participant on this occasion as on previous ones. Second it was
intended to arouse social prejudice against women who have a number of
sexual partners. The invasion of the personal life of a woman who might
already be traumatized by the assault could be a successful tactic, in that it
might lead to a strong emotional reaction which might make her evidence
less convincing, or it could lead to a refusal to cooperate, which can have
a strong negative effect on the woman's case, and indeed is unlawful. It is
questionable whether the information gained by this tactic can be justified
when balanced against the trauma and humiliation of the woman.

Questioning by lawyers concerning minute details of the sexual assault
can similarly be used as an interpersonal tactic rather than a genuine pursuit of essential information, humiliating and traumatizing the woman.
Women's groups have made strong representation on these issues of cross-
examination. In Australia some judges have been subject to criticism for
their handling of sexual assault cases – for the insensitivity of their comments, or for perceived bias in favour of male defendants, in particular
failing to prevent coercion and humiliation of women who have been physi-
cally abused.

Conclusion

From the well documented instances discussed in this chapter, the logical conclusion is that the way language is used in the justice system can disadvantage people who traditionally are less powerful, or already disadvantaged in other ways: children, minority ethnic groups including indigenous people, the less educated or those of lower socioeconomic status, the deaf and abused women. This situation is self-evidently unjust, and law without justice is merely a mechanism for oppression. These types of disadvantage, which have deep social roots, cannot be remedied only by linguistic means. However there are measures that can be taken to improve the situation. I argue in Gibbons (1994: 195) that just treatment does not mean the same treatment, but rather recognizing difference, and developing measures to cope with these differences. Some of these measures are discussed in the next chapter.

7

Bridging the Gap

In broken English, the client tried to tell the judge that she did not speak or understand well. He told her to be quiet and listen to him. He then proceeded to ask her questions which in her anxious state she did not understand . . . eventually he resorted to a sort of pidgin English which, somehow, she made sense of. Greatly pleased, the Judge said 'you see, you can speak English when you want to'.

National Italian Australian Women's Association submission to the Australian Commonwealth Attorney General's Department, quoted in Commonwealth Attorney General's Department report (1991)

Introduction

In the previous chapter we saw clear and sometimes harrowing examples of the problems that can arise in communication between representatives of the legal system, and people who do not have a full command the language of the legal system. Three problems arise from these data. First there is a problem in the communication of ideas, of conceptual content which may be communicated inaccurately or partially. Second there is a problem of coercion – vulnerable people may be pressurized or manipulated into saying something other than what they believe to be the truth. Third, there is a problem of trauma. The legal process is difficult for most people. For more vulnerable people, it may produce unnecessary and unjustifiable suffering, particularly if they encounter the more coercive and emotionally stressful forms of interrogation. Children, as Brennan (1994) notes, may be 'abused again'.

These issues again raise the problem of injustice in the legal system, and what measures can be taken to mitigate it. While perfection is unachievable, continual vigilance and effort is needed to reduce, as far as possible, the likelihood of injustice. A major part of this chapter is concerned with legal interpreting and translation, but the problems of other minorities are also discussed, particularly measures to avoid the three problems outlined in the first paragraph above.

Measures to Reduce Communication Problems

The previous chapter dealt with various problems that can arise with a range of groups in society. There are various approaches to solving such problems, all of which may be useful in different circumstances.

Information

First there is the issue of informing all participants of fundamental differences in communication patterns and the possible problems and issues that may arise from them. There are many legal professionals of good will, and when they become aware that the sources of difficulties are cultural or linguistic rather than an intent to frustrate, they are more likely to accept the misunderstandings and attempt to resolve them. The training of police officers, judges, lawyers and court staff is a common means to achieve such ends. There has been a substantial effort to provide such training in many countries, including Australia, Canada and the USA, for instance basic training at the New South Wales Police Academy includes information on Aborigines in the legal system provided by an Aboriginal staff member. In light of the difference in the comprehension among children of counsellors' questions compared to lawyers questions, efforts have also begun in many jurisdictions to educate lawyers in appropriate ways to interact with children.

Addressing disadvantage produced by social class is difficult, since it does not involve visible minorities, but the social and economic structures of society. As with indigenous minorities, there is a strong case for greater education of all participants in the justice system, and for the vetting of judges to ensure that they will not allow social stereotyping to cloud their judgment or the judicial process. Police officers will similarly benefit from careful selection and education.

More difficult, but still valuable, is the provision of counselling services for minorities who become involved with the law, so that they can increase their understanding of the legal system and its operation.

Mediation

The second approach involves the establishment of mediation and advocacy by people who understand both sides. An example of this in Australia was the creation of the Aboriginal Legal Services, consisting of people with expertise in the law and Aboriginal culture, including Aboriginal field officers, and non-Aboriginal and Aboriginal lawyers. There are also Aboriginal court liaison officers in some states. Similarly police services around the world have established liaison officers to help to resolve problems when ethnic minorities come into contact with the police: often such officers are recruited from a relevant minority group.

When children are questioned by police or lawyers, it is becoming increasingly common to involve a child counsellor who is empowered to intervene when s/he becomes aware that the child is miscommunicating or suffering. Some jurisdictions also allow the presence of a mediator in cases involving accusations of sexual assault. In various police services there are also officers with particular responsibility for cases involving children and sexual assault, charged with avoiding insensitive treatment or questioning of children or sexual assault victims.

The issue of second language speakers will be handled largely in the section on interpreting, but it is worth recording the importance of allowing the interpreter a role as a cultural as well as a linguistic intermediary.

Modifying legal procedures

A third approach is to modify legal procedures to make them less alien, incomprehensible and threatening to people of different cultures. One significant step taken in the Northern Territory of Australia was the establishment of the Anunga Rules which significantly include the right to the presence of a 'friend' or advocate at all times during police questioning, which helps to reduce the occurrence of gratuitous concurrence. There can also be specific guidelines on formulating questions and ensuring comprehension. As we shall see in the next part of this chapter, it also important to enshrine the use of interpreters for people who have a limited proficiency in the standard courtroom language, not only those who cannot speak it at all. Concerning specific courtroom procedures, recommendations from Criminal Justice Commission of Queensland report (1996: 24) are that witnesses be allowed to give evidence-in-chief in narrative form, and that leading questions be subject to greater control by the judge. Cultural sensitivity can also be made grounds for objecting to questions in court.

The problems of children in the legal system are becoming more widely appreciated, and legal systems have adopted a range of measures to handle the problem of children in court, particularly in sexual assault cases. Perhaps the most important of these is the admission of video-taped interviews with young children performed by a counsellor. Lawyers are sometimes unhappy with these, as they believe the evidence may be biased by the counsellor, and cannot be tested. Another means of reducing the trauma of courtroom appearance is the use of video links to a less threatening environment where the child can answer questions put by people whom s/he sees on a television screen. As in many areas like this, important measures are lawyer training and consequent enhanced awareness of lawyers of the impact of their language, and a more interventionist approach from judges to inhibit aggressive questioning. One useful means of overcoming a child's inability or unwillingness to give a verbal description of abuse is to use dolls or puppets. Sometimes these are used as an interview partner, and often anatomical dolls are used as non-verbal communication aids in a child's description of physical or sexual abuse. Another non-verbal communication technique is the use of drawings of the human body in which the child can identify the parts involved. Some kind of assessment of the child's suggestibility may also be required. The psychological literature (for instance Raskin and Yuille 1989: 196) suggests that interviews, particularly video taped interviews with children and other persons who might be vulnerable or suggestible, should follow the **cognitive interview** format described in chapter 4.

Sexually abused women form another group who may need protection, particularly from further trauma during the interrogation process. Guidelines have been introduced in some jurisdictions (in the USA for instance they are called 'rape shield laws') which prevent counsel asking women about their previous sexual experience as a tactic to discredit them, and which attempt to restrain questioning on details of the assault, relying instead as far as possible on other evidence, such as medical reports. Less direct means of obtaining information, such as sworn statements, tend to be resisted by counsel unless they can be 'tested' through cross-examination. Indeed there is still debate concerning the balance between protecting witnesses, and protecting the accused through rigorous testing of evidence.

Legal Interpreting and Translation

Introduction

There are two main issues that arise in the interpreting and translation area: (1) when (and indeed whether) interpreters and translators are required for legal purposes, and if interpreters are needed, what access there is to an adequate level of interpreting/translation; (2) what the processes of legal interpreting and translation look like.

In the field of translation/interpreting, the normal distinction between these two terms is that **translation** is the process of turning a written text in the source language into a **written text** in the target language, while **interpreting** has the same task to perform with **speech**. Although there is a substantial degree of commonality between the two activities, there is no single agreed word in English that covers both. In legal contexts the term **interpretation** is reserved for the mostly monolingual process of deriving meaning from operational documents – see chapter 2; in other words **interpreting** is done by interpreters, and **interpretation** is done by lawyers.

Access to interpreters and translators

Why interpreters are needed and are not used

When a person who knows nothing of the language of the legal system comes into contact with it, it is difficult to find any rational argument for denying that person access to an interpreter or translator. If such mediation is denied, two main issues arise: poor communication between the second language speaker and the police or lawyers may impede the discovery of the full facts of the case; second, the second language speaker is denied the right to adequately communicate his/her version of events, understand the legal process and participate in it. There is an evident danger of injustice resulting from these two factors. This has led to both international and national legislation on the right to an interpreter/translator (see the next section). Furthermore, the earlier chapters of this book showed that the level of language proficiency required in legal proceedings is beyond that required for everyday conversation. Some control of more complex grammar and 'high' register may be needed. This means, in turn, that interpreters are required not only for people with no command of the language used for legal purposes, but also for those with a limited command. Determining the level of language proficiency beyond which an interpreter is not required is an issue that has plagued discussion and action concerning the use of interpreters.

Legal translation and interpreting are often not used in courts, police stations and prisons when they appear to be needed. Carroll (1995) documents the radical under-use of interpreters in Australian courts. Jacquemet (1996: 169–76) also discusses the problems faced in court by speakers of Italian regional languages, who are officially obliged by the 'Italian only rule' to speak standard Italian, a language that many of them command poorly. Nowhere do the judges (or indeed Jacquemet) consider the possibility that an interpreter would be able to transmute the unacceptable to the acceptable, while giving the witnesses the opportunity to use the full range of their language to communicate their testimony. The question is why?

The Australian Commonwealth Attorney-General's Department in 1991 put out a report called *Access to Interpreters in the Australian Legal System* and, as part of that report, they enquired of judges and lawyers the reasons for not using interpreters and translators in court (Commonwealth Attorney General's Department 1991: ch. 3). The reasons given were the following:

1. if the second language speaker has some knowledge of the language of the legal system, the time taken during the interpreting process provides an advantage in terms of extra time for thinking and developing a response;
2. the use of an interpreter makes it harder to gauge the credibility of a witness, since the non-verbal information such as facial expression, eye contact, tone of voice and hesitation is altered during interpreting;
3. the interpreter may modify the content of what is said, and not simply act as a conduit giving 'literal interpretation' (see the section on the interpreting process);
4. the interpreter may take an active role in the courtroom, intervening in the interaction between lawyer and witness (Berk-Seligson 1990: ch. 5, provides many examples of interpreters intervening, sometimes for good communicative reasons);
5. giving a right to an interpreter affects judicial discretion in deciding whether an interpreter is needed.

The responses given to these points in the same report are in essence that they are true, but their effects need not be greatly significant. With (1) there is little evidence of this occurring, and the benefit will not be large, particularly for the poorly educated witnesses who form the majority of those using interpreters. Concerning (2) an experienced barrister can normally cope with the mediation of an interpreter. Point (3) misunderstands the nature of the interpreting process, and can be overcome to a large degree by a fully competent interpreter – any communication difficulties produced by interpreter use are likely to be less than those caused by a poorly mastered second language. (4) can be mitigated by training interpreters in the ethics of their profession. (5) makes a strong assumption about the judge's ability to assess second language proficiency. The Commonwealth Attorney General's Department report (1991: 45) remarks 'If there is any risk of injustice occurring, it is far better that is should occur by providing an interpreter to a witness who does not really need one, than by the court refusing the use of an interpreter to a witness who does not speak or understand English sufficiently to communicate properly.' Nevertheless there is continuing resistance to the use of interpreters among some lawyers.

Turning to the police, there is evidence in some jurisdictions of police resistance to using interpreters. For example in New South Wales, while facts and figures are not available since no central police records are kept concerning police use of interpreters or numbers of second language speakers interviewed, it is possible to get some idea from other sources. The 1994 and 1995 figures from the Telephone Interpreter Service and the Ethnic Affairs Commission reveal that interpreters were used less than 5,000 times per year. Figures from the NSW Bureau of Crime Statistics and Research for recent years show that around 145,000 people are charged each year. On this basis interpreter use is around 3 per cent. However, given that charges are not always laid, that witnesses as well as suspects are interviewed, and many suspects are subjected to more than one interview, the number of interviews is probably several times higher than the number of people charged. Therefore the real rate of interpreter use in police interviews is probably much lower – probably between 1 per cent and 1.5 per cent of all interviews. It should be remembered that in Sydney around half the population speaks English as a second language. To give a comparison, Carroll (1995: 66) reports that in Australian Tribunals where 'there was a reasonable use of interpreters', interpreter usage was 'around 25 percent, which may give some indication of the need for interpreters'. This comparison is rubbery, but there seems little reason to doubt that there has been gross under-use of interpreters by NSW police. Mildren (1999: 141) describes a similar situation for the Northern Territory of Australia.

When I have interviewed police officers concerning this issue, they express considerable reluctance to use interpreters. This is due to a number of reasons. The first is practical. Interviews often take place in the early hours of the morning. At this hour it can be difficult to obtain interpreters, and they make take some hours to arrive at the police station – from the police point of view such delays are clearly undesirable. The second issue is that under 'user pays' principles, the cost of interpreters is charged to the local budget – a most effective disincentive to using them. A third reason, as in the courts, is the role played by the interpreter in the interview process itself. An important element of the police interview is the reading of non-verbal signals from the interviewee, which give police officers clues as to the truth of what is said and the emotional status of the interviewee. An interpreter is of necessity interposed between the police and the interviewee, which may distort police perceptions of non-verbal signals such as facial expression, eye contact and physical movement, not to mention the difficulty of assessing voice quality in another language. As in the courtroom, the mediation of the interpreter also provides the interviewee with extra thinking time while the interpreting is taking place, which is particularly unwelcome to the police when a person is being repeatedly pressed on a point of information – in other words the police feel that the effectiveness of interrogation is reduced when they lose some control over the timing of the interview. A final source of difficulty is the perception, held by many police officers but disputed by interpreters, that the interpreter is to some degree 'on the side of', or is an advocate for the interviewee, particularly when the interpreter is a member of the same ethnic or cultural group as the interviewee.

The police in Ontario have adopted a different approach, in that they actively recruit police officers from minority language communities, and these police officers, rather than interpreting, interview and interact with witnesses and suspects in their mother tongue. This approach avoids many of the problems indicated above that are involved in using interpreters.

I have found little information on the use of interpreters in prisons. There seems to be comparatively little done in terms of the provision of formal interpreting services in prisons, except in cases where there is a large group that speaks a single second language, for instance Hispanic prisoners in some parts of California. The most common pattern appears to be one of no concession at all, or of other prisoners providing an informal interpreting service. For instance, in a report on the reception of prisoners in Mulawa women's prison in New South Wales mentioned in chapter 6, second language speakers are not offered the service of interpreters, although sometimes other prisoners may act as *ad hoc* interpreters. In Britain a 1999 report on Rochester prison by the Chief Inspector of Prisons, Sir David Ramsbotham, noted that almost half the population of Rochester Prison were second language speakers, many of them with little or no English, but they were required to sign documents they did not understand with no proper translation facilities. It also highlighted the case of one new arrival from Albania who was put in a cell with a Pole who had been told to pass on the rules of the prison 'because both names ended in an "i" ', although they had no shared language (< http://www.ncadc.demon.co.uk/>).

Given the reluctance discussed here concerning the use of interpreters/translators, one might ask what happens when they are not used. Again I have not found extensive documentation in this area. Jacquemet (1996) described a series of problems of communication in an Italian court when an interpreter was not used. The Commonwealth Attorney General's Department (1991) report gave an account from the National Italian Australian Women's Association, quoted at the beginning of this chapter, about a woman pensioner who was seeking a divorce. A clerk of the court had refused to arrange provision of an interpreter. The account illustrates problems with both communication and judicial discretion in this area.

Concerning the police, in Gibbons (1995) I document the case of a man who migrated from the Lebanon to Australia in adulthood, and spoke a limited amount of English as a second language. He was arrested by the police and charged in relation to a drug deal in his house which involved friends and relatives. Three types of document emerged from this case. The man was interviewed by the police, and the interview was recorded in typed form as a 'record of interview'. In order to obtain comparison data, I recorded and transcribed two interviews, obtaining two 'transcripts'. Soon after a third account of events was obtained by his counsel using the services of an interpreter in the form of a written 'statement'. By comparing the statement with the other two documents, it was possible to compare a version given through an interpreter, with two versions of the same events without such intervention. Three main differences emerged between the statement and the other two versions. First, the mediation of an interpreter produced a greater volume of information about the drug deal – there were many more details in the statement. Second the interpreted version was much clearer – it was difficult to envisage what had happened from the record of interview, but it was quite clear in the statement. Third, the impression of the witness was quite different. Low-level second language proficiency is similar in many ways to child language (see for example Larsen-Freeman and Long 1991), so in the non-interpreted version the man appeared immature, but in the interpreted version he appeared dignified and adult, corresponding to his adult Lebanese Arabic. The failure to use an interpreter was self-defeating for the police, because they denied themselves substantial and important information in a clear form about the drug deal. It was also unjust to the suspect, because he was unable to adequately communicate either his version of the events or his status as a mature adult.

The case of the Tongan man discussed in the previous chapter also documented many misunderstandings that could have been avoided if an interpreter had been used. In practical terms, for the police not using an interpreter had a negative result, since this interview was not admitted as evidence on the basis of the man's poor comprehension. In addition there are clear justice problems in obtaining incriminating evidence through a flawed process of interrogation.

The evidence given here does not of course prove that interpreters must always be used with second language speakers, but it gives weight to the view that interpreter services should be provided where there is a possibility of miscommunication.

The right to an interpreter/translator

Morris (1995) provides an overview of the history of the right to an interpreter, and attitudes to interpreters in Common Law legal systems.

International law

The International Covenant – Civil and Political Rights

Article 14 (3) of the international convention on human rights, which most nations have signed, states:

> In the determination of any criminal charge against him, everyone shall be entitled to the following minimum guarantees, in full equality:
> (a) To be informed promptly and in detail in a language which he understands of the nature and cause of the charge against him;
>   ...
> (f) To have the free assistance of an interpreter if he cannot understand or speak the language used in court

Provision (a) involves both the police and the courts, while provision (f) is relevant to courtroom interpreting. The convention on the rights of prisoners does not include such a right to an interpreter.

Subsequent testing in *Luedicke, Belcacem and Koc v. Federal Republic of Germany* (2EHRR 149) affirms that 'free' in (f) means completely and unconditionally free, and extends the definition to include committal hearings and the translation of all documents used in court proceedings. There is, however, no general entitlement to an interpreter if one understands the language of the court. There are other provisions which can also be understood to imply the right to an interpreter to all persons involved in court proceedings, not only the accused. Article 26 states 'All persons are equal before the law and are entitled without any discrimination to the equal protection of the law.' However, the *International Covenant – Civil and Political Rights* leaves open the issue of what **level** of comprehension and speaking ability is necessary for an interpreter to be used.

The Common Law

The basic Common Law doctrine is that there is **no** right to an interpreter, but an interpreter may be provided at the discretion of the magistrate/judge or an officer of the court. *Wigmore on Evidence* holds that 'whenever the witness's natural and adequate mode of expression is not intelligible to the tribunal, interpreting is necessary. Whether the need exists is to be determined by the trial court.' This is generally known as **judicial discretion**. In contact with the **police**, the use of an interpreter is at the discretion of the police officer in most jurisdictions. The prison system in most countries similarly does not provide the right to an interpreter.

In practice this means that the right to an interpreter varies considerably from jurisdiction to jurisdiction across the Common Law world, in courtrooms, prisons and in contact with the police. The latest information I have is that in UK the basic Common Law right prevails – there is no right to an interpreter and one is provided only if the judge deems it necessary. In Australia at the Federal level there has been an interesting development in the 1995 Federal Evidence Act, whereby there is still no basic right to an interpreter, but if an interpreter is not used with a second language speaker, it is up to the judge to justify not using an interpreter (rather than the witness having to prove that s/he needs one) – in other words the onus is reversed. Some states of Australia have the same provision, some have only the basic Common Law right, while others have stronger provision, for example South Australia has the following legislation (Evidence Act Amendment Act 1986).

14(1) Where –
  (a) the native language of a witness who is to give oral evidence in any proceeding is not English: and
  (b) the witness is not reasonably fluent in English,

the witness is entitled to give that evidence through an interpreter.

This wording is given as an example of a law whereby a second language speaker has the right to an interpreter – note the word 'entitled'. The problem is of course the determination of 'reasonably fluent in English' – who decides, and how. Quite often it is decided by a monolingual judge with little knowledge of second language comprehension problems (see the quotation at the beginning of this chapter). This issue arises in jurisdictions around the world.

In New Zealand the original inhabitants of that country, the Maori, have the right both to translation of legal documents and to interpreting in court in Maori (Lane, McKenzie-Bridel and Curtis 1999). Lane *et al.* (1999) also remark that there is a process under way to introduce similar rights for other minority language speakers.

In Canada section 16 of the Official Languages Act, 1988 provides the right to use either official language (French or English) in Federal Criminal Courts, and also states that the Federal Court has the duty to provide interpreting at the request of a party. See Steele (1992) for more information.

In the USA Benmaman (1999: 110) writes 'The fifth, sixth and fourteenth amendments of the US Constitution support the provision of due process and equal protection under the law for all residents. Such provision is denied the non-English-speaking individual when a qualified interpreter is not present in court.' Benmaman is claiming a right not just to an interpreter, but a qualified or 'certified' interpreter. In US Federal Courts such a provision exists under the Federal Court Interpreters Act (United States Code, Public Law Title 8 (1978), Title 7 (1988)). In state legal systems the situation varies, but there is a right to an interpreter under the constitution, and Benmaman (1999: 110) notes 'Certification of interpreters is also mandated in sixteen states'.

One state where the determination of the right to an interpreter is spelled out clearly is California. Part of Section 18 of the *California Rules of Court* reads as follows:

Section 18. STANDARDS FOR DETERMINING THE NEED FOR A COURT INTERPRETER

(a)   ... An interpreter is needed if upon examination by the court a party or witness is unable to speak English so as to be understood directly by counsel, court, and jury, or if a party is unable to speak or understand English sufficiently to comprehend the proceedings and assist counsel in the conduct of the case.

....

(c)   ... The examination of the party or witness to determine whether an interpreter is needed should normally include questions on the following:

(1)   Identification (for example: name, address, birthdate, age, place of birth);

(2)   Active vocabulary in vernacular English (for example: 'How did you come to the court today?' 'What kind of work do you do?' 'Where did you go to school?' 'What was the highest grade you completed?' 'Describe what you see in the courtroom' 'What have you eaten today?'). Questions should be phrased to avoid 'yes–no' replies;

(3)   The court proceedings (the nature of the charge or the type of case before the court, the purpose of the proceedings and function of the court, the rights of a party or criminal defendant, and the responsibilities of a witness).

Parts (1) and (2) above are measures of minimal social proficiency in a second language. Most immigrants would learn to cope with such questions, and certainly if they could not answer such questions, the need for an interpreter to help them with the far higher language demands of the courtroom would be beyond doubt. One could, however, ask whether this level of language proficiency is at all relevant to the circumstances. Part (3) could serve to assess the relevant level of language proficiency. However the manner in which this examination is be performed is much less explicit than the preceding section. These provisions make a substantial attempt to address the issue, but they implicitly exclude the taking of expert evidence on the issue, which from the point of view of an applied linguist, would be preferable. Compare the provision in the state of New Jersey:

(3 : 6)   **Determination of the Need for an Interpreter**

(3 : 6.1)   Any principal party in interest shall be assumed to have a bona fide need for an interpreter when:

(A) Representation is made by an attorney or by a pro se litigant that the party has limited or no proficiency in English; or

(B) The court, on it own motion, finds that a principal party in interest is hearing, speech or language-impaired or has limited or no proficiency in English.

(3 : 6.2) The court may reject a representation made under s. 3 : 6.1 only when a reliable and valid test for communicative competence has been administered by a trained examiner and the applicant has been found to be sufficiently communicatively competent in the English language.

This is perhaps the most enlightened provision in the Common Law world, in that it provides a right to an interpreter on request and introduces interpreters in cases of evident need. It reverses the Common Law onus, so that evidence must be provided that an interpreter is **not** required in doubtful cases, and such evidence shall be provided by a 'reliable and valid test . . . administered by a trained examiner', which most applied linguists would probably feel is a reasonable provision, although it may open the door to new problems concerning testing. Some lawyers also feel, however, that it opens the door to abuse of the system.

Interpreter/translator supply

There are two issues in the supply of interpreters/translators. First the availability of bilinguals who have the potential to act as courtroom interpreters. The second issue is the quality of translators/interpreters – adequate legal interpreting demands the following special knowledge and abilities: a high level of proficiency in both languages; knowledge of regional variants of these languages used in local communities; good general knowledge; and knowledge of the following: professional ethics; the legal process and legal language; and courtroom/police discourse conventions. It is for these reasons that interpreter education and interpreter certification are necessary.

Looking first at the availability of interpreters, in societies where there is a large community of speakers of a language other than that used in the legal system (for example Spanish speakers in some parts of the USA and French/English speakers in some Canadian provinces), it is likely that there will be an adequate number of bilinguals with the potential to become interpreters/translators. Where there are small numbers of speakers this may not always be the case, especially in communities with a lower level of education. The paradigm example is some Aboriginal communities in Australia, where the need for an intermediary with the legal system is urgent, but there are almost no high level bilinguals, and educational levels are below those needed to gain certification as a translator/interpreter. The results can be a severe problem for the justice system, and a lower standard of justice for the Aborigines.

Lascar (1997: 130) provides figures on the numbers of interpreters for 'languages of lesser demand' in New South Wales, dividing them into accredited and non-accredited interpreters. To give some examples, for Farsi, there are 7 accredited and 3 non-accredited interpreters. Figures for other languages, accredited and non-accredited are: Burmese none and five; Fijian none and four; Finnish three and none, respectively. The difficulty of obtaining the services of a qualified interpreter in this context are obvious. Similar situations will exist for ethnic minorities in many other parts of the world, particularly countries that have recently received immigrants.

Ibrahim and Bell (forthcoming) performed a national survey of court interpreters in the multicultural nation of Malaysia. The language of the legal system is either English or Malay, and the population contains many people who require interpreting services in one or other of these languages. They found that less than half of court interpreters had any training at all, and professional qualifications were 'very rare indeed'. Most interpreters supported a move to provide professional conditions along with mandatory accreditation.

There are systems in existence to accredit interpreters and translators, such as the Institute of Linguists in the UK, and in Australia the National Accreditation Authority for Translators and Interpreters, which provide interpreter and translator accreditation for general purposes. In the USA there is some variation between states, but there is a highly developed system of legal interpreter accreditation. In many countries specific training and accreditation for legal (rather than general) translation and interpreting is not available for all the languages needed – this includes most languages in Australia, and provision is also patchy in the UK. In countries such as the USA, New Zealand and Canada, where there is a widely spoken language other than English (Spanish, Maori and French respectively), training and certification in these languages is more viable.

One way to address the problem of interpreter/translator supply and quality is education. This can place considerable strain upon the public purse, and the returns on such expenditure are not immediately apparent in financial accounting terms. While there are substantial numbers of courses in general interpreting and translation, courses targeted to the specific demands of the legal system are much less common. For instance, for the USA Benmaman (1999: 109) writes 'While a few ongoing but limited legal interpreting programmes exist at the undergraduate level' only one university offers 'comprehensive and graduate programmes'. In Australia, likewise, legal interpreter training is available in only a few centres, and in few languages.

A final issue in the adequate supply of quality legal interpreting/translation is the pay and conditions offered to legal interpreters. In Australia, for instance, courtroom and police interpreters are mostly paid by the hour, have no career structure and their rate of pay is not substantially more than the hourly rate paid for unskilled manual work. Ibrahim and Bell (forthcoming) report a similar situation in Malaysia. In such circumstances the professionalization of legal interpreter services is unachievable.

The processes of legal interpreting and translation

Almost all the genres discussed in chapter 4 may need to be interpreted/translated, so the range of documents and discourses involved is highly varied – in itself a challenge for the interpreter/translator. The discussion here will be concerned mainly with the 'most' legal of genres – the translation of operative documents and courtroom interpreting.

Legal translation

The particular problems of legal translation have the linguistic sources discussed in the first four chapters of this book, and are therefore largely shared with interpreting. Of particular importance is the issue of technicality. The meanings of legal terms derive to a large extent from the legal system itself – they are often labels for parts of the system. Translation into a language based in another legal system can cause severe problems, because the concepts and therefore the terms may simply not exist in the legal system of the target language, or parallel terms may refer to rather different legal entities in the local legal system. Furthermore the use of everyday words with a specialist meaning can form a particular trap for the translator – for instance Vlachopoulos (forthcoming) mentions a mistaken translation into Greek of 'in consideration of' (see chapter 2). Additional challenges are posed by the other language features that characterize legal language – complex cognitive structure manifested in both complex discourse structure and extreme syntactic complexity, complex phrasal structure combined with grammatical metaphor, and formality in the lexicon. Finally there is the issue of language differences. Spanish for instance has a direct word-for-word translation equivalent of 'Judge of the High Court', but not of 'High Court Judge'. This poses problems in translating complex phrasal structures from English into Spanish. On the other hand, Spanish has many technical adjectives and adverbs, as for instance in this legal text quoted by Pardo (1996: 114) (bold typeface not in the original).

> ... en los casos de trauma existente en el lugar de trabajo provocado por las máquinas **patronales**, éstas son la cosa **riesgosa** a que alude el art. 1113 del Código Civil por cuyas consecuencias dañosas debe responder la empleadora
> . . .

> [. . . in cases of trauma occurring in the work place produced by the **employer's** machines, these are the **risk** factor alluded to in art. 1113 of the Civil Code for whose harmful consequences the employer is responsible . . .]

The two bold nouns in the English translation correspond to adjectives in bold in the Spanish. English does not have an equivalent adjective from *employer*, and *risky* is not appropriate in the context, although, as the example shows there are normally alternative linguistic resources in the target language for constructing a parallel meaning (in the translation above, English uses nouns where Spanish uses adjectives). Given the extreme precision demanded by legal texts, particularly the need to defend against hostile interpretations, the changes required by such language differences could lead to legal problems, and indeed have done so recently in the European Union.

The way that these issues are normally handled by translators is to look at the purpose of the translation, and the context of its use. For instance if the purpose of the translation is to ensure that the document is a lease and not a will, a rough translation of only parts of the document will suffice. If the document is a threatening letter to be tendered as evidence in court, the demand for care in the translation will be higher. The translation of operative documents such as leases or legislation is even more exacting if these are to function as operative documents in the target context. Translation theory acknowledges that a translation perfect for all purposes and contexts may be impossible to achieve. As Vlachopoulos (forthcoming) writes: 'a translation unit [can be] considered communicatively proficient if its rendition serves the purpose it has been translated for . . . a text need not necessarily be syntactically perfect or well formed, to function in actual communicative situations. What cannot be tolerated is a text that betrays the wish of the initiator by deviating from his objective.' Sometimes, for example, a word that has the correct propositional content can be used, even if it is from the wrong register.

Characteristics peculiar to written text (see chapter 1) are a particular concern of the translator (but not the interpreter). Taking as an example punctuation, when translating a source legal text that uses almost no punctuation, should the translator preserve this characteristic in the target language, or should the punctuation conventions of the target language prevail? The addition of punctuation may be appropriate if it does not change the legal interpretation of the target document. Another example is that certain words in English legal texts may begin with a capital letter to indicate specialized usage (see for instance the modern will quoted in chapter 1). In German all nouns begin with a capital, so in a German translation another stylistic convention (such as the use of underlining) would need to be established to translate this feature.

Another resource open to the translator is the convention used in legal documents of providing **definitions** (see chapter 2). In this case the translator can provide a definition of the source term and the translation equivalent being used in the target text.

The advantage that the translator has over the interpreter is that there is time to consider and experiment with alternative translations, and time to consult references and other texts. One context where this does not occur is when an interpreter is called upon to translate a text in court without having seen it in advance. Known as **sight translation**, this shares many of the time problems of interpreting.

Legal interpreting

1. Conditions

There are a number of settings where legal interpreting is required, including lawyers' offices, police stations and courtrooms. The last is the best documented. It can take two main forms, simultaneous interpreting and consecutive interpreting. **Consecutive interpreting** is where the interpreter waits until the speaker has finished a stretch of speech, usually a small number of sentences, then during a silent period left by the speaker, the interpreting takes place. Clearly a major factor in such interpreting is memory for what was said. **Simultaneous interpreting** is a specialized skill in which the interpreter interprets at the same time as the speaker is speaking, usually producing an interpreted version a few words behind the speaker. In courtrooms this can be done through headphones, for instance at the International Court in the Hague, or it may occur when an interpreter is providing whispered interpreting to a party in a trial to enable that party to understand court proceedings.

The physical conditions under which interpreters work vary considerably from jurisdiction to jurisdiction. In New South Wales there are various difficulties that emerge. It is not uncommon for the interpreter to be placed in the dock with the accused, which with some classes of defendant can be frightening, if not dangerous, for the interpreter. When microphones are not used acoustic conditions in the dock may not be optimal, since the dock may be placed some distance from the bench and the lawyers: if the interpreter can hear only poorly, this can cause problems and additional stress. Sometimes there is no chair for the interpreter in the dock, yet long periods on one's feet while providing the high levels of attention required for interpreting are clearly undesirable. Sometimes no form of refreshment (e.g. a glass of water) is offered, and generally no special rest conditions are provided for interpreters. Since an interpreter must interpret both the lawyer's and the client's speech, the interpreter is speaking at least twice as much as anyone else in the court. This means that some refreshment is desirable if not essential. Given the concentration and other demands made by the interpreting process, it is very difficult for an interpreter to continue for long periods, for example more than one hour. Conference interpreters are normally only expected to interpret for 20 minutes at a time.

In addition to the inherent difficulties of legal translation discussed above, interpreting, since it is an oral procedure, has the properties of oracy discussed in chapter 1. Unless the interpreter is working with a prepared typescript (in which case it is an oral presentation of a written translation), interpreting is language performance under real time constraints. In retrospect and with time to reflect on their performance, many interpreters feel that they could have provided a better version, but under real time pressures court interpreters must often use the first version that occurs to them. Moreover, Hale and Gibbons (1999) note that since bilingual cases are by nature twice as long as monolingual cases, any interruption from the interpreter that would lengthen a proceeding even more may be frowned upon. As one prosecutor said (concerning interpreted cases): 'There's no question that they delay the court proceedings. They take twice as long.' Awareness of this sentiment increases time pressure, since interpreters may feel they need to provide a speedy delivery. The more skilful and experienced interpreters are, the better they will perform under such pressures, but full legal exactitude is probably not feasible. Sometimes, in an attempt to save time, interpreters will act as a filter and omit information they consider to be redundant or irrelevant, both in the questions and in the answers, maintaining only the propositional content of the utterance. This example from Hale (1997) shows an incident where the interpreter omits the first part of the answer because it is a repetition of the question 'why did you not take any action to evict her?' (omitted matter underlined).

Source	Translation
W: Ahora, si yo no tomé ningún acto de echarla, porque yo le prometí que no la iba a echar	I: And also I had promised her that I wouldn't evict her
[Now, if I didn't take any act to throw her out, because I promised her that I wouldn't throw her out.]	

Over and above the inherent difficulties of the interpreting process, other difficulties that commonly arise are: the legal world's ignorance of the complexity of the translation process and consequent unrealistic demands on the interpreter; and any gaps in the interpreters' knowledge of the language of the law, of courtroom discourse conventions and of the law's assumptions of relevance.

One continuing problem, touched upon earlier, is the 'conduit' notion of interpreting, meaning that it consists of translating literally word for word. As a former Australian Supreme Court judge asserted:

> It cannot be overemphasised that an interpreter should interpret every single word that the witness utters, exactly as it is said, whether it makes sense or whether it is obviously nonsense; whether the witness has plainly not heard or whether, if he has heard, he has not understood. The interpreter should look upon himself rather as an electric transformer, whatever is fed into him is to be fed out again, duly transformed.
>
> (Wells 1991: 329)

Compare this comment from legal interpreters Colin and Morris (1996: 99).

lawyers not infrequently instruct court interpreters to say exactly what the witness has said – to 'translate literally'. What they should mean by this is: tell me no more and no less than the speaker has said. This is a perfectly acceptable requirement. What they should not mean is: give me a word-for-word transposition of what the speaker has said.

The metaphor of the interpreter as an 'electric transformer' fails to adequately recognize either the complexity or the importance of the task. The interpreter's job is seen as a simple word matching exercise capable of being performed by anyone who can speak two languages. This attitude can lead to a lack of appreciation of the challenge and expertise involved in interpreting, and a lack of consideration for what is needed to perform a proper job. On the one hand, interpreters are expected to render a perfectly accurate version of all that transpires in a case, on the other, they are not afforded the conditions to perform in such a manner. So it is not unusual to encounter judges who will not allow interpreters to take notes or who will become impatient if the interpreter asks for clarifications of meaning or for leave to consult the dictionary, or counsel who start asking the next question before the interpreter has finished interpreting the previous exchange. Niska (1995: 307) quotes the following example of a prosecutor overriding the interpreting (→: interruption).

I: Um, and then I don't know what happened when I caught sight of
        a policeman. I had this thing that you have for your bike.
PC: Mm a lock, was it, a lock?
I: ¿Una cerradura?
        [a lock]
W: Como candau
        [a sort of padlock]
→PC: Did this policeman approach you?
I: With a lo- a padlock

Hale and Gibbons (1999) remark that 'Although interpreters are essential in bilingual cases, they are not particularly liked by anyone in the courtroom. They are often seen as a necessary evil that is tolerated rather than welcomed.'

2. Roles

The roles that the interpreter plays in court may be varied and complex, according to Niska (1995). They include the following.

1. The primary role of the interpreter in the courtroom (and one supported by some interpreters) is seen as being a neutral conduit or machine, as noted previously. Interpreters in fact often play other roles.

2. An essential role is in reality that of a cross-cultural bridge, converting from one set of social and cultural norms and assumptions to another set.

3. This role of cross-cultural bridge can also be extended to the very particular culture and assumptions of the courtroom, sometimes it even includes the role of explainer of courtroom procedures and assumptions. Berk-Seligson (1990: 62) provides the following example of an interpreter playing this role with a woman who cannot understand that she must say the word *culpable* (guilty):

> I: ¿Podría yo decirle? [addressing defendant] Parece, tiene usted que decirle al juez que es usted culpable o que no es culpable. [May I tell her? It seems that you have to tell the judge either than you're guilty or that you're not guilty.]
> W: Sí.
>   [yes]
> I: Yes
> DC: [addressing interpreter] So she's gotta say it, tell her to say it.
> I: O sea que tiene usted que decirlo. ¡Dígalo! ¿Qué es? [You have to say it. Say it! What are you?]

4. A further role is as a supporter and advocate of one side or the other. Officially this should not happen, but sometimes it does, through necessity, pressure or belief – Cooke (1995a: 73–6) discusses the role of 'interpreter as a Shield'.

5. The interpreter can be viewed as an expert/source of cross-cultural information. Niska (1995) gives as an example an interpreter being asked 'What is the legal status of manslaughter in Italy?'

6. The role of controller of courtroom discourse. In the example above, notice that the interpreter takes control of the discourse. When an interpreter asks a lawyer to repeat a question if the lawyer has interrupted the interpreting, the interpreter in effect takes control of the turn taking – s/he decides who will speak.

3. Elements prone to change in the interpreting process

There are a certain elements which tend to be changed in the interpreting process. Among those documented in the literature are a tendency to change the reference to the primary context, in other words the changes are made in reference to the courtroom reality, not what interpreters see as the 'meat and potatoes' reality (Berk-Seligson 1990: 142), the matter that is under litigation, in other words the secondary context. Giving lower priority to the primary context in the interpreting – for instance the courtroom or police station – can lead to changes in various aspects of reference to it. Many language subtleties are lost in the translation, as interpreters will often keep equivalence of propositional content but not of social meaning. Shifts in register, for example, are common in interpreted versions of both questions and testimony (Berk-Seligson 1990; Hale 1997), where interpreters change the register to facilitate understanding on both sides. There may be changes in question form and discourse markers.

One element that may be omitted in interpreting is reference to the courtroom itself, as in the next example (in examples of interpreting underlined elements are changed/omitted).

Source	*Interpreted version*
C: Can you tell the court what happened?	I: ¿Y luego qué pasó? [And then what happened?]
C: Well, wasn't the evidence you gave the court a minute ago, that he never touched the fence?	I: ¿Pero usted no dice hace un minuto que él no tocó la reja en ningún momento? [But don't (*sic*) you say a minute ago that he did not touch the railing at any time?]

The reduction in the representation of the courtroom in these examples is not limited to the court reference however. A change is produced by the deletion of 'can you tell' in the first two cases, removing the whole notion of 'versions of events', of a secondary reality projected through a here and now primary courtroom reality. The witness is not only asked to tell the story, he is specifically being asked to tell his version of the story to the court, which is bound by rules of evidence. This layer is completely lost in the interpreting. The fact that such statements are viewed as evidence is revealed explicitly in the wording of the second example, but deleted in the interpreting. Hale and Gibbons (1999) provide other examples where projection or reported speech is not interpreted, concealing from witnesses that their testimony is being constructed in a particular way – often one of doubt as to its truth. Particular legal formulas such as 'I put it to you that . . . ' are particularly likely to be modified, yet these are established markers of a leading question (see chapter 3) with all its legal baggage.

Another element of the primary context that may not be maintained in the interpreting process is politeness or tenor. Berk-Seligson (1990: 151–4) documents various changes in the use of titles such as *sir* and *señora*, for example Berk-Seligson (1990: 133):

Source	*Interpreted version*
C: How about a moustache?	I: ¿Y bigote tenía señora? [And did he have a moustache, <u>madam?</u>]

Hale and Gibbons (1999) discuss changes in the use of personal names, pronouns, indirect structures and the word *please*.

An aspect of courtroom and police language that is sometimes subject to change in interpreting is questioning. Chapter 3 showed that questioning is a finely tuned aspect of legal language, with subtle distinctions in coerciveness and the degree to which a response is expected. This may be a challenge for interpreters because question forms vary across languages – for instance most languages lack the complex system of tag questions found in English, and the functional equivalents will not convey precisely the same finely tuned meaning. Changes in questions are documented in Berk-Seligson (1999), Rigney (1999) and Hale and Gibbons (1999). These changes are important because questioning is central and fundamental to the legal process. Cooke (1995a) feels that this is not necessarily undesirable. He writes (Cooke 1995a: 73) 'It is true that an interpreter inevitably provides some degree of shielding from such a barrage [of hostile questioning], if only through impeding the pace of questioning or through relaying the questions in a more civil (and therefore less threatening) tone of voice. Also the word-traps that can be set by counsel are commonly, often inevitably, defused in the translation.'

Another language element in the language of the courtroom process that is subject to change (Berk-Seligson 1999: 140–2) is that of 'discourse markers' (Schiffrin, 1987). These are the 'little words' such as *well, oh, but, now* and *though* that often appear at the beginning or end of a sentence. On the surface these appear insignificant, but they provide considerable information about the speaker's attitude to what is said – for instance they may serve to weaken or strengthen the speaker's commitment to it. Berk-Seligson (1999: 141) give the following example and comment.

Source	Interpreted version
W: Es una casa chica	I: <u>Well</u>, it's a small house

The defendant's answer is a clear definite statement. The interpreter's rendition, in contrast, is a hedged way of offering the information.

Hale (1999) also suggests that discourse markers may act as coercive devices in questioning. She shows that most of these devices are missed during interpreting, perhaps because they are of low salience.

Berk-Seligson (1990) discusses at length an issue that I will call **hyperprecision**. It involves the supply of redundant information to ensure that there is no debate about meaning. It is related, although not identical to over-elaboration. It usually involves the provision of redundant information, sometimes by the interpreter. Berk-Seligson (1990: 133) gives the following example.

C: All right, do you remember whether or not he had a beard at that time?

I: ¿Se ac-, se acuerda usted, eh, <u>señora</u>, si entonces en ese tiempo tenía él barba?

[Do y-, do you remember señora if at that time he had a beard?]

W: Sí tenía [He did have]

I: He did have <u>a beard</u>

C: How about a moustache?

I: ¿Y bigote <u>tenía</u>, <u>señora</u>?

[And he <u>had</u> a moustache, <u>señora</u>?]

W: No me fijé si tenía bigote pero barba sí tenía.

(I did not notice if he had a moustache but he did have a beard)

I: I did not, did not notice if he had a moustache, but <u>I noticed though that</u> he had a beard.

Notice that all the extra information here is already supplied by the context. The interpreter expands the detail in both directions that is into Spanish and into English. Notice too that in the last sentence the extra information is a form of projection. Berk-Seligson (1990: 176) found that hyperprecision is positively evaluated. Even Hispanics who understood the pre-interpreted language were affected in the same way.

There are other changes that can be attributed more directly to language differences. One example from Spanish–English interpreting is the passive, which can be problematic because the passive in Spanish differs substantially from English. Spanish rarely uses the passive voice, particularly in speech. Any changes in this area are important for the practice of the law, because the active attributes responsibility or blame for an action to the actor, while a passive need not. Compare: 'Fred broke Jim's glasses' with 'Jim's glasses were/got broken'. In the first sentence Fred is responsible for the act. In the second, no one is. Berk-Seligson also refers to this reduction of blame as 'defocusing'. Compare the discussion in chapter 1 of Goldman's work on the role of ergativity in expressing liability, in contrast to accidentality.

The system for Spanish (based in part on Berk-Seligson 1990) is shown in table 7.1.

Table 7.1 Transitivity and blame in Spanish

high transitivity (more blameworthy)	
rompí un vaso [I broke a glass]	(active)
Un vaso fue roto [a glass was broken – implied by someone]	(true passive)
rompieron un vaso [literally: they broke a glass but also: a glass was broken]	(3rd plural impersonal)
se me rompió un vaso [a glass got broken around me]	(reflexive pseudo-passive with dative of interest)
se rompió un vaso [a glass got broken – no implied agent]	(reflexive pseudo-passive)
low transitivity (less blameworthy)	

English has only three levels (see table 7.2).

Table 7.2   Transitivity and blame in English

high transitivity
(more blameworthy)
I broke a glass
A glass was broken
A glass got broken
low transitivity
(less blameworthy)

We saw previously that frequent use of the passive is a characteristic of English legalese, so the interpreter is frequently forced to decide among the Spanish alternatives, none of which is exactly equivalent in terms of both semantics and register. Berk–Seligson assumes that English passives should be interpreted as Spanish passives, calling this 'accurate translation'. However the Spanish passive is both marked and formal, unlike the 'everyday' use of the passive in English. Often the nearest equivalent in everyday Spanish is the reflexive or impersonal third person plural. Berk–Seligson observes that in her courtroom data approximately only 20 per cent of English passives are interpreted as Spanish true passives. Spanish also tends to use the active where English would use the passive. In the courtroom this can be misleading. Berk–Seligson (1990: 114) gives this example:

C: As that bottle <u>was thrown</u>, Mr Jiménez saw it and tried to get a hand on it.

I: Cuando <u>tiró</u> la botella, el señor Jiménez la vió y trató de agarrarla
      [When <u>he threw</u> the bottle, Mr Jiménez saw it and tried to grab it.]

The interpreted form involves a substantial change in blame attribution. When Berk–Seligson (1990: 184) tested for the effects of lower passive use, the results showed that the use of the active voice is more highly evaluated for intelligence and trustworthiness, perhaps because it is more direct.

There are many interesting examples of the even greater linguistic difficulties posed by interpreting between Aboriginal languages and English in Cooke (1995a, 1995b, 1995c).

Conclusion

A partial solution to these problems in the interpreting process is training. Once interpreters are made aware of these language features, and the consequences of changing them, they are less likely to ignore or modify them. Furthermore interpreter training can discuss equivalents to the features in the other language, particularly in the case of the more formulaic aspects of courtroom language. This solution entails the professionalization of legal interpreting. While in many legal systems there are observable improvements in the status and pay of interpreters, rarely are they accorded the full status and pay of a professional. Yet, as we have seen, the work done by translators and interpreters is essential to maintain justice, and sustaining a high standard of translation/interpreting is extremely difficult.

There is a move in some countries to provide more extensive training for lawyers and other legal professionals in the demands and difficulties of legal interpreting and translation. This may improve the provision of the conditions that contribute to higher standards. 'The other alternative is for all involved to view interpreting as an imperfect process in an imperfect world, and to behave accordingly. The price of this solution is a lower standard of justice' (Hale and Gibbons 1999).

8

Law on Language

the use of the human voice as an instrument in committing crimes
has been steadily increasing

Künzel (1994)

people talk themselves and others into killing people

Blain (1995)

Introduction

Previous chapters discussed various relationships between the law and language. Legislation about language is another important area of this relationship. There are a large range of areas of legislation that have to do with
language. One of these is related to language planning, and it has to do
with the right to use certain languages for public purposes, such as bank-
ing, education or in court. Following Ó Riagáin and Nic Shuibhne (1997)
and a number of other writers, this area is discussed here as **language
rights**. Another area of considerable legal debate is the Common Law
right to silence: in this case the right not to use language, rather than to
use it. On a smaller scale, there are various kinds of linguistic act, such as
perjury, that are illegal. Following Shuy (1993) these are called **language
crimes**. The chapter ends with a discussion of the possible illegality of
vilification, of abuse targeted at individuals and groups, which has been
the subject of much legislation.

Language Rights

Around the world there have been many efforts to provide rights under
law to linguistic minorities, both in the prevention of discrimination and
the right to use their language (Ó Riagáin and Nic Shuibhne 1997). The
Mercator website <http://www.troc.es/ciemen/mercator/index-gb.htm>
is a rich source of information on the largely successful attempts of Euro-

pean linguistic minorities such as the Catalans, Basques, Bretons and Welsh to gain some official legal status for their language. Welsh, for instance, is an official language for judicial and local government purposes. By contrast Romany, partly because of the diffusion of its speakers (in Euro-speak it is a 'non-territorial autochthonous language') lacks such status in most of Europe.

The European charter on minority language rights addresses three major issues: the establishment of media in a range of minority language, the importance of education in minority languages and, perhaps most interestingly from a language and law perspective, it provides the right to interact with government agencies including the legal system in the minority language (see the last paragraph of the following extract). The resolution adopted by the European parliament on 16 October 1981 reads:

1   Requests National Governments and regional and local authorities, despite the wide differences in their situations and having due regard for the degree of independence which they enjoy, to implement a policy in this field inspired by and designed to achieve the same objectives, and calls on them:

(a)   in the field of education:
to allow and promote the teaching of regional languages and cultures in official curricula right through from nursery school to university;

to allow and provide for, in response to needs expressed by the population teaching in schools of all levels and grades to be carried out in regional languages, with particular emphasis being placed on nursery schools teaching so as to ensure that the child is able to speak its mother tongue;

to allow teaching of the literature and history of the communities concerned to be included in all curricula;

(b)   in the field of mass communications:
to allow and take steps to ensure access to local radio and television in a way that guarantees consistent and effective community communication and to encourage the training of specialist regional presenters;

to ensure that minority groups receive organizational and financial assistance for their cultural events equivalent to that received by the majority groups;

(c)   in the field of public life and social affairs:

to assign in accordance with the Bordeaux declaration of the Council of
Europe Conference of Local Authorities, a direct responsibility to the
local authorities in this matter;

to promote as far as possible a correspondence between cultural regions
and the greographical boundaries of the local authorities;

to ensure that individuals are allowed to use their own language in the
field of public life and social affairs in their dealings with official bodies
and in the courts;

Another resolution of the European Parliament, 9 February 1994
(A3-0042/94) states that the parliament

3   Believes, furthermore, that all minority languages and cultures should
    also be protected by appropriate legal statute in the Member States;

4   Considers that this legal statute should at least cover the use and encour-
    agement of such languages and cultures in the spheres of education,
    justice and public administration, the media, toponymics and other sec-
    tors of public and cultural life without prejudice to the use of the most
    widespread languages, when required to ensure ease of communication
    within each of the Member States or in the Union as a whole;

5   Points out that the fact that a proportion of the citizens of a state use a
    language or have a culture which is different from the dominant one in
    that state or from the dominant one in a part or region of that state
    should not give rise to discrimination of any kind or, in particular, to any
    form of social marginalisation that would impede their access to, or
    continuance in, employment;

New member states are expected to take note of this. A good example of
the practical outcome (particularly for those who are familiar with Gal's
(1979) classic study of language shift) came with the entry of Austria into
the European Union. This was in the form of the amendment to the law
on ethnic groups published in the Austrian government bulletin
Bundesgesetzblatt of 20 July 2000, which became law on 1 October 2000. It
states that in addition to German, the Hungarian language is an official
language of administration in the regions of Oberpullendorf and Oberwart
and citizens have the right to use Hungarian in police stations and courts,
in contacts with the local government, in post offices, on the railways and
in the armed forces. Another example of this type of provision has meant

in Spain that judges who preside in minority language areas must either learn the minority language, or organize translation at their own expense.

In Canada, too, over recent decades the place of French has been strengthened, particularly in Quebec and New Brunswick. Bourhis (1984) offers an account of the legislation introduced in Quebec, which in effect establishes French as the dominant language of the province. New Brunswick is the only officially bilingual province of Canada, in which it is law that both French and English can be used for all official purposes, including education, health care and the law. In other countries there has been a bloody pursuit of minority language rights – for instance Kurdish in Turkey, and Albanian in Kosovo.

Kaplan and Baldauf (2001) note that the USA appears to be moving in the reverse direction to most western countries. Under the influence of the US English movement, it has been tending to outlaw the use of minority languages for institutional purposes, and legislation to this effect has been introduced in a majority of states of the USA. A balanced account of the debate can be found in Edwards (1994: 166–70). The arguments in favour of English only legislation are mainly concerned with the need to maintain social cohesion in an ethnically diverse nation, and are framed within a melting pot ideology. The policy militates against linguistic minorities maintaining the language element of their ethnic identity. Both Edwards (1994) and Kaplan and Baldauf (2001) feel that the dominance of English in the USA is not endangered, and find it difficult to determine concrete benefits from such legislation, while they perceive various negative outcomes in terms of social justice, because it means that adult migrants with limited English may have difficulty in accessing public services.

The Right to Silence

In the discussion of turn taking in chapter 3, it was demonstrated that silence in interaction is governed by conversational rules. This means that silence can be meaningful, a point also made by sociolinguists (Jaworski 1993; Tannen and Saville-Troike 1985). Kurzon (1998) proposes a number of possible types of silence, including unintentional silence, an inability to speak for psychological or emotional reasons or through lack of knowledge, an intentional unwillingness to speak and silence imposed by others – for example in courtroom examination witnesses are often told they must remain silent on certain issues, and in the wider community silence concerning certain issues may be legally imposed by official secrets acts. On the other hand, a witness who is not a suspect is generally obliged to answer and not remain silent. Refusal to answer questions from police or in court can be punishable by law.

Often in everyday life, if a person is accused, silence is taken as assent, as an admission of guilt. As Kurzon (1998: 58) remarks, in the case of intentional silence 'it would be generally held that the silent person is hiding something'. In the Common Law however this does not in general apply – the right to silence is a Common Law right, and in the case of suspects or those accused, no inference is allowed to be made on the basis of silence (although there is some question as to whether jurors always adhere to this, given the resistance to jury instructions mentioned in chapter 5). This right emerged originally from the notion that people should not be expected to testify against themselves, and it is embedded in the US constitution. This right is explicitly spelled out to suspects in the form of a 'caution', or in the USA a 'warning' (see chapter 5 for a discussion of the wording of these). Kurzon (1998: 51–7) presents three American and one Jamaican case in which an accused did not speak, either before or during a trial. In each case any presumption of guilt based on silence was rejected.

There have been challenges to the right to silence in Australia and elsewhere. In Britain the eleventh report of the Criminal Law Review Committee in 1972 argued strongly for silence to be interpreted as it would be in everyday life, since allowing suspects to remain silent frustrated police investigations and (p. 21) 'the present law and practice are much too favourable to the defence'. However it was not until IRA suspects began to regularly use their right to silence that the law was changed in 1988 in Northern Ireland, and later in England and Wales, to allow silence to be taken into account at trials. These changes allowed both judge and counsel to comment on and interpret silence during police or courtroom questioning, and the police caution was modified to warn suspects that if they remained silent during police interrogation they might harm their defence 'Now, the refusal to answer questions put by the police may result in such silence being taken into account when deciding on the case at trial' (Kurzon 1998: 60). In Australia the common use (perhaps abuse) of the right to silence by habitual criminals has been frequently raised, particularly by frustrated police officers, but so far the law has not been changed. The opposing view is presented with some force in Baldwin (1994), where the right to silence is seen as a primary protection for those least able to protect themselves against coercive or pressured questioning – the weaker, the less educated, the intellectually impaired.

In Roman Law countries the right to silence does not take the same form. For instance in French criminal law, while an accused does not have to answer, the court is free to draw inferences from this silence.

Ireland (1993) discusses a customary law investigation into the killing of a child where silence is regarded as a highly significant indicator of the views of the tribal chief. This contrasts with the limitations on the interpretation of silence in the Common Law tradition discussed previously.

Language Crimes

This section discusses the surprising amount of language behaviour that can be the object of legal action. There are a number of speech acts that may be illegal – in other words there are crimes committed by performing some kind of illocutionary act, such as offering a bribe; accepting a bribe; threats; extortion; perjury; suborning a person to a language crime; soliciting an illegal act (e.g. hiring a hitman); using foul language. There is not sufficient space here to discuss every possible language crime, so the discussion is limited to well documented and analysed examples. This section is strongly influenced by Shuy (1993).

Not all speech behaviour that is the object of litigation is treated as illegal. Many civil cases are concerned with breaches of contract – in essence whether or not a promise has been broken. These are handled as disputes between parties, rather than as crimes. There may also be language behaviour that is subject to regulation rather than law, and therefore is not strictly a language crime: for example Woolls and Coulthard (1998) discuss a plagiarism case where students were suspected of collaborating on a essay. Since this is related to authorship it is discussed further in the next chapter. Testimony on language crimes is a form of linguistic evidence, so it forms a bridge into the next chapter.

Methodology

There are several sources that a linguist will need to consult in order to understand whether or not a particular example of language behaviour is subject to the law. The most important of these is the legislation or regulation that applies to the case. Legislation or regulations will need to be carefully examined to see how they define the language crime. However, legislation and regulation, as we shall see, often leave such issues poorly defined, so a linguist will also need to examine common sense constructions and social consensus as to the nature of particular communicative acts – what constitutes foul language for instance. The linguist may also wish to examine other instances of language behaviour that are labelled in this way, in order to determine their characteristics. The analysis may then involve analysis of the contested language itself, of the relevant legislation and of the wider use of the particular communicative act. It may also involve the examination of similar but different (perhaps legal) acts, to see how they differ from the contested language. The linguist may need to examine the semantic detail of the act, and of the conditions that are necessary for it to be performed (see Searle (1969) for the framework of conditions under which speech acts are performed).

The speech act framework is, however, possibly misleading in that it tends to treat language behaviour only at the sentence or utterance level. Many of the verbal events in which we engage in daily life consist of a number of speech acts in sequence, which are needed together in order to perform a particular function (see for example the description in Hasan (1985) on the function of making a purchase). If such ordered sequences of speech acts become the consensus way of performing a particular function, they constitute genres of the type discussed in chapter 4. Like individual speech acts, the conditions and obligatory components of the genre will need to be established by analysis both of the legislation and of common sense notions. The detail of the analysis may involve the elements of communication presented in the Introduction: the knowledge schemas assumed by the legislation, and of those subject to the law; relevant language levels (grammar, words, etc.); and the context.

Once the exact nature of the language behaviour that is described and prescribed in legislation is determined, and the contested language has been studied, the next step is a matching process, to discover the contested language's degree of fit to the legislation, for example to see whether the contested language performed the speech act defined in the legislation. This will include once more a close examination of its semantics, involving lexical, grammatical and discoursal analysis, and of its pragmatics – whether, if it is an illegal speech act, it meets the conditions for the performance of such a speech act. It may also be necessary to take other aspects of communication into account, including non-verbal information (for instance a fist shaken under a nose strengthens the case for the speech act being a threat). Elements of the linguistic and physical context enter into the pragmatic considerations, and some understanding of the cultural context, and of the activated schemas of the participants may be required. Instances of these can be found in the examples that follow. A number of language crimes will now be examined, and some examples are given of how particular elements of language behaviour did or did not fit these categories.

Perjury

I begin with this category because Tiersma (1990) in his analysis of this language crime discusses several of the issues just mentioned. Perjury is in essence lying when giving evidence in a legal context. Tiersma (1990) discusses the Bronston case (*Bronston v. United States*, 409 US 352 (1973)), in which Bronston (B) engaged in the following exchange in court.

C: Do you have any bank accounts in Swiss banks, Mr Bronston?
B: No, sir.
C: Have you ever?
B: The company had an account there for about six months, in Zurich.

In fact Bronston previously had a large personal bank account in Switzerland for five years. Bronston's reply is truthful, but is clearly intended to mislead in the linguistic context. The original verdict was guilty, but the US Supreme Court reversed this decison because the words were literal truth. The legal model of language that underlies this second decision is linguistically ill-informed, because it does not take into account the pragmatic aspect of language. Meaning is dependent upon context. Another way of viewing the problem is to say that truthfulness is not dependent only on linguistic form, but also on the reading that the speaker intends the hearer to give the utterance (see also the section on interpretation in chapter 2). This issue is still developing in the courts, since there is a case that perjury needs to be narrowly interpreted to avoid aggressive prosecution of truthful witnesses on the grounds that they were hoping to be misunderstood.

Bribery

Shuy (1993) describes bribery as a genre which contains two possible language crimes – offering a bribe and accepting a bribe. *Black's Law Dictionary* (1990: 191) defines bribery as 'The offering, giving, receiving or soliciting of something of value for the purpose of influencing the action of an official in the discharge of his or her public duties' establishing a number of criteria for the construction of this crime. Shuy provides a description of the bribery genre which involves both crimes. It might be expanded slightly to include boundary stages (which he mentions in the body of his description), and it is necessary to add the possibility of iteration, that is of recycling through some or all of the stages. Shuy's description is based on listening to FBI tapes of many instances of bribery and bribery attempts.

A slightly revised version of the genre is shown in table 8.1 – the stages are in bold.

Shuy provides the example of a genuine completed bribery event shown in Table 8.2. In the table, the 'Extension' stage is optional, as are most of the elements in the third column. There is also the possibility of recycling to a previous stage – for instance even after completion the deal may be renegotiated, returning to the 'Proposal' stage. Clearly Acceptance, Rejection and Delay are either/or choices.

Shuy makes the important point that this is the same genre structure as a business deal. It is therefore essential to establish from the wording of the Offer that the content of the negotiation is illegal. To establish that the receiver is guilty it is also essential to show that the receiver understands and perceives the transaction as a bribe (i.e. that the perlocutionary force is that of a bribe) and that the bribe is accepted. This involves delicate analysis of conversational phenomena and the circumstances.

The example of bribery given in table 8.2 comes from a case where a con-man, Joe Hauser, was working for the FBI, and managed to involve a union leader, L. G. Moore, in corrupt operations. Moore offers Hauser the chance to involve the speaker of the Texas State House of Representatives, Billy Clayton. The bribery event begins with a confusing conversational turn from Moore (to Clayton) about who is offering money – is it 'I' or 'we'?

Moore: Can **I**, can **I** do it Joe? And **I** wanna, **we** wanna, **we** want to, and if it puts you in a bad situation you tell **me**. **We** want to make a contribution to your campaign . . .

This issue of pronoun reference is central, because it is legal for an **individual** to make a campaign contribution, but there are legal problems with **organizations** making contributions. Moore and Hauser begin the interview by proposing a scheme to save the State of Texas millions of dollars on insurance, then attempt to bribe Clayton to go along with their scheme.

Table 8.1 Bribery genre

Genre stage	Bribe offerer		Bribe receiver	
	Speech function	Elements	Speech function	Elements
Problem	Request help		Respond to problem	
	Check	conditions control of receiver	Provide	conditions control of receiver
Proposal	Present offer	service products payment money discussed	Consider offer Negotiate	service products payment money discussed
			Make conditions	
	Re-check	conditions control details	Re-check	conditions control details
	Establish trust	stories in-group language humour	Establish trust	stories in-group language humour
Completion	Agreement	handshake written contract speech act (e.g. 'It's a deal')	Agreement or	handshake written contract speech act (e.g. 'It's a deal')
			Rejection or delay	
(If agreement)				
Extension	Plan other deals Offer contacts		Plan other deals Offer contacts	

Table 8.2   Bribe event structure shown in actual bribe event

Phase	Joe Hauser	Target
Problem	We'd like to get some state business.	I will have to work out something, Joe, where you could visit with the trustees.
	Do you control Mr Gordon?	He'll go along with a lot of things I recommend.
	How do you and I develop a relationship?	I have a public relations firm . . . and I do business other than what I'm doing here.
Proposal	I can give you $2,000 now, with a 50–50 split of the commission.	Keep talking.
	I deal only with you. There's $4,000 a month possible in this.	We'll deal on a case by case basis. Can you handle X Insurance Company politics?
Completion	Here's $2,000. Let's shake hands on it. Do we have a deal?	We have a deal.
Extension		There's 50 people I can send you. I have contacts in Boston.

Source: Shuy 1993: 24

In this context, the problem is whether, in the following extract from the proposal stage of the bribery event, Clayton accepts a bribe. Note that after Clayton says 'Oh sure' Moore places $5,000 dollars on Clayton's desk.

Shuy says that Clayton does not accept a bribe. In the first offer, there is an unclear 'we', so Clayton makes a polite refusal. In the next exchange, Clayton accepts a legal $5,000 campaign contribution, framed as an 'I' event, that is as a legal personal donation. The next unclear offer of $100,000 is again met with a polite refusal. Only after this does Hauser in his statement about $600,000 make it clear that there is a bribe offer under way. This offer to split the commission is rejected in a clearly exculpatory way.

Hauser subsequently asserted that because $5,000 had changed hands in the context of a bribe offer, it was a bribe. However, it is not possible to

Hauser and Moore's proposals

Insurance proposal to save the State money	Campaign contribution	Offer to split commission	Clayton's responses
JH: There will be a saving of approximately a million dollars			. . . anytime you can save the State a buck, well By God, I'm for it.
	LGM: We want to make a contribution to your campaign		Let's get this thing and try to take care of it first . . . and uh, then, then, then, uh, then let's think about that.
	LGM: Could I, L. G. Moore . . . give you a contribution?		Oh, sure.
	LGM: We will put, I will, in your whatever you want to run. $100,000 going in and we can prepare to put a half a million		Anytime you can show me where you can save the State money I'll, by God, I'll go to battle for you. I think that's what part of my job is . . . try to save the State.
	LGM: That's all the commitment we want out of you.	JH: There's $600,000 every year. I'm keeping 600 and 600 whatever you want to do with it to get the business	. . . our only position is we don't want to do anything that's illegal or anything to get anybody in trouble and you all don't either.
			And this is as legitimate as it can be because anytime somebody can show me how we can help to save the State some money I'm going to bat for it.

Source: Shuy 1993: 48–9

change the speech act of the donation **after** the event. On the basis of Shuy's evidence, Clayton was acquitted. Note the delicacy of the analysis, with careful treatment of pronoun use and turn taking.

Threats

Threats are slippery speech acts. In order for an explicit threat to be performed, a specific future action and the participants need to be specified – for example 'I will hit you'. However, many threats are far less explicit, and may be indirect, as in these examples from Storey (1995).

- I'll get you
- Your days are numbered
- I'm watching you
- I'll stop you
- Touch that and you die

Only the last overtly offers physical violence, but it is in fact a formula used among school children. The others are all genuine threats, and one of them was followed by a murder. The following extract from *Black's Law Dictionary* definition of threat makes it clear that the context of an utterance is basic to determining whether or not a threat has been made: 'A communicated intent to inflict physical or other harm on any person or property. . . . In determining whether words were uttered as a threat the context in which they were spoken must be considered.' Shuy (1993: 108–9) mentions a case in which the expression 'How's David' was regarded as a serious threat. Therefore one must consider the physical and social context, the background in the participants' minds (their activated schemas), and the receiver's reading (i.e. the perlocutionary force) to get some idea of whether they act as threats. The following could be a threat or a warning: 'Do not carry illicit drugs – penalties are severe' (Australian Customs Leaflet). (This was in fact preceded by a performative 'Be warned'.)

Table 8.4, based on Shuy (1993), gives a means of distinguishing promises, warnings and advice from threats.

Although this provides the basics for making a decision, it may still be difficult in cases such as these: 'Beware of the Thing' (Addams family); 'It's your decision, but your husband will die if you contact the police'. In the first example, the issues of benefit or detriment and control are unclear. In the latter case, a wife who wishes her husband to die is deciding the out-

Table 8.4   A means of distinguishing promises, warnings and advice from threats

	Receiver's benefit or detriment?	Perspective of speaker or receiver?	Outcome under control of speaker or receiver?
Threat	detriment	speaker's perspective	speaker control
Promise	benefit	speaker's perspective	speaker control
Warning	?	speaker's perspective	listener control
Advice	benefit	listener's perspective	listener control

Source: Shuy 1993

come. This shows an example where the intention of the speaker (the illocution) is a threat (speaker control, receiver's detriment), but the reading given by the listener (the perlocution) is not (it is receiver's benefit and control). In legal matters it is mainly the illocution that counts. Yamanaka (1995) provides a finely detailed account of how these three elements of benefit, perspective and outcome can be determined when threats are indirect. He notes (Yamanaka, 1995: 46) for instance that 'August 27 is approaching' can only be a taken as referring to the receiver's detriment (and therefore be a threat) in the context of a previous utterance concerning that date.

The example in table 8.5 is part of a childish shouting match, where two grown men were 'one-upping' each other. The question is whether threats were being made.

Shuy gave evidence, first that was no threat on the basis of Tyner's specific denials of duress and threats in 4, 6 and 12. Questions remain over exchanges 8 and 15. Using the evidence from previous analyses of one-upping behaviour, Shuy convinced the jury that these were examples of Tyner 'one-upping' Blackburn. This, then, is an example of the process of examining and comparing other language behaviour, and finding an alternative reading. Shuy also noted that they were not explicit threats, since neither a concrete action nor an agent was suggested. Shuy also testified that another supposed threat made by Tyner was so indirect that it was clearly open to a range of interpretations. Tyner was acquitted.

Conspiracy

Conspiracy, like incitement (see Shuy 1993) is linguistic behaviour that may be associated with any crime. It is not the crime that is at issue, but

Table 8.5   Possible threats from Tyner

Blackburn's complaints	Tyner's responses
1 I was under duress.	I don't care what Vernon told you.
2 I don't appreciate you settin' me up like that.	O
3 I don't know why ya'll trying to pull these games.	It ain't games.
4 You'd have one hurt over just one little ol' share.	I wouldn't have you hurt, Michael.
5 You were gonna have me killed over one share.	Why don't you just leave?
6 I signed under duress.	No, I don't think there was any duress.
7 You just want to fuck me out of this money don't you.	Nope.
8 If I have to hire me a body guard to take care of me, I'll do it.	You can't hire enough body guards to take care of you Blackburn.
9 Well you were gonna sell it under the table.	NO, no, no, no, no.
10 I've seen too many done that way.	You haven't seen shit, man.
11 Don't send David over to set me up.	Just leave.
12 You accosted me in my own home.	No I didn't accost you.
13 You made it appear that you would if I didn't do what you told me to do.	No.
14 If you'd treat people the way they ought to be treated.	Oh, have I mistreated you, poor little baby.
15 Well I can hide where he can't find me.	You can't hide forever.
16 You don't scare me Don Tyner.	Well then just leave, baby.

Source: Shuy 1993: 106–7

the agreement to commit a crime. For conspiracy to be entered into, evidence is required that a party did in fact enter into such an agreement. Green (1990) documents a case where a young man was accused of conspiracy to distribute cocaine. A major piece of evidence was a covert recording of a conversation with an FBI agent and a drug dealer. The question in this case was whether the young man truly participated and was truly aware that a drug deal was taking place. Green shows through a careful and detailed discourse analysis of pronoun use, and the man's contributions to the discussion, including markers of cooperation (such as 'yeah'), answers to questions, topic management, clarification requests, interruptions and turn taking, as well as some of the incomprehension markers discussed in chapter 7, that he never actively participated in the deal itself, and that he may not have been aware that a drug deal was taking place, indeed that he was not in fact engaged in the conversation at all, and was not even attending to it – leaving it to the other participants. This testimony was not admitted by the judge, but was successfully used by the young man's attorney, and he was acquitted.

Vilification

Vilification is defined in the *OED* as 'speak ill of, defame'. I am using it here as a cover term for offensive language, and two forms of defamation, defamation targeted at groups, and defamation targeted at individuals or entities, usually called slander, libel or defamation. All these types of vilification can involve the tort 'intentional infliction of emotional distress'.

Offensive language

The situation in Australia is particularly interesting, and well documented on this issue. The NSW 1988 Summary Offences Act states:

(1) A person shall not –

. . .

(b) use offensive language in or near, or within hearing from, a public place or a school.

(2) It is sufficient defence to a prosecution for an offence under this section if the defendant satisfies the court that the defendant had a reasonable excuse for conducting himself or herself in the manner alleged in the information for the offence.

The maximum punishment for this offence was up to 3 months in prison, only changed to a fine in 1993. The question asked by Walsh (1995) is 'What is offensive?' The test proposed by the courts is 'whether reasonable persons in the relevant place and at the relevant time, and in the circumstances there and then prevailing, would be likely to be seriously alarmed or seriously affronted'. It is noticeable that this test depends on the immediate context, including the participants and their schemas. It provides little real information, leaving it open to the judgment of the judge concerning who is a reasonable person, and what is likely to alarm or affront them. There is also a defence of a 'reasonable excuse', for instance if someone drops a hammer on their foot.

The extreme discretion within this legislation is dangerous, since in 1993 Amnesty International reported that it was used overwhelming to imprison or fine Aborigines, who were twenty-seven times more likely to go to prison than other Australians. To a lesser extent the same is true for younger and working class people. Around 5,000 people a year were found guilty of this offence in the mid 1990s. In part this form of behaviour is a product of cultural differences concerning swearing (Cowlishaw 1988: 173, 194–5). There is also the likelihood (in Australia and elsewhere) that swearing, like a range of taboo language behaviours, carries less weight in a second language – the use in English of Latin words for sexual organs, rather than the (originally non-offensive) Anglo-Saxon terms, is an example.

Taylor (1995) provides a detailed description of swearing in Australian English, including the conditions under which it may occur. He also documents the hypocrisy surrounding the offence, showing that the law makers, high ranking politicians of both the left and right, use the more offensive swearwords (sometimes in public) with impunity (as did the American president Lyndon B. Johnson), and that the law enforcers, the police, use such language to people that they subsequently arrest for using it to them: for example one Aboriginal man was charged for saying to police 'Don't tell me to get fucked', clearly responding to the police use of the term. Langton (1988) provides more examples.

Defamation: slander and libel

Slander and libel are both forms of defamation, and in broad terms the difference between them is that slander involves ordinary speech, while libel involves publication, mostly in written form. *The Oxford English Dictionary* defines slander as 'false report maliciously uttered to person's injury', and *Black's Legal Dictionary* defines defamation as 'An intentional false communication, either published or publicly spoken, that injures another's reputation or good name'. These definitions contain three issues (1) whether the report is **true or false**; (2) whether the report is 'malicious' – in other words whether any harm is **intentional**; and (3) whether the report **harms** the other person's **reputation**. In principle all three conditions need to be met for the act to take place, and the level of any compensation would depend mainly on the extent of harm. Looking at how these apply in English law, concerning **truth**, proof of truth or falsehood often involves minute attention to the language of the report under examination. However, another element of English law is that the defamation can be by implication or **innuendo**. Such **innuendo** need not conform to any legal notion of construction, it can be 'what meaning would be attached to the words by a reasonable man' who knew the relevant facts (Gatley 1998). A defence based on the notion that facts published are true is also risky, because if the case is found against the publisher, extra damages are awarded for repeating the defamation.

The Common Law does not agree with the *OED* on the second issue of **intention** – my (limited) understanding is that intention is not always necessary for defamation to take place. For example, in the case of *Cassidy v. Daily Mirror Newspaper* [1929] 2 KB 331 at page 354 Russell LJ held that 'the liability of libel does not depend on intention of the defamer, but on the fact of defamation'. Indeed a publisher can be held liable even when unaware of the defamatory nature of a report – in *Lee v. Wilson and MacKinnon* (1934) 51 CLR at page 288: 'It might be thought therefore, than in any event, this warranted or required some investigation of the actual intention of the publisher. But his liability depends upon mere communication of the defamatory matter to a third person. The communication may be quite unintentional, and the publisher may be unaware of the defamatory matter.' Finally, proving **harm** to one's reputation is quite difficult, but such proof is not always required – it is often assumed on a common sense basis, or it is regarded as sufficient that the text **could** harm the person's reputation. Interestingly, exactly the same position has been arrived at in some Roman Law jurisdictions, such as Chile (Montero Brunner 1996).

In the USA it is difficult and less common for a person to be successfully sued for slander since the constitutional right to free speech is often taken to override other considerations. In the other main branch of the Common Law, derived from Britain, slander and libel are still actively pursued in court. A well-known recent example is the so-called McLibel case, in which McDonalds sued two British environmental activists over a brochure in which they made certain claims about McDonalds' food, and the activities that lie behind its production. The case led to intense media coverage. The two accused conducted their own defence, which they based mainly on the truthfulness of their claims. On a number of issues they were exonerated, but on others they were found liable.

Group Vilification

The debate on vilification, and on the extent to which it should be legally controlled, is by no means simple. Apart from the difficulty of proving vilification, it involves a balance between two major competing values of a civilized society – freedom of speech and freedom from vilification and distress.

These competing values will both be briefly described. Looking first at the freedom of speech case, Freedman and Freedman (1995) say in their introduction concerning the USA 'Along with the Equal Protection Clause, the greatest safeguard of minority rights in this country is the First Amendment's guarantee of freedom of speech and association – an essential limitation on the power of the majority to impose its will on any minority.' For those who support democracy, it is important to recognize that freedom of speech, particularly public criticism, is essential. A common action of dictatorial and corrupt rulers is to restrict freedom of speech. Limitations placed on freedom of speech impugn the judgment of speakers and therefore tend to be intensely resented, perhaps doing more harm than good to minority groups. Smolla (1993) argues that hate speech is more effectively battled through persuasion and education on the values of tolerance, civility and respect for human dignity rather than through punishment and coercion. Leets and Giles (1997) write 'Deprecating speech is a rape of human dignity that needs to be vigorously confronted, but perhaps not through the heavy hand of the law'. Restrictions on freedom of speech open the door to further limitations, and to abuse by their extension to restrict behaviour other than that intended. It is important to take into account the possible consequences of suppression of freedom of speech, of the risk involved in not allowing prejudices and misrepresentation to be publicly aired where they can be publicly refuted, of the danger of forcing them underground to fester. Those who say this price (i.e. loss of freedom of speech) must be paid, need to keep a reckoning of the cost.

The opposing view is that vilification can have profoundly undesirable consequences. It is argued that it can cause emotional pain among its targets, and hate-filled words can lead to hate-filled action. Therefore, in order to justify legislation on vilification, it is necessary to provide evidence that words can wound, and that hate language can lead to hate action. The remainder of this section on group vilification will examine such evidence, then the issues involved in attempting to frame legislation to control racist language will be addressed.

Group vilification, sometimes inaccurately referred to as 'hate speech' (it is in fact often written), is used to denigrate people not only on the basis of their biological race, but also their political nationality, cultural ethnicity, age, physical condition, disability, religion, gender and sexual orientation. I will concentrate on racial vilification as the form of vilification most widely legislated against, but the issues are similar across all forms of vilification. van Dijk (1987) provides a useful account of racist language. In some countries there are institutions charged with pursuing cases of vilification.

Speech act understandings

This section is based in part on the proposal in Celis (1999). Legal discussion of vilification usually involves three participants, a speaker, an intended hearer and the 'reasonable person'. It also involves issues of the speaker's intended speech act (the illocution), and the reading of this that might be made by the intended hearer, or the reasonable person (the perlocution). These variables interact in various ways. The clearest and simplest cases are the following three.

1. The speaker may not intend to hurt the hearer (the illocution), and a 'reasonable person' would interpret the illocution in this way (perlocution). This is clearly not defamation

2. The speaker may not intend to hurt the hearer (illocution), but a 'reasonable person' would interpret the illocution as hurtful (perlocution) so the speaker is guilty of not taking reasonable care.

3. The speaker intended to hurt the hearer (illocution), and a 'reasonable person' would interpret the illocution as hurtful (perlocution). This is vilification.

However, there may be problem cases.

4. The speaker intended to hurt the hearer (illocution), and a 'reasonable person' would interpret the illocution as hurtful (perlocution), but the hearer felt no hurt. It could be hard to justify this as a case of vilification.

5. The speaker may not intend to hurt the hearer (illocution), and a 'reasonable person' would interpret the illocution in this way (perlocution), but a particular type of hearer has particular sensibilities which cause that hearer to be hurt by the language.

An issue in the last type of case (which is the type that tends to be tendentious and widely reported) is whether the speaker was, or could reasonably be expected to be aware of these sensibilities, since the law provides for penalties for both deliberate harm, and for unintentional harm. An issue in unintentional harm is whether reasonable care was taken to avoid the harm.

As with offensive language, there is a problem with the 'reasonable person'. In judgments it often seems that reasonable person readings are in fact a reading of the degree to which, within a particular speech community, a particular meaning has been linked to a particular language form, in Givón's (1985) terms 'grammaticised'.

Can words wound?

Tajfel's social identity theory (Tajfel and Turner 1979) reveals that in order to maintain a positive social identity, social groups may engage in out-group derogation and in-group favouritism. This can be manifested (sometimes quite subtly) in various ways which have the potential to cause emotional distress. One is by linguistic divergence (see Giles and Coupland 1991: 60–126). This can be a group phenomenon, such as the development of a distinctive accent, or slang (e.g. teenagers) which marks membership of the in-group and distances the out-group; or an individual phenomenon, for example in conversation, code-switching to a variety that the outsider does not speak. This would be difficult to bring to court. A second means is the use of linguistically constructed categories: for instance on one occasion my careful 'speakers of English as a second language' was translated by a journalist as 'migrants'. In Australia 'Australian culture' often means 'Anglo-

Australian', excluding even the original inhabitants of Australia, the Aborigines ('Ozzie tucker' means anglo food, not bush food). This may be the unconscious expression of an ideology, in which case it is an indirect expression of prejudice and is probably not actionable, but it can also be used deliberately to wound. The third and most extreme way of distinguishing the in-group from the out-group is direct vilification. This is illegal in many but not all countries. The most noteworthy exception is the USA, where constitutionally protected freedom of speech overrides protection against racial vilification.

The issue arising is how we can demonstrate that these forms of language behaviour, both direct and indirect vilification, cause **harm** to the receiver. Can we prove (particularly in court) that words wound? There are a range of types of harm. The most serious form of harm occurs when the receiver internalizes and believes the derogatory stereotype and inferiority expressed in the racist language. This might be hard to prove (although Lambert, Frankel and Tucker (1966) provide clear evidence of French Canadians of that era internalizing negative stereotypes of themselves). Other long-term effects might be: sleeplessness, nightmares, depression, hypertension and reduced self-esteem. The latter could be testified to in court by a doctor or psychologist. Short-term effects could include: embarrassment, humiliation, fear, anger, shame, hurt, anxiety, etc., to which the victim would need to testify.

The law also distinguishes between intentional acts and unintentional acts that are a result of a lack of care, which may still be culpable, but less so than intentional acts. See also Goldman (1993) on the importance of establishing **intention** as part of culpability.

A third legal issue is establishing the **severity** of the vilification – some legislation prescribes a level of severity before an offence is committed, and punishment or monetary compensation may also reflect the severity of the act.

An interesting attempt was made in Leets and Giles (1997) to examine various of these issues. The studies used a social psychological approach, with various stimulus materials containing racist language and questionnaires which were completed by university students. An important finding was the response to the following questions:

In general how painful is it for you to have people treat you *without* dignity?
In general, do you think psychological pain is worse than physical pain?
In general, is psychological pain harder to endure than physical pain?

The first question scored 6.48 on a 7-point scale. In other words, to be treated without dignity is extremely painful. The subjects also found psychological pain both harder to endure and worse than physical pain. On this evidence, words wound.

Leets and Giles (1997) first study involved the use of scenarios, involving two levels of intentionality (directness), and two levels of severity. The second study used a clip from the film 'The Joy Luck Club' in which the racism was more covert. In both studies subjects indicated high levels of the following: displeasure at having their identity attacked; anxiety after hate speech; social harm; group harm and individual harm. They indicated low levels of acceptance and tolerance of hate speech.

With regard to whether the respondent was Asian or not, the difference was that the Asians saw unintentional racist speech as more harmful than the intentional type, while the non-Asian subjects felt the reverse. (In other words, the recipients of racism find it more difficult to cope with people who do not realize that they are being racist, the racism that arises from flawed understanding rather than malice.) This is in conflict with the legal position, since criminalizing unintentional behaviour is problematic. Overall the studies provide empirical support for the notion that vilification is psychologically harmful.

Can hate language lead to hate action?

In Blain's (1995) words, do 'people talk themselves and others into killing people'? The answer to this question can be found in history. Blain documents the long history in Europe of a negative construction of the Jews. As early as the fifteenth century in Austria they were depicted as eating Aryan children. There was also a well established nineteenth-century negative stereotype of the ghetto Jew. In much of the adult and children's literature of the Nazi era ethnic groups are portrayed in terms of Germanic myth: the Germans are portrayed as 'Ubermensch' (supermen) and Aryan knights, while the Jews are described as 'sly', 'egotistical' and 'cunning'. This develops into the portrayal of Jews as 'Untermensch' (subhuman) and 'racial monsters'. Other terms used are 'criminal', 'parasite', 'germ', 'maggot on an open wound' and the 'Antichrist'. They are portrayed in both word and image as 'vermin'. A normal response to parasites, germs, maggots and vermin is to kill them. This is the verbal means by which a basis for genocide can be constructed. However, while Jews are constructed negatively, their genocide is constructed positively – the word 'killing' is never used in the bureaucratic structures used to carry out the Holocaust. Instead we read of 'The Final Solution to the Jewish Problem' (*die Endlosung der Judenfrage*). The bureaucrats consistently refer to 'evacuation' and 're-settlement' to the extermination camps. The crematorium was a 'bakery'. (There are parallels in more recent language – particularly the terms 'ethnic cleansing' and 'collateral damage'.) By this linguistic means the use of violence, including hate action, can be masked and responsibility evaded. Fergenson (1995) gives additional psychological evidence of the link between language, thought and violence.

The fundamental choice, therefore, is which is the lesser of two evils: the danger to democracy posed by a reduction in freedom of speech or the pain suffered by the receiver of hate language, and the racial violence hate language can engender. In many countries the latter considerations are taken to be more significant, and legislation to control hate language has been introduced.

Constructing legislation

The preceding two sections provide the two bases on which legislation can be constructed – incitement to racist violence and harm to the receiver of hate messages. Article 4 of the *International Convention on the Elimination of All Forms of Racial Discrimination* (1965), to which most nations are signatories, reads:

> States Parties condemn all propaganda and all organizations which are based on ideas or theories of superiority of one race or group of persons of one colour or ethnic origin, or which attempt to justify or promote racial hatred and discrimination in any form, and undertake to adopt immediate and positive measures designed to eradicate all incitement to, or acts of, such discrimination and, to this end, with due regard to the principles embodied in the Universal Declaration of Human Rights and the rights expressly set forth in Article 5 of this convention, *inter alia*:
>
> (a) Shall declare an offense punishable by law all dissemination of ideas based on racial superiority or hatred, incitement to racial discrimina tion as well as all acts of violence or incitement to such acts against any race or group of persons of another colour or ethnic origin, and also the provision of any assistance to racist activities, including the financing thereof;
>
>   . . .

This Article is explicit in the obligation it places on signatories to enact legislation banning racial vilification and incitement to racist violence. It is noteworthy that there is no explicit reference to intention, or to the need for proof of harm. The extent to which legislation based on this has been enacted varies from state to state. Early British legislation on racial vilification focused on incitement to racist violence. The USA opted out of this provision. Australia also placed a reservation on its ratification, stating freedom of speech concerns, and the relevant provisions of the Commonwealth Racial Discrimination Act were rejected by the federal parliament and never placed into law, on the basis of free speech concerns. However various states in Australia have put legislation in place. For example, the New South Wales legislation reads in part:

> **Racial vilification unlawful**
> 20c. (1) It is unlawful for a person, by a public act, to incite hatred towards, serious contempt for, or severe ridicule of, a person or group of persons on the ground of the race of the person or members of the group.
>   . . .

Many European nations have considerably stronger legislation, including France and Germany.

Conclusion

Both individual and group vilification are phenomena of social and linguistic importance. Both reveal concerns about intention, harm and truth, and more work on their definition and proof is a present and future need. There is an unfinished debate about the balance between freedom of speech on the one hand, and sparing people emotional pain and the increased likelihood of racist violence on the other.

9

Linguistic Evidence

linguistic and sociolinguistic methods are rightly called scientific . . .
[but] legal professionals . . . think of us as unscientific because we
cannot be as dogmatic as other sciences

Eades (1994b)

Introduction

This chapter discusses the presentation of evidence on language, sometimes called 'forensic linguistics' narrowly defined. Much of this work is
done (1) in court and (2) by linguists, but neither of these provisions is
absolute. I have, for example, provided police with linguistic evidence to
help them eliminate a person as the possible writer of a threatening letter,
and this did not involve the provision of evidence in court. Sometimes
telephone technicians provide evidence on language, but they are not
usually trained linguists.

Linguistic evidence is mostly provided in two broad categories: evidence
on communication and evidence on authorship. Within both categories it
is helpful to classify the linguistic evidence by the linguistic levels we have
used throughout this book: phonology, lexis, grammar, discourse, register,
genre and sociolinguistic variation. The examples in this chapter are drawn
both from the experience of others and from my own work. The objective
of this chapter is to illustrate the possibilities of linguistic evidence, not to
report every case in the literature.

I have not included a separate entry here concerning linguists' contributions to the interpretation of legislation that deals with non-linguistic issues. The reason for this is that such expert evidence is rarely sought or
used. Lawyers generally do not accept that linguists have relevant expertise in this area, which they regard as part of their domain. As noted
previously, this perception is probably to some extent misguided.

The Ethics and Admissibility of Linguistic Evidence

There are three issues that challenge the admissibility of expert evidence from linguists: expertise, validity and reliability. The **expertise** issue involves proving that the linguist has knowledge, and can present information that is outside common sense knowledge. In legal terms this is referred to as 'the rule of common knowledge'. Concerning the evidence that the linguist may present, there are two common scientific criteria that need to be applied. First **validity** – can the linguist offer information that is relevant and precisely targeted at a disputed issue in the case? In other words, can linguists and linguistics do the job. In the language of the legal system this may be referred to as 'the rule of ultimate issue'. Secondly, concerning **reliability**, is the information based on scientific methods, such that it can be trusted. This might include scientific notions such as testability, replicability and falsifiability. It often has to do with the type of methods used. These three issues, expertise, reliability and validity, are central to professional ethics and to the admissibility of linguistic evidence. Green (1990: 261–74) provides a detailed justification of how and why linguistics can meet these criteria, based on the uncommon knowledge and expertise of linguists, the relevance of their contribution, and the reliability of their methods.

As Bowe and Storey (1995: 188–9) point out 'While many people are quite capable of identifying or eliminating unknown speakers in a[n earwitness] line-up, they are generally unable to say why. ... Linguistically trained analysts on the other hand are in a position to give a detailed description of differences or similarities noted in two voice samples, together with an explanation of how and why these differences or similarities occur.' However, it can be difficult to convince judges that the linguist can offer particular insights. Although the study of language has a history that reaches back to ancient Greece, ancient India, ancient China and beyond, it is only over the last century that linguistics has become fully established as a separate discipline. Since judges are often classically trained and conservative in background, linguistics will rarely have formed part of their education, and they will often not have appreciated the degree to which linguistics is exceptional among the humanities for its rigour, technicality and objectivity. The literature is full of cases in which linguists are not permitted to provide evidence – for example, Shuy (1993: xx) mentions some rejection of his evidence on the validity issue, and there is an extensive discussion of the problem in Eades (1997). Jensen (1995) provides an interesting and detailed description of the courtroom process through which she passed in order to have herself accepted at an expert, and to establish that linguistics is a genuine field of expertise, and that it was relevant to an issue at stake in the trial – in other words to establish the expertise, validity and reliability of her linguistic evidence. In Roman Law systems there may be a process through which people may go in order to be accepted once and for all as an expert witness: in Chile for instance one becomes an *experto oficial* of the courts. This involves careful checking of the expert's credentials, and then entry into a register of such experts. In Common Law systems, the police often maintain such lists, but usually there is no such system for courts.

While Common Law systems share basic concerns about establishing the expertise of witnesses, they vary somewhat in their legislation, and in how they handle the issue of expert evidence. In the USA Rule 702 of the Federal Rules of Evidence states 'if scientific, technical, or other specialized knowledge will assist the trier of fact to understand the evidence or to determine a fact in issue, a witness qualified by knowledge, skill, experience, training, or education may testify thereto in the form of an opinion or otherwise'. The issues are therefore those of expertise and validity. However, scientific method (reliability) is also frequently used as a basis to challenge evidence. Rule 403 also seeks to exclude evidence that is so wrapped up in scientific method that it cannot be challenged. More recently the Daubert decision has given judges more power to exclude testimony by purported experts, if judges feel that it does not have what they believe to be a reasonable scientific foundation.

Like Britain in the previous decade, in Australia in the 1990s there were changes in national and most state legal systems to make it easier to tender expert evidence. In the Federal and NSW Evidence Acts, the field of expertise rule has been changed to allow evidence which derives from 'specialised knowledge based on a person's training study or expertise'. On this criterion there is little question concerning the admissibility of evidence from qualified linguists.

However, this leaves open the definition of 'qualified linguist'. The International Association of Forensic Linguists has as an admission criterion the possession of a postgraduate qualification in linguistics (there are other grades of membership for those who do not wish to practice as forensic linguists). The International Association for Forensic Phonetics, which as its name implies specializes in forensic uses of phonetics, has rigorous criteria for membership and a strict code of practice, which are available through their website <http://www.iafp.net/>.

The two sections which follow cover two main areas in which a linguist may be able to offer evidence – communication issues and authorship. The sections follow a pattern of presenting the linguistic information and the type of methodology used, followed by descriptions of actual cases wherever possible.

Evidence on Communication

I have placed this issue here, because some of the literature on linguistic evidence makes the assumption that the field is confined to authorship. This section will demonstrate that this is not the case. It may, for instance, involve linguists presenting evidence on the issues discussed in chapter 5, on the difficulty of understanding legal language, and on the matters in chapter 7 on linguistic disadvantage suffered before the law, and on the language proficiency of second language speakers. Evidence on communication also includes evidence on whether a particular language crime has been committed (see the previous chapter). Shuy (1993) documents many cases where he has offered expert evidence in this area.

Methodology

We have seen earlier that communication involves three critical elements: the linguistic forms; the situation in which the communication takes place; and the 'behind the eye' knowledge of the participants. Miscommunication can be caused by poor linguistic construction; by wordings that are clear in principle, but are inappropriate to the context to the extent that they are difficult or impossible to grasp; or by differences between the knowledge base of the speaker/writer and the hearer/reader: Aborigines, lawyers and linguists frequently experience the frustration of saying something that they believe is clear, but is not understood or is misunderstood by people who do not share their knowledge base. Effective communication involves choosing the best **wording** to communicate an intended **meaning** to a particular **participant** in a particular **context**, taking into account the effects of distance from context (see the discussion of 'decontexualization' in chapter 1). Evidence from linguists is often concerned with what a text means, and whether a participant or group of participants can understand a particular text. Deciding what a text means can also involve decoding unclear texts or elements of text. Related to this are trade name issues – in essence, what is communicated by a trade name. There are in fact two types of trade name disputes. First there are those that relate to whether a name can be used as a trade name at all, since it may be viewed as a more general generic term referring to origin, nature, type, value or quality of the product, rather than to a particular brand. Okawara, in her work on Japanese trade names, proposes that certain brand names have in effect turned into generic names. Second, there is the issue of whether trade names are sufficiently similar to be confused, or to show that a trade name has in some way been used by people other than those to whom it is licensed.

Therefore in communication cases forensic linguistic methodology will involve examination of some or all of these four aspects. The linguist in particular will tend to examine the **wording** – the linguistic resources used in the communication. This usually entails a careful analysis of any of the linguistic features of the communication that may be problematic, including sounds, words, grammar and discourse, and their interaction with the social context. This may be analysis of linguistic complexity per se, or it may involve the analysis of interaction (perhaps using Conversational Analysis techniques) for discoursal evidence such as inappropriate responses which can indicate communication breakdown, as in the case of the young Tongan man discussed in chapter 6. The linguist will also usually need to provide an analysis of the **meanings** that the linguistic forms might or might not be expressing. Another aspect concerns the language proficiencies of the **participants**. Sometimes an assessment of aspects of their language proficiency relevant to the communication will needed. If some participants do not control the language elements found in the relevant text(s), then communication is endangered. One means of resolving this is (if feasible) to test the participants' comprehension of the relevant texts. Finally the **context** may need to be examined, for instance the level of background noise may need to be assessed for its effects on communication. The best way to see what all this means in practice is to examine cases.

Grapho-phonology

One case involved two trade names which were similar but not identical: Alkeran and Arclan. The trade names referred to drugs, one of which was being introduced into the Australian market. The makers of the other drug were worried about any confusion between the two drugs, since their drug, if misprescribed, could be life threatening. They were attempting through their lawyers to persuade the other company to change the name of its drug to avoid any possibility of confusion. They needed evidence that there was some possibility of the differences between the names of the two drugs being neutralised. It was not necessary to state with certainty that the drugs would be confused, only to say that there was a possibility of this. The written forms are quite distinct, so the only possible area of confusion is their pronunciation. An important factor in this is that a substantial proportion of the Australian population speak English as a second language – the 'participant' issue.

The most likely feature that would differentiate the pronunciation of the names of the two drugs Alkeran and Arclan is the initial vowel, which in their most likely Australian pronunciations [ælkəræn] and [ɑklæn] seem quite distinct. However the [æ–ɑ] vowels of *had* versus *hard* are quite close in Australian English, and there is a low probability pronunciation of Alkeran as [ɑlkəræn]. Another difference which distinguishes the two words is the extra [ə] sound (the first and last vowel sound of *banana*) in Alkeran. In English it is common for the [ə] sound to be added or lost in consonant clusters. For example, in the word *secretary* it is variable, with some speakers saying [sekrətri] and others [sekrətəri] or [sekrəteri]. This means that the [ə] could be lost in Alkeran, meaning that a possible pronunciation is [ɑlkræn]. The remaining difference is the 'l' and 'r' sounds. The sounds 'r' and 'l' are widely variable in the languages of the world, and are frequently substituted the one for the other. Note for instance Spanish *milagro* from *miraculum*, and *palabra* from *parabole*, where they are reversed. In English, *marble* is sourced from Latin *marmor* and *turtle* from Latin *turtur* – in both cases a change from final 'r' to 'l', and the words *peregrine* and *pilgrim* both have the same source. Notice too the loss of 'l' and 'r', respectively, in the Australian pronunciation, but not the spelling of *almond* and *Armand* (compare the drug names). Speakers of Chinese, Japanese, Gikuyu and other languages may confuse these sounds in English. Aside from this phonetic detail, there is psycholinguistic evidence that words that are not in frequent use, but are of this level of similarity, may be confused.

Since there are similarities between the two words, and the sounds that distinguish them are unstable, it is possible that native speakers of English could confuse them, particularly as these words are not in common usage, and might not be fully internalized by speakers. The substantial minority of Australians who speak English as a second language would be at even greater risk of confusion. Although a confusion between the two words is unlikely, it cannot be ruled out, and any such confusion could be life threatening.

This is an example where expert linguistic evidence is of value because a linguist can provide information about which sounds are relatively unstable, and about their history of sound change. It is also a good example of a communication rather than an authorship issue. In the pronunciation area, phoneticians can also give evidence in cases where phonetic ambiguity or error has led to miscommunication. They can testify to mismatch between English spelling and pronunciation, particularly vowels (in part a consequence of the great vowel shift). People are also often unaware of what articulatory features distinguish consonants, including place and manner of articulation.

Concerning the written language, Oyanadel and Samaniego (1999) describe the means they used in several trade name cases, where an existing trade name holder challenged a new trade name, for example *Sal de Fruta* vs. *Sal Disfruta*. At the grapho-phonic level they examined both the likely pronunciations of the two names, and did a comparison of the typeface, colour and spatial organization of the new trademark.

Writing or print can also cause communication problems. Although I have not read of individual cases, there will have been expert evidence in court on how handwriting can be read, on the legibility of handwriting, typefaces and actual handwritten or print material. In a case involving a Malaysian politician, discussed below, the fact that there were public notices in Malay was discounted in court because evidence was given that the Malay version was given in small letters at ankle height, so the likelihood of it being read and understood was small.

Transcription

An area of miscommunication can be at the interface of written and spoke language – in the transcription of testimony and surveillance material by police and courts. A number of linguists have testified on this. I have had to correct police transcripts of interviews on a number of occasions on the basis of the audio tapes, and have testified to this in court. Prince (1990: 281–3) gives some powerful examples of omissions and errors in the transcripts of FBI surveillance tapes which make elements of recorded conversations appear incriminating, when they may not be so. For example she suggests (Prince 1990: 283) that a

'change . . . from 'Do you <u>know</u> anything?' to 'Do you <u>need</u> anything?' quoted from . . . local gamblers to the . . . chief of police, inserts an implicature of collusion, of special 'shared knowledge' between them. This tape and transcript were shown to the jury on the first day of the trial. In the evening paper, this message was cited in a front-page article under the headline 'Tape Ties [gambler] to Ex-Chief'.

This demonstrates the possible negative impact of mistranscription.

Eades (1996) identifies various areas where changes take place in courtroom transcripts. She discusses shifts in language variety (from Aboriginal to standard English), register (colloquial to formal), the failure to represent the chronology of speech – particularly overlaps, the omission of unlicensed contributions (for example from the public gallery), and of discourse markers (see chapter 7), hesitation phenomena and inaudible fragments. Of particular interest is the fact that the lawyer's **third part** is often omitted, for example the underlined segment in the following extract was omitted in the courtroom transcript.

C: ... You went straight to your two-way radio.
P: Yes
C: <u>Yes</u>. And you made the call straight away to the other police officers?
     ...

While this omission does not change the propositional content, it manifests power in the relationship, since only more powerful parties normally use third parts like this. Eades also mentions the omission of repetition.

Lexis

This category concerns words, their use, their frequency and the company they keep (collocation). Lexical information is particularly important in the meaning and communication arena, although it may also have identificatory potential. A related issue is the role of linguists in interpreting legislation, discussed in the *Washington Law Journal* (73, 3; see also the discussions of 'interpretation' in chapter 2). There have been contributions from linguists to courts which have discussed the meaning of legislation, although the legal profession is not comfortable with this intervention (see Solan 1995).

One case involving meaning/communication is documented by McMenamin (1993). The issue was the meaning/communicative intent of the words *syndrome*, *accident* and *disease* in an insurance policy. McMenamin (1993) testified on behalf of parents whose child died of Sudden Infant

Death Syndrome (SIDS) at the age of 18 months. The child's life was protected by the father's life and accident insurance, which included the statement 'The plan pays a benefit for losses resulting from any kind of accident . . .'. The insurance company denied the claim initially, saying that the policy did not cover deaths from illness or disease.

McMenamin's reading of the medical literature and dictionary definitions revealed that *syndrome* is distinguished from *disease* in that a *syndrome* groups together patterns of incidents, but there is no explanation in terms of physical malfunctioning, particularly that caused by bacteria, viruses, etc., while *diseases* exist at a specific time in a specific person, between health and either restored health or death (*syndromes* do not share this quality). As McMenamin says ' "disease' is a temporally bound state between health and death. A diseased person either gets well or becomes chronically diseased and dies. SIDS is something a healthy infant either has or does not have. The result, even with a 'near-miss', is health or death, nothing in between.' Hence SIDS cannot be classified as a disease.

Turning now to the definition of *accident*, this is an event that is sudden, unintentional and usually undesirable. It need not involve trauma or violence. The expression *near miss* is regularly used with SIDS. Therefore SIDS shares the characteristics of an accident, but not of an *illness* or a *disease*. As a result of McMenamin's analysis, the insurance company paid out.

A methodology suggested by Coulthard (1994a) for this type of work is the use of corpora and concordancing. Such computer based techniques may permit the rapid retrieval of all occurrences of a particular word in a large number and range of texts, revealing the company they keep, and thereby much of their usual meaning. Coulthard reports that Sinclair was able to testify concerning the normal meaning of the word *visa* by examining 5 million words of text from *The Times* newspaper, supplemented by reference to the Birmingham Corpus of 28 million words. This approach provides good evidence on the popular or everyday understanding of words, and could be used in other areas, such as trademark disputes, where there may be an argument as to whether a word like 'hoover' is a proper name or not, and defamation, to determine whether certain words are understood as defamatory or not in the wider population (a principal issue in defamation).

Another 'communication' example comes from the work with police cautions discussed in chapter 5. At a *voir dire* I testified that a second language speaker with restricted English proficiency was unlikely to understand the word 'inducement' which formed part of the right to silence caution (see chapter 7). In consequence the court ruled that the person involved could not understand his right to silence, and therefore the police interview was ruled inadmissible.

In examples such as the last, it is clearly important to look not only at the words of the text for comprehension, but also at their match with the 'behind the eye' knowledge of the person who is to understand them. It may be necessary to develop techniques to investigate this match.

One such case involved a prominent Malaysian politician who was charged in Australia with attempting to export illegally a large sum of foreign currency. The facts of the case were that he had brought the money in to buy a house, but the sale could not be completed, so he was taking the money back to Malaysia – there was no illegal intent or money laundering involved.

The man had signed two Australian customs forms *B72 (7/95) Traveller's Statement*, and an International *Currency Transfer Report*, which required him to declare such sums of currency, which he had failed to do. The two forms posed various communication problems. The first sentence of the relevant part of the *Traveller's Statement* reads:

> You MUST file a currency report with Customs if you have $5000 or more
> Australian currency or foreign equivalent.

The expression 'foreign equivalent' is complex, in part because it seems to be a reduced form for 'equivalent sum in foreign currency'. If we ask 'Is the equivalent foreign?' this throws up the oddness of this form of expression. Additionally *equivalent* is semantically an adjective, but here it used (grammatically metaphorically) as a noun. The same expression is used in the other form. A second language speaker with a less than native proficiency may have problems with these two crucial words. There were also many other grammatically metaphorical words. Furthermore, at the point where he had to fill in the amount of currency he was carrying, the wording was

> 'Total amount $A———'

The most likely meaning to attach to this is 'the total amount OF Australian dollars', although the intention is to ask the value IN Australian dollars of any currency carried. This is potentially misleading. His response to this was to write in the amount of Australian dollars he was carrying.

It was not possible to examine directly the man's understanding of these particular customs forms, since by the time I came into the case he was entirely aware of their meaning. However, during an interview recorded with him, a range of non-standard grammatical and lexical features appeared in his speech. Therefore, to examine the accused's vocabulary level, a lengthy vocabulary reading test section was taken from a validated international test battery. This section examined specifically the type of formal written vocabulary found in the forms, although it was somewhat simpler. The man failed this test.

In court, evidence on both aspects was given: first concerning the difficult and possibly misleading language of the forms; and second concerning the man's level of language proficiency. The case was made that there was a mismatch between the language demands of the forms and the man's level of language proficiency such that he may not have understood them. This evidence was admitted and contributed to a not guilty verdict.

Grammar

Morphology
Lentine and Shuy (1990) describe their role as expert witnesses in the *McSleep Inns* case. These were a new line of budget motels, and the Mc-prefix was supposed to indicate the frugality and cleanliness associated with the Scots. However, the name was challenged by the McDonald's hamburger chain, who claimed a proprietary interest in the Mc- prefix, because of their use of it in McFries, McNuggets, etc. In other words they were claiming exclusive rights to the productive use of a prefix, despite its long history in Scottish surnames. Lentine and Shuy did a trawl of magazines, and came up with the following extant productive commercial uses of the Mc- prefix, with a source that was not 'McDonalds'.

The case was lost despite this evidence.

McThrift Motor Inn	Budget motel with a Scottish motif
McAuto	Subsidiary of the McDonnell–Douglas Corporation
McBooks	Bookstore named after its owners McCarthy and McGovern
McTek	Computer discount stores specializing in Macintosh products
McRides	Morris County RIDES, a ride-sharing programme

Syntax
Levi (1994) discusses a class action brought by recipients of Aid to Families with Dependent Children against the Illinois Department of Public Aid, because a notice sent to them was so incomprehensible that it failed in its constitutional task of informing the recipients of their rights. Levi (1994: 8) gives the following two examples to illustrate the syntactic and lexical difficulties of the notice.

1. 'If your AFDC financial assistance benefits are continued at the present level and the fair hearing decides your AFDC financial assistance reduction was correct, the amount of AFDC assistance received to which they were not entitled will be recouped from future AFDC assistance payments or must be paid back if the AFDC case is cancelled.'

    Equivalent to
    If X happens and then Y happens, then either Z will happen [expressed in very complex terms including a negative and a relative clause] or – if R has also happened – then Q must happen.

This example has seven clauses in an extremely complex chain of semantic relations which are revealed in the *Equivalent to* passage below; it has six passive verbs without expressed agents, making it unclear who is doing what to whom, for instance is it the same person who is 'recouping' and 'paying back' – presumably not; notice the complex noun phrases 'your AFDC financial assistance reduction' and 'future AFDC assistance payments', remembering in addition that AFDC stands for 'Aid to Families with Dependent Children' which already contains the notion of financial assistance.

2. 'If you do not request a new hearing date and do not appear at the scheduled hearing date, your appeal will be dismissed, unless you show good cause for failure to appear.'

The complexity in Example 2 derives largely from its highly compounded negation, overtly in 'not request', and 'not appear', but also less overtly in 'dismissed', 'unless' (= if not), and 'failure to'. The *Equivalent to* section might be rewritten as 'If *not* X and *not* Y, then *not* Z if *not* Q cause *not* P' – it contains five negative expressions. Chapter 5 referred to psycholinguistic research that has shown that comprehension difficulties increase in proportion to the number of negative expressions contained in a single sentence.

The verdict was that IDPA were ordered to pay 20 million dollars to the plaintiff class, and to rewrite the letter so that it was comprehensible. In this case then the language proficiency of the reader was not raised, since it could be assumed that this level of syntactic complexity would be problematic for any reader (with the possible exception of a lawyer).

In the US Steel case reported in Labov and Harris (1994), the authors demonstrated that black steel workers failed to receive just compensation for previous discrimination from their employer, because the release put out by US Steel Co. was worded in a misleading and technical fashion. Labov and two of his colleagues provided evidence from grammatical analysis and readability measures which demonstrated the linguistic complexity and difficulty of the text (the 'wording' and 'meaning' issues). He then took into account the 'participants', in this case the steel workers. He took two versions of an element of the contested letter:

1. 'there was no question about his getting **any** back pay'
2. 'there was no question about his getting **the** back pay'.

He embedded these in a scenario question about the likelihood of the person receiving back pay (see Labov and Harris (1994) for details), which he then tested on people of a similar social background. The issue was whether there was any difference in people's interpreting the sentences negatively (he would **not** get back pay) or positively (he **would** get back pay). There was a statistically significant difference: the use of 'any' biased people to the negative interpretation. This was the original wording, so Labov was able to testify that the letter was biased (intentionally or not) in favour of the company, which did not want to pay the back pay. This, therefore, is a good example of how subtle linguistic analysis and testing can be used to examine the meaning of language forms for particular participants in a particular contextual frame. The case was lost, but the judge took the linguistic evidence seriously.

In another trade name case, Oyanadel and Samaniego (1999) gave evidence concerning brands of baby cream. An old established brand was 'Hipoglos', a name derived from a technical term for fish oil. A new brand came onto the market called 'Fasaglos', FASA being an acronym for the company name. Oyanadel and Samaniego were able to testify that '-glos' is not a productive morpheme in Spanish, in other words it is not used generally as the last part of words to make new words – it had been taken directly from 'Hipoglos'. The evidence was accepted, and the trade name 'Fasaglos' was rejected.

Discourse

In a case involving the violent death of a man, the NSW Police Service requested me to listen to four tape recorded conversations between a male voice and a female voice (M and F hereafter), in order to decode the secret language the woman used on occasions. The most likely reason for doing so was to conceal what was being said. This view is supported by the content of the concealed and surrounding language, by the sometimes strained voice quality, and by a 'framing' move in one tape 'I'm going to say something'. The police needed an impartial witness to decode this language and present the findings in court.

The first, seemingly incomprehensible sample of the secret language that I heard sounded like this.

[bəpəkəpos əpin əp√ kəp√pəpω əpov məp√nθs]

After careful listening, repeated many times, and with the meaning clues provided by the clear language context, the language became clear. It used a type of strategy that is found in children's secret languages, or 'pig latin', of placing a neutral vowel plus 'p' before each vowel. So *take* becomes [təpeik], and *inside* becomes [əpinsəpɑid]. This strategy makes the language difficult for outsiders to understand initially. However, once the code is cracked, on later hearings the speech is clear. This analysis was supported by the fact that on some occasions the voices repeated elements stated initially in the secret language in plain English – as is the case with 'going' in the last turn of the following extract. A transcription of a section of the tape containing the secret language follows. The plain English is in normal script, the secret language is in **bold**, and the translation of the secret language is placed underneath in *italics*. Normal English spelling rather than a phonetic transcription is used in order to make the text more accessible.

F: Yeah, um. Just be nice you know for a few months. Bite your tongue, do anything erm she wants, be really nice to her, let her not clean up and that, and erm

b(ep)ec(ep)ause (ep)in (ep)a c(ep)oup(ep)le (ep)of m(ep)onths
because in a couple of months

y(ep)ou c(ep)an t(ep)ake (ep)off.
you can take off.

(ep)and n(ep)ot t(ep)ell h(ep)er wh(ep)ere y(ep)ou (ep)are g(ep)o(ep)ing.
and not tell her where you are going.

M: (*Belch*)
F: . . . I'm just so nervous of

g(ep)o(ep)ing (ep)ins(ep)ide
going inside

M: Alright then
F: You know, it's, it's worth it. Anything is better than going

(ep)ins(ep)ide
inside

This case is interesting, because it deals with intentional rather than unintentional barriers to communication. The methodology, as in many cases involving the decoding of an unknown language or script, is to work out the meaning of elements from their context (in this case their linguistic context), then to attempt to discover how the language encodes those meanings, particularly where there are repeated language elements. One problem that I had in court was proving that my interpretations of what sounded like gobbledygook were in fact correct. The strategy that I selected was to attempt to teach the jury to understand the language, so that they could follow it themselves.

An example of a written text involved decoding a suicide note for a family, who wished to understand the dead man's last thoughts. The man was obviously mentally disturbed, and probably under the influence of drugs when he wrote the note, in which he used a mixture of drawings (for example a drawing of an eye for 'I'), spatial relations, and unclear handwriting to communicate. I was able to arrive at a possible interpretation for the family, using the decoding techniques mentioned above.

Pronoun reference is another aspect of discourse on which a linguist may be able to testify. Prince (1990) discusses the meaning of the pronoun *we*, which is ambiguous in standard English, in that it can mean 'you and me' or 'other people and me'. Therefore she has testified to the fact that someone agreeing with another speaker's statement 'We killed that X' need not mean that the hearer was involved in the killing.

Sociolinguistics

This section must begin by pointing out that much of the preceding material could be seen as falling within the ambit of sociolinguistics, and sociolinguistic evidence. For instance, the US Steel case was partly an example of a mismatch between sociolects. Secret language, such as that described above, are part of the study of sociolinguistics. Even more important, however, is the part that sociolinguists play when giving evidence on the difficulty of understanding register, in particular legal register, such as the police cautions described in chapter 5.

Eades (1993, 1995b) makes a convincing case for the poor communication that may occur between speakers of Aboriginal English and the legal system, particularly in the area of pragmatic differences between the two varieties. She shows how, on a number of occasions, people who have been proved to be innocent have been imprisoned on the basis of police interviews and courtroom testimony where a significant degree of cross cultural communication difficulties were in play, and she has presented linguistic evidence on this miscommunication. Eades has (among other issues) testified concerning two of the issues discussed in chapter 6: the difficulties of Aborigines faced with direct questioning, and 'gratuitous concurrence'.

Oyanadel and Samaniego (1999) mention an interesting case in which they provided analysis of sociolinguistic issues of 'language planning', and language boundaries in interaction with issues of vocabulary. A regulatory board in Chile ruled that all medicine must be labelled in Spanish. Three questions arose: (1) What is the exact distinction between proper names and common nouns – since the first could be left intact, but the latter would need to be translated. (2) Where does Spanish end and English begin, given the extensive loans from English into Chilean Spanish in recent decades, many of them unmodified in the written form (e.g. top, full, sundae, pie, etc.) (3) What is labelling? Could slogans be left untranslated?

Evidence on Authorship

The basic issue here is whether Person A produced text Z. The term 'author' is used here in its full original sense of the person who produced a painting, a spoken utterance, or a written text. So the text produced by the author (or authors) may be spoken or written, may vary in length from a grunt to a book, and sometimes the issue may be whether the person produced all of a text or only parts of it. A common type of case is when there are two possible authors of a text, and the task it to decide between them.

The basic methodology is to obtain comparison texts definitely produced by the imputed author, and then compare them with the questioned text for similarities and differences. Such similarities need to be identificatory, in other words they need to be language features that differentiate possible authors. It is often easier to demonstrate that a person did **not** produce a particular text. For instance if a speaker has a deep voice, but a voice on tape is high, it is not difficult to show that it is unlikely that they were produced by the same speaker. Sure positive identification is much harder to achieve, and often the findings will be probabilistic rather than absolute. The consequence is that evidence on negative identification is more likely to be unqualified, while positive identification will often involve some form of probability statement (for discussion of some scales of probability see Sjerps and Biesheuvel 1999; Broeders 1999). The detail on methodology will be discussed in each section.

Speech sounds

This area, which is by far the most developed area of linguistic evidence, can involve much detail and technicality. Within the bounds of this book it is not possible to enter into it in depth. Readers interested in greater coverage, particularly if they wish to examine evidence, should consult the various specialized issues of the journal *Forensic Linguistics*, and books such as Hollien (1990, 2001), Baldwin and French (1990) and Nolan (1983). Hollien (1990) has had a major influence on this section.

Speech varies on many parameters, including the following, which can be used for speaker identification, as the issue of 'authorship' is generally called at this language level (they can also affect 'communication'). These might be called **identificatory features**.

- speaking fundamental frequency (SFF or F_0): this is the heard pitch – does the voice sound high, low or medium? Most clearly heard in vowel sounds;
- articulation: any idiosyncrasies in vowels/consonants?;
- general voice quality: creaky, breathy, squeaky, gravelly, etc.;

- prosody;
- timing: fast/slow, choppy/smooth;
- intonation patterns;
- intensity: how loud;
- dialect/sociolect: regional or class accent;
- speech impediments: defective 'r', etc.;
- idiosyncratic pronunciations: e.g. shripsophenia (for schizophrenia);
- idiosyncratic language patterns: grammar, words, etc.;
- unusual use of stress/emphasis.

There are two ways in which speaker identification can be done: by ear or by a machine. The field of ear identification is sometimes called **earwitnessing**.

Earwitnessing
Hollien (1990: 197) provides the following set of variables that affect the likely reliability of earwitnessing.

> Most of the following are considered to be among those positive relation-ships associated with the perceptual identification task.
>
> 1.   Speakers who are known to the listener are the easiest to identify by voice, and the accuracy here can be quite high.
> 2.   If the listeners' perception of a talker's speech characteristics are reinforced from time to time, correct identification will decay more slowly than if appropriate stimulation is not provided. This relation ship holds both for listeners who know the talker and those who do not.
> 3.   The larger the speech sample – and the better its quality – the more accurate will be the aural-perceptual identification.
> 4.   Listeners can be quite variable in their ability to make speaker recog-nition judgments, but some are naturally quite good at it.
> 5.   Listeners appear to be successful in using a number of the 'natural' characteristics found within speech/voice in the identification task.
> 6.   Phonetic training and task organization appear to aid in successful identifications.

Hollien also points out that the converse of these relationships applies – identification is less certain if the speaker is not familiar, if the listener has not heard the speaker recently, if the number of speakers is large, if the signal is of poor quality, and if voices are similar. Hollien has performed a number of experiments that give evidence of these assertions, one of which, for example, (Hollien 1990: fig 9.2) showed a very large advantage in identification for listeners who knew the speaker, compared with those who did not. Attempts by speakers to disguise their speech only reduced the accuracy of identification from nearly 100 per cent to around 80 per cent among listeners who knew them well. The experiment also demonstrated the advantage of training in identification, and revealed quite large differences between listeners who seemed to have natural ability in this area, and those who did not. In earwitness lineups people listen to voices, recorded or live, without seeing the speaker, preferably in conditions similar to the original hearing, and see if they can distinguish a suspect from the other voices (some of which should be 'sound-alikes'). It should be noted that earwitness identification by an untrained listener who does not know the speaker is even less reliable than eyewitness identification (Nolan 1994). Therefore this type of evidence often places weight in the evidentiary scales, rather than being conclusive.

In one case, I was asked to compare recordings of two voices, one of a man making a 000 emergency telephone call, the other of a suspect undergoing a police interview. In both recordings there was a defective 'r' sound which occurred only between vowels (the 'speech impediment' factor). The police had not noticed this important identificatory speech feature, which, along with other speech features such as sociolect, enabled us to be fairly certain that the suspect had made the emergency call, and was therefore involved in the arson. However, it is important to notice that authorship could not be guaranteed.

Bowe and Storey (1995: 199, case 6) mention a case in which 'Although the client's voice quality, sociolinguistic characteristics and some features of pronunciation were very similar to those of one of the speakers on the tape, his intonation patterns were quite different. Because there were no apparent contextual motivations for such a difference in intonational style Storey concluded that it was a different speaker.' In this case, unlike most, intonation was the deciding factor.

Analysis by machine
Machine Speaker Identification is familiar to many people in the form of 'voiceprints' – properly termed 'spectrograms'. Unfortunately inflated claims were made for the reliability of these, particularly by the FBI in America, and they became somewhat discredited. However, with the increasing sophistication of machine analysis, and its more careful use, it has re-emerged as an important tool in forensic linguistics. It usually involves the machine

measurement of the physical properties of speech sounds such as amplitude, duration and frequency, and the display of these on a screen, with the possibility of a print out. Computing may then be used to analyse them for various vectors, such as voice onset and vowel formants. Hollien suggests that the following machine detectable **vectors** can be effectively used in combination in speech identification (no single one provides sufficient information, but too many vectors reduces the effectiveness of the technique as a result of statistical relations).

- Long-term speech spectra: an averaged reading of the amount of the full range of frequencies that appear in a person's speech over a period of time.
- Speaking Fundamental Frequency (SFF): this is a measurement of the underlying pitch (high or low) of the human voice. For more detail see Hollien (1990).
- Vowel Formant Tracking (VFT): there are certain dense patterns of sound picked up for vowels such as /i/ /a/ /u/ (and the cluster /na/) which can be identificatory. Formants F1, F2 and F3 are the most important.
- Temporal (TED): this involves measurements of the time involved in speaking, including the total speech time – time taken to read an utterance of specific length; the speech to silence ratio – the amount of time acoustic energy is present; speech rate – number of syllables per minute; and consonant vowel duration. The last three measures are divided by the first to obtain a TED score.

Hollien (1990) gives evidence of high levels of reliability when these four measurements are combined. However, Bowe and Storey (1995: 191), while acknowledging Hollien's contribution, caution that 'the reliability of these electronic methods is still very debatable'. Hollien (1990) suggests that machines can be used not only for identification and communication purposes (including speech enhancement and decoding), but also to detect stress and to authenticate recordings. He discusses the identification of the electronic 'signatures' left by telephones, tape recorders and other electrical devices.

In the early years of spectrographic analysis, Tosi and his colleagues found that a trained and experienced 'voiceprint analyst' could get high levels of accuracy in identification, claiming up to 99 per cent. However, even their own experiments showed that when voice samples were collected at different times (the normal forensic situation) error levels rose to 18 per cent. Other work reported by voiceprint supporters reported error rates of 30 per cent and 41 per cent. Subsequent experiments by mainstream phoneticians showed error rates of 12–51 per cent in ideal laboratory conditions of recording (not the normal forensic situation when voices are often recorded over the telephone, or with background noise, etc.), and better results from earwitnessing (see for example Baldwin and French (1990).) When speakers deliberately mask their voices, error rates rise to 40 –78 per cent. Hollien also points out that many of the 'voiceprint analysts' used in the heyday of the movement were unable to interpret spectrograms properly – he writes 'I have reluctantly come to the conclusion that many of them are not familiar enough with the relevant concepts and knowledge to be able to carry out speaker identification tasks of any type'. Hollien (1990) provides spectrograms of a particular utterance, where two different speakers had almost identical spectrographic profiles, and a single speaker produced markedly different profiles. A trained phonetician may be able to provide probabilistic data on speaker identification from spectrograms, but identification becomes particularly difficult if one of the samples for analysis is recorded in such a way that much of the signal is affected: see the following section.

The range of other speech features given earlier that may be identificatory included voice quality characteristics such as creakiness or breathiness. Klasmeyer and Sendlmeier (1997) discuss the machine detectable acoustic traces of these. Certain of these speech characteristics are below the level of awareness, or are dependent on the shape of the vocal tract, and are therefore are very difficult to simulate. As in other areas, negative identification is often easier than positive identification.

Sources of degradation in the message
A message which is recorded and played back has the following possible sources of degradation (in other words these instruments may not fully and equally transmit the full range of wavelengths of human speech or other sounds of forensic interest). A system is only as good as its weakest link. Optimal performance from these is hard to obtain in a laboratory, and even harder in a courtroom.

● the microphone: only the very best microphones are equally sensitive to all the wavelengths of human speech; most remove or reduce certain of them.

- the amplifier: the energy produced by the diaphragm on a microphone is tiny so it must be amplified before recording; amplifiers also tend not to be entirely faithful;
- the recording head;
- the recording medium: usually tape, but increasingly digital encoding;
- the playback head;
- the amplifier;
- the speaker.

Other possible sources of problems are:

- noise: ambient or from the recording machine;
- multiple voices;
- filtering produced by telephones;
- the acoustic properties of the situation where the recording takes place.

There are 'filter' techniques that can be used to reduce or enhance bandwidths which are affected by the recording process or noise. Hollien suggests a technique where a 'filtered' and 'non-filtered' version of the recording are made, and they are played simultaneously, one into each ear of the hearer. This seems to greatly enhance people's ability to understand distorted or degraded speech.

Writing

I include in this category handwriting, typeface and other surface characteristics of a text such as the width of margins. Handwriting is an old established field of identification, although the widespread use of type/print has rendered it less useful. The survey of the field in Found, Dick and Rogers (1994) indicates that handwriting analysis is still of identificatory potential, although its certainty varies from case to case. There are features which distinguish groups or communities of writers: **class features, individual features** and **idiosyncratic features**. It is the combinations of these three types that lead to the possibility of identification. The methodology of handwriting analysis involves general features such as the size and slope of handwriting, along with detailed analysis of each of the stroke marks used to construct individual letters, looking for consistent patterns. There is also an emerging area of identification of printers and computer programs.

Other possible identificatory aspects of writing are spelling and punctuation. Eagleson (1994) shows how these features contributed to the identification of the writer of a letter which purported to be a suicide note. Police believed the letter had been written by the woman's husband, who was suspected of murdering her. Eagleson compared samples of the husband's and the wife's writing, and was able to show a range of spelling features that were found in the disputed letter and the man's other writing, but not in the woman's writing, particularly 'assult' (for assault), 'carring' (carrying), 'thier' (their), and 'treat' (threat).

Words

Uses of a particular word or words may contribute to the identification of an author, for instance it may be possible to say that a person is unlikely to know a word that occurs in a language sample, and is therefore unlikely to be the author of that sample. For example there may be technical or specialized vocabulary that a person is unlikely to know, or in the case of a second language speaker, there may be words beyond his/her current level of development. Coulthard (1997) and elsewhere has presented evidence that when police fabricate evidence, they sometimes slip into the vocabulary of police jargon and indulge in over-elaboration as discussed in chapters 2 and 3. This type of evidence identifies the author as the police rather than the suspect. Coulthard (1994a) also showed that corpora and concordancing based methodologies can be used for this kind of work. He showed that an incriminating word in one police statement occurred much more frequently than is normal, and in a range of contexts that demonstrated that the text was much more likely to have been fabricated than spontaneously produced.

Another type of forensic work, sometimes known as 'Stylometry' is based on word counts. It is associated particularly with the Rev A. Morton and involves counting the frequency of occurrence of particular types of word, most commonly 'nouns beginning with a vowel' and 'two/three letter words'. These frequencies are then compared for different texts using a statistical method called Q Sum. It is said that these features vary among authors. Stylometry has been attacked on two main issues, its reliability and its validity. Reliability in this case refers to the issue of whether analytic techniques are used correctly. In stylometry, statistics are often used inappropriately (Smith 1994), and even Bissell (1995: 59), a supporter of stylometry, writes 'word-count analysis, using cusums or other techniques, can form only part of an investigation into authorship'. Validity is the issue of whether an approach can be seen to be doing what it purports to do. There is little basis for assuming that the use of nouns beginning with a vowel varies consistently between individuals, indeed most linguists would assume that this feature would vary within the writing of an individual. (In speech, of course, initial consonant deletion (of 'h' for instance) could increase the number of initial vowels, and words do not contain three letters but a sequence of speech sounds, so the method is largely irrelevant.) For these reasons stylometry is currently not regarded as sufficiently dependable for forensic uses, and its use as evidence is subject to challenge. As with 'voiceprints' its appearance of scientific objectivity may be misleading.

Morphology

In one case in which I was involved, a police record of an interview purported to be a 'verbatim' transcript. It reported a low proficiency second language speaker using a past continuous tense ('was/were -ing'). The man in question consistently used either no tense marking at all, or a simple past tense (-ed) on a limited set of verbs. The past continuous tense was several language acquisition stages beyond the man's proficiency level, so I was able to say that it was unlikely that this was his own wording, and this feature along with a number of others cast doubt on the fidelity of the record. Jensen (1995) reports a similar case where the transcript, on language acquisition grounds, was most unlikely to be a faithful record of the interviewee's speech. The problem that arises with this type of evidence is whether it is possible that the speaker is artificially depressing his/her language level during the recording with the linguist. There are various measures that can be taken to address this problem, including interviews of considerable length (at least 30 minutes), topics that emotionally engage the interviewee so that monitoring of speech is reduced (Labov 1972), and careful analysis afterwards. I have found that subjects cannot consistently depress their language level in such circumstances, and have detected several attempts to do so (and in consequence refused to be involved in the cases).

Discourse

Coulthard (1994b) gave evidence at the appeal of the Birmingham Six in the UK, which showed on the basis of the nature of the discourse that the police records of interview contained fabrication. For instance, they contained repeated reference to a 'white plastic bag' in that full form, rather than beginning with the full form, and then using only 'bag' thereafter, which would be normal in spoken discourse. This hyper elaboration is typical of legal language, rather than everyday speech. Another feature was that the man consistently referred to his friends by their first name, or their first name plus surname, while in the contested samples, they were referred to by surname only. Coulthard also examined a range of other features. The Birmingham Six were subsequently released and paid compensation.

Sociolinguistics

Variations in all the areas mentioned above (speech sounds, words, syntax, etc.) are associated with different geographical regions, that is dialect (e.g. Queensland English); with socioeconomic status, that is sociolect (e.g. cultured English); and with different uses of language, that is register (e.g. the language of the courtroom). Linguists have analysed many of these variations. There is a substantial literature on the forensic use of evidence on dialect differences. As a number of people speak any dialect, such evidence is typically not used to provide identification, unless the speaker is one of a small number of speakers (e.g. who said a particular sentence in a room containing four people). The most common use of such evidence is negative, that is saying that particular speech is not the voice of a certain person on the basis of dialectal or sociolectal evidence. Labov and Harris (1994) describe the Prinzivalli case, in which Labov says that there was no doubt that Prinzivalli could not have made a bomb threat phone call because the bomb threat voice had an unmistakable New England (Boston area) accent, while Prinzivalli had an equally unmistakable New York accent. His main problem was convincing the court of this (see Labov and Harris for a clear exposition). The evidence was accepted and Prinzivalli was acquitted.

Chambers (1990) discusses a case in which the historical claim of a group of indigenous Canadians to a particular area of land was strongly supported by evidence from dialectologists based on both morphological and lexical evidence.

In one case the *Australian Refugee Review Tribunal* asked me to tell them whether a man was a speaker of Canadian English. On the basis of some distinctive features, I was able to tell them that the accent came from the West of Canada or the North West of the USA, but lacked the local knowledge to tell them from which side of the border the man came. This is a good example of linguists needing local experience of accents (preferably as a native) in order to accurately identify them.

Milroy (1984) discusses cases where the identification of regional dialects was involved, including one where he was able to identify two different accents in telephone calls, neither of which belonged to the convicted man. Milroy did not believe that either accent was feigned, since they were consistently sustained for substantial periods of time. This bring us to the important issue of whether people can convincingly fake or assume a dialect or accent that is not their own. There are recent examples of people in films producing convincing versions of accents not their own – notice for instance Merryl Streep in 'The French Lieutenant's Woman' producing a convincing British accent (but later failing in her attempt at an Australian accent). Ash (1988) had Philadelphia speakers attempt to disguise their voices, but found that none of them could consistently disguise their vowels in such a way as to prevent their identification as Philadelphia speakers. Markham (1999) discusses experiments using phonetically trained judges and some assumed accents, and concludes (Markham 1999: 298) 'there is wide variation in the ability of even highly motivated and perhaps phonetically talented speakers convincingly and consistently to create natural-sounding accent reading for dialectal accents other than their own'.

Plagiarism

One interesting, and increasingly common, variant of work on authorship is plagiarism. For example one case in which I was involved determining whether parts of a questionnaire had been copied without the permission of the original author, or even an attribution to him. The difficulty in such a case is that it requires careful study of a range of other questionnaires to assure that there was not a common source of influence on both.

Oyanadel and Samaniego (1999) mention that in a case in which they gave evidence, the text that had been produced by plagiarism contained information that was only available to the writer of the source text. This was clear evidence of its derivative nature.

Woolls and Coulthard (1998) describe the use of various computer programs, particular concordancing programs, which reveal the degree of lexical overlap between texts. In particular they show that the essays of three students suspected of collaborating shared five times more vocabulary than those of other students. They were also able to show a number of sentences that were shared in only slightly modified form by the three writers, by using an abridgement program.

Author profiling

It may often not be possible, and in some cases it may not be necessary, to provide language based identification of a particular person. However, another forensic service that linguists may be able to provide is a profile of the speaker or writer. Speech in particular may give broad band indicators of a person's age, sex, social class, level of education and regional origins. Sometimes the use of jargon may even indicate a person's likely profession or avocation. This type of evidence may be more useful to police investigation, for instance for the elimination of suspects, than in court.

In the Yorkshire Ripper case the phonetician Stanley Ellis was able to locate the accent of a hoax caller to a particular neighbourhood of Sunderland (Chambers 1990: 22). In one case of a threatening call to an insurance company, certain generationally marked expressions revealed that the caller was probably less than thirty, the voice quality indicated that it was probably a male, and despite extensive foul language the vocabulary revealed that the writer was probably well educated. The main suspect shared these characteristics, while the other suspects did not, so the company was able to strengthen its convictions concerning the likely caller.

Another case involved the writer of the ransom letter in the kidnapping (well known in Australia) of Kerry Whelan. The letter contained inside information that could only have come from the kidnapper, so it was not a hoax letter. The writer of the letter consistently used the plural 'we' to refer to the kidnappers. The writer used 'Australian' in 'You are not our first Australian target', when the natural thing in Australia is to assume this, and also demanded payment in US dollars. The style of parts of the letter was telegraphic, and there were a number of spelling errors. The overall impact of these features was to construct an image of a 'professional foreign gang'. This was, however, contradicted by the Australian local knowledge in the mention of 'new plastic notes'. The spelling errors were found almost entirely in the early paragraphs of the letter, which may indicate that they were a deliberate strategy that was not adhered to later. The writer also revealed that s/he was a highly proficient and probably well educated user of English, by using many expression like the following: 'dire consequences', 'breaching a rule', 'implicitly followed', 'remote transmitting devices' and 'means of tracing the money'. These contradictions raised the possibility that the writer was attempting to mask the fact that s/he was an Australian native speaker, and that the ransom letter was a deliberate attempt to mislead the police. Here profiling gave useful information concerning the background of the writer.

The man who was later charged with the kidnapping had a background in radio advertising. A clever police officer noticed that there were resemblances between the telegraphic style of the ransom letter and the scripts used in radio advertising, so I and the other linguist in the case, Robert Eagleson, were asked to compare the ransom letter with some examples of such scripts for signs of 'intertextuality'. This phenomenon is one where the characteristics of a text or text type are in some way reproduced in another text or text type. In this case, whether some characteristics of radio advertisement scripts were manifested in the ransom letter. The ransom letter and the radio advertising scripts shared the following features (examples on the left are from the ransom letter, and on the right are from radio advertisement scripts).

1. typed entirely in capital letters
2. very short paragraphs, consisting roughly of a single unit of information
3. many 'minor clauses' without a main verb, e.g.

NO RADIOACTIVE DUSTS.   THREE DRAWS TONIGHT, COMMENCING AT 7.15

NO DYES   NO WAITING
NO PAPER CORRENCY

4. a lack of conjunctions linking ideas, e.g.

TAKE CARE THIS IS YOUR   THE CELEBRATIONS DON'T
ONLY MEANS OF EVER   STOP NOW. THEY
SEEING HER ALIVE AGAIN   CONTINUE

5. sentences beginning with *and*, *then* and *but*
6. extensive use of simple commands, e.g.

| BE READY TO LEAVE WITH THE MONEY AT ANY TIME | CALL AMAZING CLEAN |

DO NOT UNDERSTIMATE OUR CAPABILITIES

DON'T FORGET THE POKER MACHINE PROMOTION STOP DREAMING!

While is possible that these resemblances are coincidental, and a result of an attempt to produce clear direct and spoken-like language in both cases, it seems unlikely that so many features would be shared. It seems possible that the writer of the ransom letter had experience of scripts for radio advertising, so this is a possible example of language pointing towards the writer's profession. However, without a database of ransom letters which would show how common these feature are in such letters, it was impossible to arrive at an estimate of the degree of likelihood, and it is unlikely that such evidence would be accepted in court.

Conclusion

Language evidence is a fascinating area of applied linguistics that is growing rapidly. The journal *Forensic Linguistics* contains many more case studies, and further developments of the basic framework presented in this chapter. However, the warnings that were presented in the earlier section on the ethics and admissibility of linguistic evidence are important – there have already been some notable failures as well as considerable successes. Like many of the other topics discussed in this book, linguistic evidence is of social importance, in this case because it may reveal problematic miscommunication, or contribute to the conviction of the guilty and the freeing of the innocent.

References

American Civil Liberties Union (1997) *ACLU Briefing Paper Number 2* (Washington, DC: Department of Public Education).

Anderson, R. C. (1984) The role of the reader's schema in comprehension, learning and memory. In R. C. Anderson, J. Osborn and R. J. Tierney (eds), *Learning to Read in American Schools: Basal Readers and Content Texts* (Hillsdale, NJ: Erlbaum).

Anderson, R. C. and Pearson, P. D. (1988) A schema-theoretic view of basic processes in reading comprehension. In P. Carrell, J. Devine and D. Esky (eds), *Interactive Approaches to Second-Language Reading* (Cambridge: Cambridge University Press) pp. 37–55.

Ash, S. (1988) Speaker identification in sociolinguistics and criminal law. In K. Ferrara, B. Brown, K. Walters and J. Baugh (eds), *Linguistic Change and Contact* (Austin, TX: Department of Linguistics, University of Texas) pp. 25–33.

Atkinson, J. M. and Drew, P. (1979) *Order in Court: The Organisation of Verbal Interaction in Judicial Setting* (London: Macmillan).

Auburn, T., Drake, S. and Willig, C. (1995) 'You punched him, didn't you?': versions of violence in accusatory interviews. *Discourse and Society*, 6 (3), 353–86.

Austin, J. L. (1963) *How to Do Things with Words* (Oxford: Oxford University Press).

Baldwin, J. (1993) Police interview techniques: establishing truth or proof. *British Journal of Criminology*, 33 (3), 325–52.

Baldwin, J. (1994) Police interrogation: What are the rules of the game? In D. Morgan and G. Stephenson (eds), *Suspicion and Silence: The Right to Silence in Criminal Investigations* (London: Blackstone Press) pp. 66–76.

Baldwin, J. and French, P. (1990) *Forensic Phonetics* (London: Pinter).

Barber, C. L. (1962) Some measurable characteristics of modern scientific prose. In F. Behre (ed.), *Contributions to English Syntax and Philology* (Götesburg: Almqvist and Wiksell) pp. 21–43.

Baynham, M. (1995) *Literacy Practices: Investigating Literacy in Social Contexts* (London: Longman).

Bell, A. (1997) Language style as audience design. In N. Coupland and A. Jaworski (eds), *Sociolinguistics: A Reader and Coursebook* (Basingstoke: Macmillan) pp. 240–50.

Benmaman, V. (1999) Bilingual legal interpreter education. *Forensic Linguistics*, 6 (1), 109–14.

Bennett, W. L. and Feldman, M. S. (1981) *Reconstructing Reality in the Courtroom* (London: Tavistock Publications).

Bentham, J. (1838) *The Works of Jeremy Bentham*, ed. J. Bowring (Edinburgh: William Tait).

Berk-Seligson, S. (1990) *The Bilingual Courtroom Court Interpreters in the Judicial Process* (Chicago, IL: University of Chicago Press).

Berk-Seligson, S. (1999) The impact of court interpreting on the coerciveness of leading questions. *Forensic Linguistics*, 6 (1), 30–51.

Berry, M. (1981) Systemic linguistics and discourse analysis: a multi-layered approach to exchange structure. In M. Coulthard and M. Montgomery (eds), *Studies in Discourse Analysis* (London: Routledge and Kegan Paul) pp. 120–45.

Bhatia, V. K. (1987) Textual mapping in British legislative writing. *World Englishes*, 6 (1), 1–10.

Bhatia, V. K. (1993) *Analysing Genre: Language Use in Professional Settings* (Harlow: Longman).

Bhatia, V. K. (1994) Cognitive structuring in legislative provisions. In J. Gibbons (ed.), *Language and the Law* (London: Longman) pp. 136–55.

Biber, D. (1988) *Variation Across Speech and Writing* (Cambridge: Cambridge University Press).

Bissell, D. (1995) *Statistical Methods for Text Analysis by Word-Counts* (Swansea: European Business Management School, University of Wales).

Black, H. C. (1990) *Black's Law Dictionary*. (6th edn) (St Paul, MN: West).

Blain, M. (1995) Group defamation and the Holocaust. In M. H. Freedman and E. M. Freedman (eds), *Group Defamation and Freedom of Speech: The Relationship between Language and Violence* (Westport, CT: Greenwood Press) pp. 45–68.

Bourhis, R. Y. (ed.) (1984) *Conflict and Language Planning in Quebec* (Clevedon: Multilingual Matter).

Bowe, H. and Storey, K. (1995) Linguistic analysis as evidence of speaker identification: Demand and response. In D. Eades (ed.), *Language in Evidence Issues Confronting Aboriginal and Multicultural Australia* (Sydney, NSW: University of New South Wales Press) pp. 187–200.

Bower, G. H., Black, J. D. and Turner, T. J. (1979) Scripts in memory for text. *Cognitive Psychology*, 11, 177–220.

Brennan, M. (1994) Cross-examining children in criminal courts: Child welfare under attack. In J. Gibbons (ed.), *Language and the Law* (Harlow: Longman) pp. 199–216.

Brennan, M. and Brown, R. (1997) *Equality before the Law: Deaf People's Access to Justice* (Durham: Deaf Studies Research Unit, University of Durham).

Brière, E. J. (1978) Limited English speakers and the Miranda Rights. *TESOL Quarterly*, 12 (3), 235–45.

Broeders, A. P. A. (1999) Some observations on the use of probability scales in forensic identification. *Forensic Linguistics,* 6 (2), 228–41.

Brown, G. (1990) *Listening to Spoken English* (Harlow: Longman).

Brown, P. and Levinson, S. (1978) Universals in language use: politeness phenomena. In E. Goody (ed.), *Questions and Politeness* (Cambridge: Cambridge University Press) pp. 56–311.

Brown, R. and Gilman, A. (1960) The pronouns of power and solidarity. In T. Sebeok (ed.), *Style in Language* (New York, NY: John Wiley) pp. 253–77.

Bull, R. and Carson, D. (1995) *Handbook of Psychology in Legal Contexts* (Chichester: Wiley).

Bülow-Møller, A. M. (1991) Trial evidence: overt and covert communication in court. *International Journal of Applied Linguistics,* 1 (1) 38–60.

Carlen, P. (1976) *Magistrate's Justice* (Oxford: Martin Robertson).

Carroll, J. (1995) The use of interpreters in court. *Forensic Linguistics,* 2 (1), 65–73.

Cavagnoli, S. and Wölk, J. (1997) *Einführung in die italienische Reschssprache – Introduzione all'italiano giuridico* (Munich/Vienna/Bern: Beck/Manz/Stämpfli).

Celis, C. R. (1999) Linguistic measurement of proximity of harm. Unpublished Ph.D. proposal. Department of Linguistics, University of Chicago.

Chabun, W. (1997) Glossary of 'Copspeak' terms, *Calgary Crime Stoppers* (Calgary: Website <http://crimestoppers.iul-ccs.com/glossary.html>).

Chafe, W. (1985) Linguistic differences produced by differences between speaking and writing. In D. L. Olson, W. Torrance and A. Hildgard (eds), *Literacy, Language and Learning* (Cambridge: Cambridge University Press) pp. 105–23.

Chafe, W. and Tannen, D. (1987) The relation between written and spoken language. *Annual Review of Anthropology,* 16, 383–409.

Chambers, J. K. (1990) Forensic dialectology and the Bear Island land claim. In R. W. Rieber and W. A. Stewart (eds), *The Language Scientist as Expert in the Legal Setting: Issues in Forensic Linguistics* (New York, NY: New York Academy of Sciences) pp. 19–31.

Charrow, R. P. and Charrow, V. (1979) Making legal language understandable: A psycholinguistic study of jury instructions. *Columbia Law Review* (79), 1306–74.

Christie, M. and Harris, S. (1985) Communication breakdown in the Aboriginal classroom. In J. Pride (ed.), *Cross-Cultural Encounters: Communication and Mis-Communication* (Melbourne, Vic.: River Seine) pp. 81–109.

Cicourel, A. V. (1976) *The Social Organization of Juvenile Justice* (London: Heinemann Education).

Clark, H. H. (1996) *Using Language* (Cambridge: Cambridge University Press).

Coates, A. (1964) *Myself a Mandarin: Memoirs of a Special Magistrate* (Hong Kong: Heinemann Educational Books (Asia) Ltd).

Coldrey, J. (1987) Aboriginals and the criminal courts. In K. M. Hazlehurst (ed.), *Ivory Scales: Black Australia and the Law* (Sydney, NSW: University of New South Wales Press) pp. 81–92.

Colin, J. and Morris, R. (1996) *Interpreters and the Legal Process* (Winchester, England: Waterside Press).

Commissioner of Police (1998) *Code of Practice for Custody, Rights, Investigation,*

Management and Evidence (CRIME). (Sydney, NSW: New South Wales Police Service).

Commonwealth Attorney General's Department (1991) *Access to Interpreters in the Australian Legal System* (Canberra: Australian Government Publishing Service).

Conley, J. M., O'Barr, W. M. and Lind, E. A. (1978) The power of language: presentational style in the courtroom. *Duke Law Journal*, 1375–99.

Cooke, M. (1995a) Aboriginal evidence in the cross-cultural courtroom. In D. Eades (ed.), *Language in Evidence: Issues Confronting Aboriginal and Multicultural Australia* (Sydney, NSW: University of New South Wales Press) pp. 55–96.

Cooke, M. (1995b) Interpreting in a cross-cultural cross-examination: An Aboriginal case study. *International Journal of the Sociology of Language*, 113, 99–111.

Cooke, M. (1995c) Understood by all concerned? Anglo/Aboriginal translation. In M. Morris (ed.), *Translation and the Law* (Amsterdam: John Benjamins) pp. 37–63.

Cooper, L. S. (1997) Police jargon: How to talk like a cop (Denver: Website <http://members.aol.com/HeartODnvr/cop1.html>).

Coulson, N. J. (1971) *A History of Islamic Law* (Edinburgh: Edinburgh University Press).

Coulthard, M. (1994a) On the use of corpora in the analysis of forensic texts. *Forensic Linguistics*, 1 (1), 26–43.

Coulthard, M. (1994b) Powerful evidence for the defence: an exercise in forensic discourse analysis. In J. Gibbons (ed.), *Language and the Law* (Harlow: Longman) pp. 414–27.

Coulthard, M. (1997) A failed appeal. *Forensic Linguistics*, 4 (2), 287–302.

Coulthard, M. (2001) Power and control in the re-presentation of evidence. Paper at Discourses on Discourse Conference. 9 November 2001. University of Technology, Sydney.

Cowlishaw, W. (1988) *Black, White or Brindle: Race in Rural Australia* (Cambridge: Cambridge University Press).

Cox, M. and Tanford, S. (1989) Effects of evidence and instruction in civil trials: An experimental investigation of rules of admissibility. *Social Behaviour*, 4, 31–55.

Criminal Justice Commission of Queensland (1996) *Aboriginal Witnesses in Queensland's Criminal Courts* (Brisbane: Criminal Justice Commission).

Cross, R. (1979) *Evidence* (5th edn) (London: Butterworth).

Crystal, D. and Davy, D. (1969) *Investigating English Style* (London: Longman).

Cunningham, C., Levi, J., Green, G. and Kaplan, J. (1994) Plain meaning and hard cases. *Yale Law Journal*, 103 (6), 1561–1625.

Danet, B. (1980) 'Baby' or 'fetus': language and the construction of reality in a manslaughter trial. *Semiotica*, 32, 187–219.

Danet, B. (1984) The magic flute: a prosodic analysis of binomial expression in legal Hebrew. *Text*, 4 (1–3), 143–72.

Danet, B. and Bogoch, B. (1994) Orality, literacy, and performativity in Anglo-Saxon wills. In J. Gibbons (ed.), *Language and the Law* (London: Longman) pp. 100–35.

Danet, B. and Kermish, N. C. (1978) Courtroom questioning: a sociolinguistic perspective. In L. N. Massery (ed.), *Psychology and Persuasion in Advocacy* (Washington, DC: Association of Trial Lawyers of America, National College of Advocacy) pp. 413–41.

David, R. and Brierly, J. E. C. (1985) *Major Legal Systems in the World Today* (London: Stevens).

Davies, E. C. (forthcoming) Register distinctions and measures of complexity in the language of legal contracts. In J. Gibbons, V. Prakasham and K. V. Tirumalesh (eds), *Justice and Language* (Delhi: Longman Orient).

De Seife, R. J. A. (1994) *The Shari'a: An Introduction to the Law of the Islam* (San Francisco: Austin and Winfield).

Derham, D., Maher, F. and Waller, L. (1991) *An Introduction to Law* (Sydney: Law Book Company).

Diamond, S. S. and Levi, J. N. (1996) Improving decisions on death by revising and testing jury instructions. *Judicature,* 79 (5), 224–32.

Dickens, C. (1893) *Bleak House* (London: Chapman and Hall).

Drew, P. (1990) Strategies in the contest between lawyer and witness in cross-examination. In J. N. Levi and A. G. Walker (eds), *Language in the Judicial Process* (New York: Plenum) pp. 39–64.

Duarte i Monserrat, C. (1993) *Llengua i Administració* (Barcelona: Columna Edicions).

Duarte i Montserrat, C. and Martínez, A. (1995) *El Lenguaje Jurídico* (Buenos Aires: A–Z editora).

Dumas, B. K. (1990) An analysis of the adequacy of federally mandated cigarette package warnings. In J. N. Levi and A. G. Walker (eds), *Language in the Judicial Process* (New York: Plenum) pp. 309–42.

Dumas, B. K. (2000) US pattern jury instructions: problems and proposals. *Forensic Linguistics* 7 (1), 49–71.

Eades, D. (1992) *Aboriginal English and the Law: Communication with Aboriginal English-Speaking Clients: A Handbook for Legal Practitioners* (Brisbane: Queensland Law Society).

Eades, D. (1993) The case for Condren: Aboriginal English, pragmatics and the law. *Journal of Pragmatics,* 20 (2), 141–62.

Eades, D. (1994a) A case of communicative clash: Aboriginal English and the legal system. In J. Gibbons (ed.), *Language and the Law* (London: Longman) pp. 234–64.

Eades, D. (1994b) Forensic linguistics in Australia: an overview. *Forensic Linguistics,* 1 (2), 113–32.

Eades, D. (1995a) Language and the law: White Australia vs Nancy. In M. Walsh and C. Yallop (eds), *Language and Culture in Aboriginal Australia* (Canberra: Aboriginal Studies Press) pp. 181–90.

Eades, D. (ed.) (1995b) *Language in Evidence: Linguistic and Legal Perspectives in Multicultural Australia* (Sydney: University of New South Wales Press).

Eades, D. (1996) Verbatim courtroom transcripts and discourse analysis. In H.

Kniffka, S. Blackwell and M. Coulthard (eds), *Recent Developments in Forensic Linguistics*. Frankfurt am Main: Peter Lang, pp. 241–54.

Eades, D. (1997) Language in court: the acceptance of linguistic evidence about Indigenous Australians in the criminal justice system. *Australian Aboriginal Studies*, 1, 15–27.

Eades, D. (2000) *I don't think it's an answer to the question*: Silencing Aboriginal witnesses in court. *Language in Society*, 29: 161–95.

Eagleson, R. D. (1991) The Plain English Movement in Australia and the United Kingdom. In E. R. Steinberg (ed.), *Plain Language Principles and Practice* (Detroit: Wayne State University Press) pp. 30–42.

Eagleson, R. (1994) Forensic analysis of personal written texts: A case study. In J. Gibbons (ed.), *Language and the Law* (Harlow: Longman) pp. 363–73.

Edwards, J. (1994) *Multilingualism* (London: Routledge).

English, P. W. and Sales, B. D. (1997) A ceiling or consistency effect for the comprehension of jury instructions. *Psychology, Public Policy, and Law*, 3, 381–401.

Evans, K. (1983) *Advocacy at the Bar* (London: Blackstone).

Fairclough, N. (1989) *Language and Power* (London: Longman).

Feak, C., Reinhart, S. and Sinsheimer, A. (2000) A preliminary analysis of law review notes. *English for Specific Purposes*, 19, 197–220.

Felker, D. B., Pickering, F., Charrow, V. R., Holland, V. M. and Redish, J. C. (1981), *Guidelines for Document Designers* (Washington, DC: American Institutes for Research).

Fergenson, L. R. (1995) Group defamation: from language to thought to action. In M. H. Freedman and E. M. Freedman (eds), *Group Defamation and Freedom of Speech: The Relationship between Language and Violence* (Westport, CT: Greenwood Press) pp. 71–85.

Ferguson, C. A. (1964) Diglossia. In D. Hymes (ed.), *Language in Culture and Society* (New York: Harper and Row).

Finkel, N. J. (1995) *Commonsense Justice: Jurors' Notions of the Law* (Cambridge, MA: Harvard University Press).

Finkel, N. J., and Groscup, J. L. (1997) Crime prototypes, objective vs. subjective culpability, and a commonsense balance. *Law and Human Behaviour*, 21, 209–30.

Fishman, J. A. (1967) Bilingualism with and without diglossia; diglossia with and without bilingualism. *Journal of Social Issues*, 23 (2), 29–38.

Found, B., Dick, D. and Rogers, D. (1994) The structure of forensic handwriting and signature comparisons. *Forensic Linguistics*, 1 (2), 183–96.

Freedman, M. H. and Freedman, E. M. (eds) (1995) *Group Defamation and Freedom of Speech: The Relationship between Language and Violence* (Westport, CT: Greenwood Press).

Gaete, C., Ilabaca, P., Meza, E. and Zúñiga, L. (1999) Brève acercamiento al COA feminina. *Cuadernos de Lenguaje*, 1, 13–21.

Gal, S. (1979) *Language Shift – Social Determinants of Linguistic Change in Bilin-*

gual Austria (New York: Academic Press).

Gardner, R. (1994) Conversation analysis transcription. *Australian Review of Applied Linguistics, Series S, Number 11*, 185–91.

Garfinkel, H. (1967) *Studies in Ethnomethodology* (Englewood Cliffs, NJ: Prentice Hall).

Gatley, J. C. C. (1998) *Gatley on Libel and Slander* (9th edn) (London: Sweet and Maxwell).

Gibbons, J. (1981) A tentative framework for speech act description of the utterance particle in conversational Cantonese. *Linguistics*, 18 (9/10), 763–75.

Gibbons, J. (1990) Applied linguistics in court. *Applied Linguistics*, 11 (3), 229–37.

Gibbons, J. (1994) (ed.) *Language and the Law* (Harlow: Longman).

Gibbons, J. (1995) What got lost? The place of electronic recording and interpreters in police interviews. In D. Eades (ed.), *Language in Evidence: Linguistic and Legal Perspectives in Multicultural Australia* (Sydney: University of New South Wales Press).

Gibbons, J. (1996) Distortions of the police interview process revealed by videotape. *Forensic Linguistics*, 3 (2) 289–98.

Gibbons, J. (1999) Register aspects of literacy in Spanish. *Written Language and Literacy*, 2 (1), 63–88.

Gibbons, J. (2001) Legal transformations in Spanish: an 'audiencia' in Chile. *Forensic Linguistics*, 8 (1), 24–43.

Giles, H., and Coupland, N. (1991) *Language: Context and Consequences* (Pacific Grove CA: Brooks/Cole).

Giles, H. and Powesland, P. (1975) *Speech Style and Social Evaluation* (London: Academic Press).

Givón, T. (1985) Function, structure and language acquisition. In D. Slobin (ed.), *The Cross-Linguistic Study of Language Acquisition* (Hillsdale, NJ: Lawrence Erlbaum) pp. 1005–28.

Goldman, L. R. (1986a) The presentational style of women in Huli disputes. *Pacific Linguistics*, 24, 213–89.

Goldman, L. (1993) *The Culture of Coincidence: Accident and Absolute Liability in Huli* (Oxford: Oxford University Press).

Goldman, L. (1994) Accident and absolute liability in anthropology. In J. Gibbons (ed.), *Language and the Law* (Harlow: Longman) pp. 51–99.

Goodrich, P. (1987) *Legal Discourse* (London: Macmillan).

Goodrich, P. (1988) Modalities of annunciation: an introduction to courtroom speech. In R. Levelson (ed.), *Law and Semiotics*, vol 2. (New York: Plenum Press) 143–65.

Gowers, E. (1948) *Plain Words* (London: Her Majesty's Stationery Office).

Gowers, E. (1954) *The Complete Plain Words* (London: Her Majesty's Stationery Office).

Green, G. M. (1990) Linguistic analysis of conversation as evidence regarding the interpretation of speech events. In J. N. Levi and A. G. Walker (eds), *Language in the Judicial Process* (New York: Plenum Press) pp. 247–77.

Greenwood, J. M., Horney, J., Jacobovitch, M.-D., Lowenstein, F. B. and Wheeler, R. R. (1983) *A Comparative Evaluation of Stenographic and Audiotape Methods for US District Court Reporting* (Washington, DC: Federal Judicial Center).

Grice, H. P. (1975) Logic and conversation. In P. Cole and J. Morgan (eds), *Speech Acts* (New York: Academic Press) pp. 41–58.

Gudjonsson, G. H. (1999) *The Psychology of Interrogations, Confessions and Testimony* (Chichester: John Wiley).

Gumperz, J. (1982) Fact and inference in courtroom testimony. In J. Gumperz (ed.), *Language and Social Identity* (Cambridge: Cambridge University Press) pp. 163–95.

Gunnarsson, B.-L. (1984) Functional comprehensibility of legislative texts: Experiments with a Swedish act of parliament. *Text*, 4 (1–3), 71–105.

Gustafsson, M. (1984) The syntactic features of binomial expressions in legal English. *Text*, 4 (1–3), 123–41.

Hale, S. (1997) The treatment of register variation in court interpreting. *The Translator*, 3 (1), 39–54.

Hale, S. (1999) Interpreters' treatment of discourse markers in courtroom questions. *Forensic Linguistics*, 6 (1), 57–82.

Hale, S. and Gibbons, J. (1999) Varying realities patterned changes in the interpreter's representation of courtroom and external realities. *Applied Linguistics*, 20 (2), 203–20.

Hall, P. (1998) 'Do you agree that you then said, "It's like this, she did fall down the stairs . . . " ': Electronically recorded interviews with suspect persons (ERISP) register or merely situation? Unpublished BA Honours thesis, Macquarie University.

Hall, P. (forthcoming) Prone to distortions? undue reliance on unreliable records in the NSW Police Service's formal interview model. In J. Gibbons, V. Prakasam and K. V. Tirumalesh (eds), *Language and Justice* (Delhi: Longman Orient).

Halliday, M. A. K. (1985) *Spoken and Written Language* (Geelong, Victoria: Deakin University Press).

Halliday, M. A. K. and Hasan, R. (1985) *Language, Context and Text: Aspects of Language in a Social-Semiotic Perspective* (Geelong, Victoria: Deakin University Press).

Haney, C. and Lynch, M. (1994) Comprehending life and death matters. *Law and Human Behaviour*, 18, 411–36.

Harris, P. (1984) *An Introduction to Law* (London: Weidenfeld and Nicolson).

Harris, S. (1984) Questions as a mode of control in magistrates' courts. *International Journal of the Sociology of Language*, 49, 5–27.

Hasan, R. (1985) The structure of a text. In M. A. K. Halliday and R. Hasan (eds), *Language, Context and Text: Aspects of Language in a Social-Semiotic Perspective* (Geelong, Victoria: Deakin University Press) pp. 52–69.

Hayes, S. (1993) *People with an Intellectual Disability and the Criminal Justice System: Appearances before Local Courts* (4) (Sydney: New South Wales Law Reform Commission).

Heller, M. and Freeman, S. (1987) First encounters – the role of communication in the medical intake process. *Discourse Processes*, 10, 369–84.

Heritage, J. (1984) *Garfinkel and Ethnomethodology* (Cambridge: Polity).

Hiltunen, R. (1984) The type and structure of clausal embedding in legal English. *Text* (107), 108–9.

Hiltunen, R. (1990) *Chapters on Legal English: Aspects Past and Present of the Language of the Law* (Helsinki: Suomalainen Tiedeakatemia).

Hollien, H. (1990) *The Acoustics of Crime: The New Science of Forensic Phonetics* (New York: Plenum).

Hollien, H.(2001) *Forensic Voice Identification* (New York: Academic Press).

Howe, P. M. (1990) The problem of the problem question in English for Academic Legal Purposes. *English for Specific Purposes*, 9 (3), 215–36.

Huckin, T. N., Curtin, E. H. and Graham, D. (1991) Prescriptive linguistics and plain English: The case of 'whiz-deletions'. In E. R. Steinberg (ed.), *Plain Language Principles and Practice* (Detroit: Wayne State University Press) pp. 67–80.

Hutchby, I. and Wooffitt, R. (1998) *Conversation Analysis* (Cambridge: Polity Press).

Ibrahim, Z. and Bell, R. (forthcoming) By trial and error: A report on a national survey on the situation and perceptions of court interpreters in Malaysia. *Jurnal Bahasa Moden.*

Inbau, F. E., Reid, J. E. and Buckley, J. P. (1986) *Criminal Interrogation and Confessions* (Baltimore: Williams & Wilkins).

Ireland, E. M. (1993) When a chief speaks through his silence. *PoLAR: Political and Legal Anthropology Review*, 16, 19–25.

Jackson, B. (1988) *Law, Fact and Narrative Coherence* (Roby: Deborah Charles Publications).

Jackson, B. (1990) Semiotics and the problem of interpretation. In P. Nerholt (ed.), *Law Interpretation and Reality: Essays in Epistemology, Hermeneutics and Jurisprudence* (Dordrecht: Kluwer) pp. 84–103.

Jackson, B. S. (1991) Narrative models in legal proof. In D. R. Papke (ed.), *Narrative and Legal Discourse: A Reader in Storytelling and the Law* (Liverpool: Deborah Charles Publications) pp. 158–78.

Jackson, B. S. (1994) Some semiotic features of a judicial summing up in an English criminal court. *International Journal for the Semiotics of Law*, 7 (20), 201–24.

Jackson, B. S. (1997) Who enacts statutes? *Statute Law Review*, 18 (3), 177–207.

Jacquemet, M. (1996) *Credibility in Court: Communicative practices in the Camorra trials.* (Cambridge: Cambridge University Press).

Jaworski, A. (1993) *The Power of Silence: Social and Pragmatic Perspectives* (Newbury Park, CA: Sage).

Jefferson, G. (1984) Notes on a systematic deployment of the acknowledgment tokens 'yeah' and 'mm hm'. *Papers in Linguistics*, 17 (2), 197–216.

Jensen, M.-T. (1995) Linguistic evidence accepted in the case of a non-native speaker of English. In D. Eades (ed.), *Language in Evidence* (Sydney: University of New South Wales Press) pp. 127–46.

Kaplan, R. B. and Baldauf, R. B. (2001) Not only English: 'English-only' and the world. In R. D. González and I. Melis (eds), *Critical Perspectives on the Official English Movement*, vol. 2: *History, Theory and Policy* (Champaign-Urbana, IL: NCTE/Laurence Erlbaum).

Kintsch, W. (1988) The role of knowledge in discourse comprehension: A construction-integration model. *Psychological Review* (95), 163–82.

Klasmeyer, G. and Sendlmeier, W. F. (1997) The classification of different phonation types in emotional and neutral speech. *Forensic Linguistics*, 4 (1), 104–24.

Körner, H. (1992) *Legal Interviews: Solicitors and Clients from Non-English Speaking Background*, report to the Faculty of Education, University of Sydney.

Kramer, G. P., Kerr, N. L. and Carroll, J. S. (1990) Pretrial publicity, judicial remedies, and jury bias. *Law and Human Behaviour*, 14, 409–38.

Künzel, H. (1994) On the problem of speaker identification by victims and witnesses. *Forensic Linguistics*, 1 (1), 45–57.

Kurzon, D. (1986) *It is hereby performed . . . : Explorations in Legal Speech Acts* (Amsterdam: John Benjamins).

Kurzon, D. (1996) 'To speak or not to speak': the comprehensibility of the revised police caution (PACE). *International Journal for the Semiotics of Law*, IX (25), 3–16.

Kurzon, D. (1997) 'Legal language': varieties, genres, registers, discourses. *International Journal of Applied Linguistics*, 7 (2), 119–39.

Kurzon, D. (1998) *Discourse of Silence* (Amsterdam/Philadelphia: John Benjamins).

Labov, W. (1969) The logic of nonstandard English. *Georgetown Monographs on Language and Linguistics*, 22, 1–31.

Labov, W. (1972) *Sociolinguistic Patterns* (Philadelphia, PA: University of Pennsylvania Press).

Labov, W. and Harris, W. A. (1994) Addressing social issues through linguistic evidence. In J. Gibbons (ed.), *Language and the Law* (Harlow: Longman) pp. 265–305.

Labov, W. and Waletzky, J. (1967) Narrative analysis. In J. Helm (ed.), *Essays on the Verbal and Visual Arts* (Seattle, WA: University of Washington Press) pp. 12–44.

Lakoff, R. (1975) *Language and Women's Place* (New York: Harper and Row).

Lambert, W. E., Frankel, H. and Tucker, G. R. (1966) Judging personality through speech: a French–Canadian example. *Journal of Communication*, 16 (4), 305–21.

Lane, C. (1985) Mis-communication in cross-examination. In J. B. Pride (ed.), *Cross-Cultural Encounters: Communication and Mis-Communication* (Melbourne: River Seine) pp. 196–211.

Lane, C. (1993) 'Yes, I don't understand': Yes, no and European–Polynesian miscommunication in New Zealand. *Journal of Pragmatics*, 20, 163–88.

Lane, C., McKenzie-Bridel, K. and Curtis, L. (1999) The right to interpreting and translation services in New Zealand courts. *Forensic Linguistics*, 6 (1), 115–35.

Langton, M. (1988) Medicine square. In I. Keen (ed.), *Being Black: Aboriginal culture in 'settled' Australia* (Canberra: Aboriginal Studies Press) 201–25.

Larsen-Freeman, D. and Long, M. H. (1991) *An Introduction to Second-Language Acquisition Research* (London: Longman).

Lascar, E. (1997) Accreditation in Australia: An alternative means. In S. E. Carr, R. Roberts, A. Dufour and D. Steyn (eds), *The Critical Link: Interpreters in the Community* (Amsterdam: John Benjamins) pp. 119–30.

Law Reform Commission of Victoria (1987) *Plain English and the Law. Report No. 9* (Melbourne: F. D. Atkinson Government Printer).

Leets, L. and Giles, H. (1997) Words as weapons – when do they wound? Investigations of harmful speech. *Human Communication Research,* 2 (2), 260–301.

Lentine, G. and Shuy, R. (1990) 'Mc': meaning in the marketplace. *American Speech,* 65 (4), 349–66.

Lerm, H. (1997) Language manipulation in court cross-examination: 'how powerful is thy sword'. In K. Müller and S. Newman (eds), *Language in Court* (Port Elizabeth, South Africa: Vista University) pp. 167–81,

Levi, J. (1993) Evaluating jury comprehension of Illinois capital sentencing instructions. *American Speech,* 65 (4), 20–49.

Levi, J. (1994) Language as evidence: The linguist as expert witness in North American courts. *Forensic Linguistics: The International Journal of Speech Language and the Law,* 1 (1), 1–26.

Liberman, K. (1981) Understanding Aborigines in Australian courts of law. *Human Organization,* 40, 247–55.

Lieberman, J. and Sales, B. (1997) What social science teaches us about the jury instruction process. *Psychology, Public Policy, and Law,* 3, 589–664.

Liebes-Plesner, T. (1984) Rhetoric in the service of justice: The sociolinguistic construction of stereotypes in an Israeli rape trial. *Text,* 4 (1–3), 173–92.

Lind, E. A. and O'Barr, W. (1979) The social significance of speech in the courtroom. In H. Giles and R. St Clair (eds) *Language and Social Psychology* (Oxford: Basil Blackwell) pp. 66–87.

Loftus, E. (1979) *Eyewitness Testimony* (Cambridge, MA: Harvard University Press).

Lyons, J. (1977) *Semantics* (London: Cambridge University Press).

Maher, L., Roumeliotis, V., Webster, C. and Moore, H. (1998) *A Report on the Needs and Services for NESB Women at Mulawa* (Sydney, NSW: NSW Department of Corrective Services).

Maley, Y. (1985) Judicial discourse: the case of the legal judgment. In J. E. Clark (ed.), *The Cultivated Australian: Festschrift in Honour of Arthur Delbridge* (Hamburg: Helmut Buske Verlag) pp. 159–73.

Maley, Y. (1994) The language of the law. In J. Gibbons (ed.), *Language and the Law* (London: Longman) pp. 3–50.

Maley, Y. and Fahey, R. (1991) Presenting the evidence: Constructions of reality in court. *International Journal for the Semiotics of Law,* IV (10), 3–17.

Markham, D. (1999) Listeners and disguised voices: the imitation and perception of dialectal accent. *Forensic Linguistics*, 6 (2), 289–99.

Martin, J. R. (1990) Literacy in science: learning to handle text as technology. In F. Christie (ed.), *Literacy for a Changing World* (Hawthorn, Victoria: Australian Council for Educational Research) pp. 79–117.

Martin, J. R. (1992) *English Text: System and Structure* (Amsterdam/Philadelphia: John Benjamins).

Mather, L. and Yngvesson, B. (1982) *The Politics of Informal Justice* (New York).

Matoesian, G. (1993) *Reproducing Rape: Domination through Talk in the Courtroom* (Chicago: Chicago University Press).

Matoesian, G. (1997) 'You were interested in him as a person?' Rhythms of domination in the Kennedy Smith rape trial. *Law and Social Inquiry*, 22 (1), 55–91.

Mauet, T. A. (1996) *Trial Techniques* (3rd edn) (Boston, MA: Little, Brown).

Maynard, D. W. (1991) Narratives and narrative structure in plea bargaining. In D. R. Papke (ed.), *Narrative and the Legal Discourse: A Reader in Storytelling and the Law*. (Liverpool: Deborah Charles Publications) pp. 102–31.

McCauley, P. J. (1991) *Eternal Light* (London: Victor Gollancz).

McMenamin, G. R. (1993) *Forensic Stylistics* (Amsterdam: Elsevier).

Mellinkoff, D. (1963) *Language of the Law* (Boston, MA: Little, Brown).

Mendoza-Denton, N. (1995) Pregnant pauses: silence and authority in the Anita Hill–Clarence Thomas hearings. In K. Hall and M. Bucholtz (eds), *Gender Articulated: Language and the Socially Constructed Self* (New York: Routledge) pp. 51–66.

Michaels, S. and Collins, J. (1984) Oral discourse styles: classroom interaction and the acquisition of literacy. In D. Tannen (ed.), *Coherence in Spoken and Written Discourse* (Norwood, NJ: Ablex).

Mildren, D. (1999) Redressing the imbalance: Aboriginal people in the criminal justice system. *Forensic Linguistics*, 6 (1), 137–60.

Milroy, J. (1984) Sociolinguistic methodology and the identification of speakers' voices in legal proceedings. In P. Trudgill (ed.), *Applied Sociolinguistics* (New York: Academic Press) pp. 51–72.

Montero Brunner, F. (1996) El delito de injuria. Thesis. Facultad de Derecho, Santiago, Pontificia Universidad Católica de Chile.

Morris, R. (1995) Pragmatism, precept and passions: the attitudes of English-language legal systems to non-English speakers. In M. Morris (ed.), *Translation and the Law* (Amsterdam: John Benjamins) pp. 263–79.

Mumby, D. K. (1988) *Communication and Power in Organizations: Discourse Ideology and Domination* (Norwood, NJ: Ablex).

Niska, H. (1995) Just interpreting: Role conflicts and discourse types in court interpreting. In M. Morris (ed.), *Translation and the Law* (Amsterdam and Philadelphia: John Benjamins) pp. 293–316.

Nofsinger, R. E. (1991) *Everyday Conversation* (Newbury Park, CA: Sage).

Nolan, F. (1983) *The Phonetic Bases of Speaker Recognition* (Cambridge: Cambridge University Press).

Nolan, F. (1994) Auditory and acoustic analysis in speaker recognition. In J. Gibbons (ed.), *Language and the Law* (Harlow: Longman) pp. 326–45.

NSRA (1983) *English* (Vienna, VA: National Shorthand Reporters Association).

O'Barr, W. M. (1982) *Linguistic Evidence: Language Power and Strategy in the Courtroom* (New York: Academic Press).

O'Barr, W. and Conley, J. (1990) *Rules versus Relationships: The Ethnography of Legal Discourse* (Chicago, IL: University of Chicago Press).

O'Connor, P. E. (1994) 'You could feel it through the skin': Agency and positioning in prisoners' stabbing stories. *Text*, 14 (1), 45–75.

Oddie, C. (1988) The psychodynamics of courtroom behaviour. In P. J. van Koppen, D. J. Hessing and G. van den Heuvel (eds), *Lawyers on Psychology and Psychologists on Law* (Lisse: Swets and Zeitlinger) pp. 27–34.

Okawara, M. H. (forthcoming) Legal Japanese viewed through the Unfair Competition Prevention Law. In J. Gibbons, V. Prakasham and K. V. Tirumalesh (eds), *Justice and Language* (Delhi: Longman Orient).

Ong, W. J. (1982) *Orality and Literacy: The Technologizing of the World* (London: Methuen).

Ó Riagáin, P. and Nic Shuibhne, N. (1997) Minority language rights. *Annual Review of Applied Linguistics*, (17), 11–29.

O'Toole, M. (1994) Lawyers' response to language constructing law. In J. Gibbons (ed.), *Language and the Law* (Harlow: Longman) pp. 188–91.

Oyanadel, M. and Samaniego, J. L. (1999) Aplicaciones de la lingüística al campo legal. Paper presented at the XIII Congreso de la Sociedad Chilena de Lingüística, SOCHIL, La Serena, Chile.

Pardo, M. L. (1994) La ficción jurídica desde la lingüística: Actos de habla y ficción. *Revista de Llengua y Dret*, 22, 25–43.

Pardo, M. L. (1996) *Derecho y Lingüística Como se Juzga con Palabras* (Buenos Aires: Ediciones Nueva Vista).

Pauwels, A., D'Argaville, M. and Eades, D. (1992) Problems and issues of cross-cultural communication in legal settings. In A. Pauwels (ed.), *Cross-Cultural Communication in Legal Settings* (Melbourne: Language and Society Centre, National Languages and Literacy Institute of Australia, Monash University) pp. 77–105.

Pearson, B. A. and Berch, R. W. (1994) Video depositions: linguistic endorsement and caveats. In J. Gibbons (ed.), *Language and the Law* (Harlow: Longman) pp. 171–87.

Penman, R. (1992) Plain English: wrong solution to an important problem. *Australian Journal of Communication*, 19 (3) 1–18.

Pennington, N. and Hastie, R. (1992) Explaining evidence: tests of the story model for juror decision making. *Journal of Personality and Social Psychology*, 62, 189–206.

Pennington, N. and Hastie, R. (1993) The story model for juror decision making. In R. Hastie (ed.), *Inside the Juror: The Psychology of Juror Decision-Making* (New York: Cambridge University Press).

Perkins, K. (1987) The relationship between nonverbal schematic concept formation and story comprehension. In J. Devine, P. L. Carrell and D. E. Eskey (eds), *Research on Reading English as a Second Language* (Washington, DC: TESOL) pp. 151–71.

Philips, S. U. (1982) The language and socialization of lawyers: Acquiring the 'cant'. In G. Spindler (ed.), *Doing the Ethnography of Schooling* (New York: Holt, Rinehart and Winston) pp. 176–209.

Philips, S. U. (1985) Strategies of clarification in judges' use of language: from the written to the spoken. *Discourse Processes*, 8, 421–39.

Philips, S. U. (1998) *Ideology in the Language of Judges: How Judges Practice Law, Politics, and Courtroom Control* (New York: Oxford University Press).

Phillips, T. (1985) Beyond lip-service: discourse development after the age of nine. In G. Wells and J. Nicholls (eds), *Language and Learning: An Interactional Perspective* (London: Falmer Press) pp. 59–82.

Pomerantz, A. (1984) Agreeing and disagreeing with assessments: Some features of preferred/dispreferred turn shapes. In J. M. Atkinson and J. Heritage (eds), *Structures of Social Action: Studies in Conversation Analysis* (Cambridge: Cambridge University Press) pp. 57–101.

Pratchett, T. (1996) *Feet of Clay* (London: Victor Gollancz).

Pratchett, T. (1988) *Witches Abroad* (London: Victor Gollancz).

Prince, E. F. (1990) On the use of social conversation as evidence in a court of law. In J. N. Levi and A. G. Walker (eds), *Language in the Judicial Process* (New York: Plenum Press) pp. 279–89.

Raskin, D. C. and Yuille, J. C. (1989) Problems in evaluating interviews of children in sexual abuse cases. In S. J. Ceci, M. P. Toglia and D. F. Ross (eds), *Perspectives on Children's Testimony* (New York: Springer Verlag) pp. 184–207.

Rasmussen, R. K. (1995) Why linguistics? *Washington University Law Quarterly*, 73 (3), 1047–56.

Redish, J. C. (1986) The Plain English Movement. In S. Greenbaum (ed.), *The English Language Today* (Oxford: Pergamon).

Redish, J. C. and Rosen, S. (1991) Can guidelines help writers? In E. R. Steinberg (ed.), *Plain Language: Principles and Practice* (Detroit: Wayne State University Press) pp. 83–92.

Renton, D. (1975) *The Preparation of Legislation: Report of a committee appointed by the Lord President of the Council* (London: Her Majesty's Stationery Office).

Rigney, A. C. (1999) Questioning in interpreted testimony. *Forensic Linguistics*, 6 (1), 83–108.

Robinson, L. (1994) *Handbook for Legal Interpreters* (North Ryde: Law Book Company).

Rosch, E. (1973) On the internal structure of conceptual categories. In T. E. Moore (ed.), *Cognitive Development and the Acquisition of Language* (New York: Academic Press).

Russell, B. (1975) *My Philosophical Development* (London: Unwin).

Sacks, H., Schegloff, E. A. and Jefferson, G. (1978) A simplest systematic for the organization of turn-taking for conversation. In J. Schenkein (ed.), *Studies in the Organization of Conversational Interaction* (London: Academic Press) pp. 7–55.

Saywitz, K. J. and Moan-Hardie, S. (1994) Reducing the potential for distortion of childhood memories. *Consciousness and Cognition, 3,* 408–25.

Schacht, J. (1964) *An Introduction to Islamic Law* (Oxford: Clarendon Press).

Schank, R. C. and Abelson, R. P. (1977) *Scripts, Plans, Goals and Understanding* (Hillsdale, NJ: Erlbaum).

Schegloff, E. (1973) Opening up closings. *Semiotica,* 8, 289–327.

Schegloff, E., Jefferson, G. and Sacks, H. (1977) The preference for self-correction in the organisation of repair in conversation. *Language,* 53, 361–82.

Scherer, K. (1979) Voice and speech correlates of perceived social influence in simulated juries. In H. Giles and R. StClair (eds), *Language and Social Psychology* (Oxford: Basil Blackwell) pp. 88–120.

Schiffrin, D. (1987) *Discourse Markers* (Cambridge: Cambridge University Press).

Scotton, C. M. (1976) Strategies of neutrality: language choice in uncertain situations. *Language,* 52, 919–90.

Searle, J. (1969) *Speech Acts* (Cambridge: Cambridge University Press).

Searle, J. R. (1976) The classification of illocutionary acts. *Language in Society,* 5 (1), 1–23.

Severance, L. J., Greene, E. and Loftus, E. F. (1984) Toward criminal jury instructions that jurors can understand. *Journal of Criminal Law and Criminology,* 75, 198–233.

Severance, L. J. and Loftus, E. F. (1982) Improving the ability of jurors to comprehend and apply criminal jury instructions. *Law and Human Behavior,* 17, 153–97.

Shuy, R. (1993) *Language Crimes: The Use and Abuse of Language Evidence in the Courtroom* (Oxford: Blackwell).

Shuy, R. (1998a) Ten unanswered language questions about Miranda. *Forensic Linguistics,* 4 (2), 175–96.

Shuy, R. (1998b) *The Language of Confession, Interrogation, and Deception (Empirical Linguistics)* (Thousand Oaks, CA: Sage).

Simpson, J. (1994) Confidentiality of linguistic material: the case of Aboriginal land claims. In J. Gibbons (ed.), *Language and the Law* (Harlow: Longman).

Sinclair, J. M. and Coulthard, R. M. (1975) *Towards an Analysis of Discourse: The English used by Teachers and Pupils* (London: Oxford University Press).

Sjerps, M. and Biesheuvel, D. B. (1999) The interpretation of conventional and 'Bayesian' verbal scales for expressing expert opinion: a small experiment among jurists. *Forensic Linguistics,* 6 (2), 214–27.

Smith, V. L. (1993) When prior knowledge and law collide: Helping jurors use the law. *Law and Human Behavior,* 17, 507–36.

Smith, W. (1994) Computers, statistics and disputed authorship. In J. Gibbons (ed.), *Language and the Law* (Harlow: Longman) pp. 374–413.

Smolla, R. (1993) *Free Speech in an Open Society* (New York: Vintage Books).

Snedaker, K. H. (1991) Storytelling in opening statements. In D. R. Papke (ed.),

Narrative and the Legal Discourse: A Reader in Storytelling and the Law (Liverpool, UK: Deborah Charles Publications) pp. 132–57.

Solan, L. M. (1993a) When judges use the dictionary. *American Speech*, 50 (1), 50–7.

Solan, L. M. (1993b) *The Language of Judges* (Chicago: University of Chicago Press).

Solan, L. M. (1995) Judicial decisions and linguistic analysis: Is there a linguist in the court? *Washington University Law Journal*, 73 (3), 1069–83.

Solomon, N. (1996) Plain English: from a perspective of language in society. In R. Hasan and G. Williams (eds), *Literacy in Society* (Harlow: Longman) pp. 279–307.

Steele, G. J. (1992) Court interpreters in Canadian criminal law. *Criminal Law Quarterly*, 34 (2), 218–51.

Steinberg, E. R. (ed.) (1991) *Plain Language: Principles and practice* (Detroit: Wayne State University Press).

Stone, M. (1984) *Proof of Facts in Criminal Trials* (Edinburgh: W. Green and Son).

Storey, K. (1995) The language of threats. *Forensic Linguistics*, 2 (1), 74–80.

Stratman, J. F. (1994) Investigating persuasive processes in legal discourse in real time: cognitive biases and rhetorical strategy in appeal court briefs. *Discourse Processes*, 17, 1–57.

Stygall, G. (1994) *Trial Language: Differential Discourse Processing and Discursive Formation* (Amsterdam and Philadelphia: John Benjamins).

Swales, J. (1990) *Genre Analysis: English in an Academic Research Setting* (Cambridge: Cambridge University Press).

Swales, J. and Bhatia, V. (1983) An approach to the linguistic study of legal documents. *Fachsprache*, 5 (5), 98–108.

Tajfel, H. and Turner, J. C. (1979) An integrative theory of intergroup conflict. In W. C. Austin and S. Worchel (eds), *The Social Psychology of Intergroup Relations* (Monterey, CA: Brooks/Cole) pp. 33–53.

Tannen, D., and Saville-Troike, M. (eds) (1985) *Perspectives on Silence* (Norwood, NJ: Ablex).

Taylor, B. (1995) Offensive language: a linguistic and sociolinguistic perspective. In D. Eades (ed.), *Language in Evidence: Issues Confronting Aboriginal and Multicultural Australia* (Sydney: University of New South Wales Press) pp. 219–58.

Tiersma, P. M. (1990) The language of perjury: 'literal truth', ambiguity and the false statement requirement. *Southern California Law Review*, 63, 373–431.

Tiersma, P. (1993) Linguistic issues in the law. *Language*, 69, 113–37.

Tiersma, P. M. (1995) Dictionaries and death: do capital jurors understand mitigation? *Utah Law Review*, 1, 1–49.

Tiersma, P. M. (1999) *Legal Language* (Chicago: The University of Chicago Press).

Trosborg, A. (1995) Statutes and contracts: An analysis of legal speech acts in the English language of the law. *Journal of Pragmatics*, 23 (1).

Trosborg, A. (1997) Contracts as social action. In B.-L. Gunnarson, P. Linell and

B. Nordberg (eds), *The Construction of Professional Discourse* (Harlow: Addison Wesley Longman) pp. 54–75.

van Dijk, T. (1987) *Communicating Racism* (Newbury Park, CA: Sage).

van Dijk, T. (1993) Principles of critical discourse analysis. *Discourse and Society*, 4, 249–83.

Vargas, D. M. (1984) Two types of legal discourse: Transitivity in American appellate opinions and casebooks. *Text*, 14 (1), 9–30.

Vlachopoulos, S. (forthcoming) Translating the untranslatable? The impact of cultural constraints on the translation of legal texts. In J. Gibbons, V. Prakasham and K. V. Tirumalesh (eds), *Justice and Language* (Delhi: Longman Orient).

Walker, A. G. (1990) Language at work in the law: The customs, conventions, and appellate consequences of court reporting. In J. Levi and A. G. Walker (eds), *Language in the Judicial Process* (New York: Plenum) pp. 203–44.

Walker, A. G. and Warren, A. R. (1995) The language of the child abuse interview: asking the questions, understanding the answers. In T. Ney (ed.), *True and False Allegations of Child Sexual Abuse* (New York: Brunner/Mazel) pp. 153–62.

Wallace, C. (1990) *Reading* (Oxford: Oxford University Press).

Walsh, B. (1995) Offensive language: A legal perspective. In D. Eades (ed.), *Language in Evidence: Issues Confronting Aboriginal and Multicultural Australia* (Sydney: University of New South Wales Press) pp. 203–18.

Walsh, M. (1994) Interactional styles in the courtroom. In J. Gibbons (ed.), *Language and the Law* (Harlow: Longman) 217–33.

Watson, A. (1991) *Roman Law and Comparative Law* (Athens, GA: University of Georgia Press).

Weaver, C. (1988) *Reading Process and Practice: From Socio-Psycholinguistics to Whole Language* (Portsmouth, NH: Heinemann Educational).

Wells, W. A. N. (1991) *An Introduction to the Law of Evidence* (Adelaide, SA: A. B. Caudell).

Wodak-Engel, R. (1984) Determination of guilt discourse in the courtroom. In C. Kramarae, M. Schulz and W. O'Barr (eds), *Language and Power*. Beverly Hills, CA: Sage. pp. 89–100.

Woolls, D. and Coulthard, M. (1998) Tools for the trade. *Forensic Linguistics*, 5 (1), 33–57.

Yamanaka, N. (1995) On indirect threats. *International Journal for the Semiotics of Law*, 8 (22), 37–52.

Zaragoza, M. S., Graham, J. R., Hall., G. C. N., Hirschman, R. and Ben-Porath, Y. S. (eds) (1995) *Memory and Testimony in the Child Witness* (Thousand Oaks, CA: Sage Publications).

Index of Legal Cases and Legislation

Index